WHAT THEN *IS* THEOLOGY?

Academic Introductions
for Beginners

WHAT THEN *IS* THEOLOGY?

An Introduction to
Christian Theology

WILLEM J. OUWENEEL

PAIDEIA
PRESS

PAIDEIA PRESS,
P.O. Box 500, Jordan Station,
Ontario, Canada L0R 1S0
www.paideiapress.ca

Library & Archives Canada
ISBN 978-0-88815-270-1

2nd printing cover design and layout by Steven R. Martins,
project manager, Paideia Press

Printed in the United States of America

"Jesus answered them, 'you are wrong, because you know neither the Scriptures nor the power of God.'" (Matthew 22:29)

"'[E]verything written about me in the Law of Moses and the Prophets and the Psalms must be fulfilled.' Then he opened their minds to understand the Scriptures" (Luke 24:44-45).

"[A]s for you, continue in what you have learned and have firmly believed, knowing from whom you learned it and how from childhood you have been acquainted with the sacred writings, which are able to make you wise for salvation through faith in Christ Jesus. All Scripture is breathed out by God and profitable for teaching, for reproof, for correction, and for training in righteousness, that the man of God may be complete, equipped for every good work" (2 Timothy 3:15-17).

Table of Contents

About the Author

Willem J. Ouweneel (1944) earned his Ph.D. in biology at the University of Utrecht (The Netherlands, 1970), his Ph.D. in philosophy at the Free University in Amsterdam (The Netherlands, 1986), and his Ph.D. in theology at the University of the Orange Free State in Bloemfontein (Republic of South Africa, 1993). Among many other things, he has been professor of the Philosophy of Science for the Natural Sciences at the University for Christian Higher Education in Potchefstroom (Republic of South Africa, 1990-1998), and professor of Philosophy and Systematic Theology at the Evangelical Theological Faculty in Leuven (Belgium, 1995-2014. He is a prolific writer (mainly in Dutch, and has preached in more than thirty countries. Several times he was a candidate for Dutch Christian political parties.

Foreword

This book is Volume 3 of a series of Christian introductions to various academic disciplines intended for beginners. Of the volumes which have been published so far, the first is on Christian philosophy and the second on Christian political thought. Our intention is not to put together a series of scholarly books, with many learned footnotes and extensive bibliographies, but instead one of an accessible nature, suitable (I hope) for students in the last years of high school, or the first years of college or university, as well as for the general interested public.

Those who do wish to find references to the literature cited may find them in my far more extensive—albeit Dutch—work *De glorie van God* (Heerenveen, NL: Medema, 2013), the last of a twelve-volume series on Evangelical Dogmatics. The present study is a kind of summary and simplification of the philosophical part of that volume. The book itself was an elaboration and updating of part of my theological dissertation (Bloemfontein, South Africa, 1993).

Some "introductions to theology" tell you that theologians study the Bible. They then go on to list the various disciplines contained therein, and give you a description of these disciplines. They are like guides showing you around in a palace. And there is nothing wrong with that. But the present introduction is different. It is more like a chemist taking you into his laboratory, and showing you what he is doing. That is, the purpose of this book is to analyze the phenomenon of theology as such.

This is a much harder job than just guiding you around. For one thing, it demands some basic knowledge of fundamental philosophical ideas. Therefore, for a proper understanding of the present introduction to Christian theology, I highly recommend that you begin by reading the first volume of this series, *Wisdom for Thinkers: An Introduction to Christian Philosophy*. Many ideas in the present volume will be hard to understand without knowledge of the first volume, which forms the foundation for this whole series.

Although this book is intended to be a relatively simple introduction, I am afraid it is not so simple after all. It will really demand much of the beginner. But remember, there is a prize at the end of the race. This is a better understanding of one of the most fascinating phenomena you may ever come across: theology.

Bible quotations in this book are usually from the English Standard Version. When other translations are used, this is indicated.

Willem J. Ouweneel
Zeist (The Netherlands)
January 2014

Chapter One
AN INTRODUCTION TO THE INTRODUCTION

This book is supposed to be an introduction to Christian theology. Such an introduction must itself first be introduced. We will immediately need to answer some vital introductory questions. The first one, of course, is: What is theology? Many people today use the term in a rather sloppy way. They speak of the "theology" of the Apostles Paul, John and Peter, or of the "theology" of the various Gospel writers, etc. What they mean is merely the biblical doctrine(s) of Paul, or Peter, or Luke, or John. Is that the same as "theology"? That is the question. You may even wonder whether they ever presented "biblical doctrines" as such. They addressed *practical problems*, and in this context touched upon doctrinal issues. The two are not the same.

Indeed, what the Gospel writers and the other apostles were occupied with was something very different from what is done at present-day theological faculties, as I will explain further down. What staff members do at theological faculties is to practice theology as a science, a theoretical enterprise—a very special science indeed, yet a science like so many others. The apostles did not do any "science"; strictly speaking, they did not even develop certain well-defined and circumscribed "doctrines." They *preached the truth*, usually because of very practical issues that arose among the early Christians.

Even when Paul uses the word "doctrine" it is in this very practical sense. A beautiful example of this is 2 Timothy 3:10, where he speaks of "my doctrine" (KJV), not as something that has to be "studied" but as something that has to be "followed" (cf. ESV, you "have followed my teaching"). Paul is not teaching a kind of "science"—whether you call it theology, or whatever—but guidelines that have to be worked out in practical Christian life.

Even in the Letter to the Romans, what he teaches is not so much some abstract "doctrine of justification" but rather how we can become just (righteous), and learn to live as such.

In this book, I am using the word *science* in a very broad sense, including not just the natural sciences but also the humanities, such as psychology, sociology, economics, and, as I mentioned before, theology. "Science," in the broad way in which I am using the word, is what the Germans call *Wissenschaft*, and the Dutch *wetenschap*. Scientific (academic, scholarly) theology is an academic discipline, something practiced at theological faculties.

"Christian" Theology?

The second question we will have to answer is: What is *Christian* theology? For some readers, this may sound like a silly question, because the only theology they know is done by Christians. However, this does not hold for *all* theology. Nowadays, a Jewish *yeshiva*, that is a school for rabbinical studies, is often called a theological seminary, for example, the Jewish Theological Seminary of America in New York. Nowadays, Muslims also have their "theological" seminaries in various countries. In a broad sense, the Greek word *theologia* could be interpreted as the study of "divine matters," and such study could be undertaken by people from many different religions.

There is another reason why "Christian" theology is not at all a self-evident matter. What is actually meant is a theology that studies Christian doctrine, but this is not always done by Christians. I know people who are very interested in the Bible and the ancient world, as well as the history of ideas it involves, but who are not Christians. I once had a neighbor who was an agnostic, but he told me that when he was young, he had considered studying theology because he was enraptured by the fascinating world of the Bible. Eventually he studied Egyptology instead. But if he had chosen theology, he would not have been the only agnostic to do so. (There were even some atheists who had made the same choice!)

If you think that agnostic theologians could not be "good" theologians, it really depends on your definition of "good" theology. Purely academically speaking, some agnostic or very liberal theologians may be "better," i.e., of a higher academic standard, than some Bible-believing theologians. In this "horizontal" respect, a Muslim or an atheist could be a "successful" theologian—in the sense of a scholar of Christian doctrine—if he (or she) correctly plays the *language game* of theology (to borrow Ludwig Wittgenstein's terminology) and correctly applies the appropriate hermeneutical rules and theological methods. In short, this academic obeys the rules implied in the structure of academic theology. One example of this is the German theologian Rudolf Bultmann (1884-1976), who was extremely liberal in his beliefs. Yet, his scholarly commentary on the Gospel of John is, academically speaking, so outstanding that no serious New Testament scholar who works on the Gospel of John can avoid this commentary.

From a strictly structural point of view, the "good" theologian is the one who is academically outstanding. However, when it comes to matters of faith, we have to say that the Muslim or the atheist is doing *apostate* theology because he works from an apostate starting-point, and not from the self-conception of the Bible as Word of God. Seen from this perspective, he is a "bad" theologian, and his achievements are definitely "unsuccessful." That is, God's blessing cannot rest upon them. All these points will be explained further below.

Still looking at this matter of a "Christian" theology, we might ask the question—as some indeed have done—why theology, even if it is understood in the sense of the study of Christian doctrine, should itself be "Christian." To some, the only thing that matters is academic standards. They consider theology to be nothing but a special form of "literary science," namely, the study of an ancient piece of literature called the Bible, as well as ancient and more recent texts directly related to the Bible. If you add to this idea the (mistaken) notion of some "neutral, objective, unprejudiced" science, then you will understand why some people even claim that the whole idea of a "Christian theology" is fundamentally wrong. Theology, as the study of the Bible, or of Christian doctrine if you like, should not be "Christianly prejudiced" but neutral, objective, and unbiased.

You see, when it comes to "Christian theology," it does not take long before we have landed in a whole bunch of problems. Is theology really nothing but "Bible study," or the "study of Christian doctrine"? Is theology "science"? And if so, what does this involve? How can you distinguish between scientific and non-scientific–or even unscientific–theology? If the Apostles Peter, John, and Paul were indeed "theologians," were they scientific, non-scientific, or *un*scientific theologians? Does it matter whether theology is "scientific" or not? Some traditional theologians have asserted that theology is nothing but carefully—and reverently—*repeating* (German *nachsprechen*; Dutch *naspreken*) what the Scriptures say. At the same time, they certainly like to call themselves "scientists," or "scholars" as most of them prefer to say; many of them are professors at academic institutes. But why would it be scientific or scholarly just to *parrot* what the Bible says (if you will excuse my phrasing it that way)? Either this is not scholarly at all, or it is in fact much more than just repeating. In what sense is it much more? What makes theology an *academic, scientific,* or *theoretical* enterprise, as opposed to our (thorough) practical reading and handling of the Bible?

Some people like to quote Paul's words here: "O Timothy, keep that which is committed to thy trust, avoiding profane *and* vain babblings, and oppositions of science falsely so called" (1 Tim. 6:20 KJV). They argue that what their *opponents* are doing is "science falsely so called," whereas what *they* are doing is proper "science." They do not even ask themselves whether that which Paul calls "science" here—modern translations have "knowledge"—has anything to do with what *we* call science today. If we call theology a "science," 1 Tim. 6:20 is of no help in understanding what the word "science" involves. What we call "science" today is something that has to meet certain *scientific (academic, theoretical) standards*. There is a whole department within philosophy devoted to the study of such academic standards, and this department is called the philosophy of science (German *Wissenschaftsphilosophie*; Dutch: *wetenschapsfilosofie*). This is the study of what makes science to be science, the study of science as compared to non-science and the study of the criteria and the proper methods of science, as well as the study of good (i.e., academically strong) science as compared to bad (i.e., academically weak) science.

AN INTRODUCTION TO THE INTRODUCTION

"Bible Study"

Let me try to explain what *scientific* theology is by comparing it with "Bible study." Many Christians have the good habit of reading the Bible regularly, and even *studying* (or meditating on) what they are reading. I mean this in the sense of pondering the text, trying to understand what it says, sometimes even consulting some dictionary, concordance, or commentary in order to acquire a better understanding of the text. They *search* the Scriptures (cf. John 5:39; Acts 17:11), and they are doing a good thing. But this daily Bible reading, or Bible *study* if you like, always has a *practical* purpose. Christians want to enter into a closer relationship with the Lord, they wish the Word to reach their *hearts* for their *edification* (cf. 1 Cor. 14:3, 26; Eph. 4:12, 16, 29), they desire to let it have a practical effect on their daily Christian lives, they would like to see their worship deepened, their spiritual growth furthered. A Christian lives by the Word of God (cf. Luke 4:4). It is his desire not only to hear the Word but to do it (cf. Luke 8:21). He *searches* the Word in order that the Word in its turn will *search* his heart (cf. Heb. 4:12).

This is all very necessary; no Christian can do without it. The Word is the food for his (or her) soul, and he (or she) cannot afford to dispense with it any more than his (or her) body can dispense with its daily bread (cf. Jer. 15:16; 1 Cor. 3:2; Heb. 5:12-13; 1 Pet. 2:2). But at the same time, it is all very practical. It has little to do with theology as we normally understand it, i.e., as a theoretical enterprise, a science. I do not mean this in a derogatory way; on the contrary. If a Christian ever has to choose between the Word as *food* and the Word as a theological study object, he should choose the former. Christians can do without science, but they cannot do without spiritual food, or they would starve spiritually.

Theology as such is not spiritual food. It is a bit like the difference between the eater and the chemist in the case of bread. The ordinary man *eats* bread every day, while the chemist appointed for this work *analyzes* bread regularly, in order to establish whether the composition of the bread still meets official standards of quality. That is a very useful job, and we should be thankful that there are chemists who regularly check our bread. But if we had to choose, we would rather *eat* the bread—with all the possible risks involved—than merely *analyze* it, and eventually starve. Theology, as the analysis of the Scriptures, is a very useful job, in a certain sense a bit like the chemist's job, but *eating* the Word is always far more important than *analyzing* it.

The tendency today is to revere science to such an extent that even ordinary Christians believe that theologians are a particularly *elevated* group of Christians. They do not see that their own eating the Word is far more important than the theologians' analyzing it. At the same time, they may be thankful that there *are* theologians who can help them to understand the Word better and to distinguish between a *healthy* dealing with the Word, as opposed to (unhealthy) heresies.

Several times, the Apostle Paul speaks of "sound doctrine" (1 Tim. 1:10; 2 Tim. 4:3; Tit. 1:9; 2:1) and "sound words" (1 Tim. 6:3; 2 Tim. 1:13). Sound, or healthy, doctrine is not just healthily balanced and harmonious in itself, it is that which *makes* you spiritually healthy. It does so in contrast with heresies, which make you spiritually unhealthy or unbalanced, and lead you astray. Theology can help us to distinguish between healthy and unhealthy doctrine, just as the chemist distinguishes between healthy and unhealthy food. Jesus tells his opponents, "You are in error because you do not know the Scriptures or the power of God" (Matt. 22:29). Theologians can help us to know the Scriptures so that we will not be in error. The Apostle Paul warns his readers time and again, "Do not be deceived," or, "Do not be misled" (1 Cor. 6:9; 15:33; Gal. 6:7; cf. James 1:16). That is, please understand correctly what Scripture means. Theology can be of tremendous help here.

Bible Schools

You may see by now that moving from *eating* the Word to *analyzing* the Scriptures, not primarily for the edification of your soul but for your mind's theoretical insight into the Scriptures, is a big step. In practice, there may be a sliding scale between the two, but that does not alter the basic difference between these two attitudes towards the Bible. But be careful! Analyzing the Word, instead of *eating* it does not automatically turn you into a theologian. *Scientific theology is much more than analyzing the Scriptures.* Let me explain.

Imagine that you love the Bible so much that you consider taking a program of study in which you will get to know the Bible much better. What do you choose: a Bible school, or a theological faculty? I will try to avoid the word "seminary" here because this term is rather vague: is it a kind of upgraded Bible school, or is it an academic institution? Never mind. If you are a practical type of person and if the purpose of your intended Bible study is practical, I recommend a Bible school. If you want to grow spiritually, if you want to do some practical Christian work afterwards, or if you want to prepare yourself for the mission field, I recommend a Bible school. Moreover, I would recommend that, if you are a Pentecostal, you go to a Pentecostal Bible school. If you are a Baptist, go to a Baptist Bible school. If you are Reformed, go to a Reformed Bible school. If you are a Lutheran, go to a Lutheran Bible school. If you are Roman Catholic, go to a Catholic seminary. You will learn, in the way of the Pentecostal, Baptist, Reformed, Lutheran, or Catholic denominations respectively, how the Bible is read and understood.

Excellent! There is nothing wrong with that. Go to a Bible school and you will learn a lot about Pentecostal, Baptist, Reformed, Lutheran, or Catholic thinking, respectively, and of course also about the basic, universal truths of Christianity as summarized, for instance, in the Apostles' Creed. If you are a Pentecostal, you might learn a lot more about the baptism with the Holy Spirit and the gifts of the Spirit than if you had *not* gone to that Bible school. If you are a Baptist, you will learn a lot more about believer's baptism, and its relation to both the local congregation and the kingdom of God. If you are Reformed, you will learn a lot more about the Covenant, about God's sovereignty, and about predestination. If you are a Lutheran, you will learn a lot more about law and gospel, or the Lutheran view of the Lord's Supper, or Lutheran church organization, or the doctrine of the Two Kingdoms. If you are a Roman Catholic, you will learn a lot more about the Church, about the papacy, about Mariology, etc. In all these cases you will greatly benefit from your study at your

WHAT THEN *IS* THEOLOGY?

Bible school or seminary. Afterwards you will feel strengthened in the power and significance of the tradition in which you were raised. Be thankful for it.

But such study has little to do with theology.

I sometimes simplify it this way. At a Bible school you learn what the Bible teaches, while at a theological faculty you learn what for many centuries people have *thought* that the Bible teaches. Please note: at a Bible school, you learn what the Bible teaches *according to the tradition to which that Bible school belongs*. But that is not a problem. Pentecostals, Baptists, Calvinists, Lutherans, Roman Catholics, and all the others have a right to teach the Bible to their young people according to their respective traditions. For many young people, that is actually enough. They feel no urge to stand back and put their tradition under criticism. They are thankful for that tradition, and happily wish to understand the Bible in the light of it. There is nothing wrong with this; *most Christians are like that*. It is not because they are not bright enough to study theology, but because they are practical people. They lack the typical theoretical, analytical vein of the academic scholar— just as so many scholars lack many practical skills.

Practical Christians are people who want to *do* something with their Pentecostal, Baptist, Reformed, Lutheran, or Catholic thinking, respectively, instead of critically analyzing their traditions as such. There is nothing wrong with such an attitude. There is nothing wrong with practical people being practical. In their study, they receive tools with which they want to work, that is, to serve, to teach, to preach, to evangelize, to do pastoral work, etc. They do not have the urge to analyze these tools, as those "weird" theologians do. (Isn't it "weird" to analyze the hammer instead of hammering with it?) But I repeat: this kind of Bible study has little to do with theology.

Theological Faculties

Later on in this book, I will give a more precise definition of what I think theology is. For the moment, I just want to explain very briefly a few aspects of what happens at a genuine theological faculty. At such a place, to be perfectly honest, nobody will tell you what the Bible teaches. Instead, the professors will give you the hermeneutical tools to find out for yourself what it teaches. (Hermeneutics is the science of interpretation; it studies the principles, rules, and methods by which you have to analyze a text.) Furthermore, the professors will tell you how the rabbis read and explained the Old Testament, how the Church Fathers read the Bible, how the great medieval thinkers, the Reformers and the Enlightenment thinkers did it, etc. The professors will explain to you why they think these interpreters interpreted the Bible in the ways they did. They will teach you how you can learn to critically evaluate all these earlier theologians. And they will also teach you how you can learn to critically evaluate your *own* thinking about the Bible.

You see, that is what *science* as a truly academic, theoretical enterprise is all about—and this includes theology. First, other than common biblical knowledge, theological knowledge must be *critical* and *well founded*. That is, as a matter of principle, nothing is taken for granted, *even if your own Christian tradition feels very strongly about doctrine A or B.* For everything you believe about the Bible the theologian needs critical arguments that are well thought through. Neither tradition, nor the authority of previous generations, nor even the authority of your professors, but sound reasoning is decisive for the theological theories you are going to hold.

Second, theology—the academic analysis of Christian doctrine —must be *systematic and coherent,* that is, it ought, as much as possible, to form a systematic, coherent whole. There is no place for loose pieces of knowledge; if they occur, they must either be integrated in the whole, or else be discarded. Theology, like any science, usually acquires its knowledge not in a spontaneous, arbitrary way, as in practical life, but in an orderly, purposeful manner through systematic investigation, that is, through critical analyses of texts. The results of this investigation are represented in theories in which the results of the various analyses have been organized with a logically meaningful coherence.

Third, theology must be *detached and unconcerned*. Science is characterized by the typical cool distance it has from its field of investigation. When we do theology, the biblical text is not there to feed us but to be analyzed. The texts of the theologians from the past are not read for our edification, but in order to be analyzed. If, for instance, you want to study ecclesiology (the study of what the church is) you are not thinking of your own congregation with which you are wholeheartedly concerned—or not very concerned at all—in a very practical way. No, you take a certain *theoretical distance:* you look at the church, or at the local congregation, in a very general (detached, unconcerned) way. You switch off all your affections, emotions, memories and prejudices, and only rationally analyze the phenomenon of the church, or the local congregation, in general.

Fourth, theological knowledge must be *reproducible.* That is, if theologians leave aside their traditional views, prejudices, preferences, affections and emotions, then it should in principle make no great difference which theologian has analyzed a certain text. Theology can never be objective in the sense of having no pre-scientific beliefs in which it is rooted. A Christian who studies theology cannot help doing so from a Christian perspective. However, theology does need to be objective when it comes to obtaining reliable results. No theologian should slant or adapt his results because the effects suit him better. Sometimes this kind of objectivity has been called "inter-subjectivity." This term means that different theologians doing the same theological work should come to similar results.

I repeat, at a Bible school the teachers tell you what this or that Bible verse means. At a theological faculty the professors give you the tools to find out for yourself what the text means. They teach you the rules according to which you must interpret the text; they might even teach you how to critically evaluate the rules themselves! They teach you how theologians throughout the ages have interpreted the text, and why they did so (depending on the various theological frameworks within which they operated). Then, finally, when you have all the necessary materials at your disposal, *you* interpret the text to the best of your knowledge, as honestly, critically, and objectively as you can.

There might be one element in my argument so far that might seem inconsistent to you. I have tried to explain in simple terms the difference between a Bible school and a theological faculty. The latter is far more objective than the former. Nevertheless, everybody knows that there are also Pentecostal, Baptist, Reformed, Lutheran, and Catholic *theological faculties*. But how can a school be a truly academic institution, and at the same time Pentecostal, Reformed, or Catholic? Well, you see, even if you wish to be a critical, detached, objective, unprejudiced theologian, you cannot help being Pentecostal, Baptist, Reformed, Lutheran, or Roman Catholic—or agnostic, or atheist, for that matter. Later on in this book (chapters 8 and 9), I will explain the term *paradigm*, which is a certain framework of thinking within which every scientist does his scientific work. If you want to be an academically "good" theologian, you must be as critical, detached, objective, unprejudiced as possible. But we will see that you inevitably work within the framework of a certain paradigm.

Practical Wisdom

Let me make it clear right from the start that theological knowledge is *not* a higher kind of Christian knowledge than the Christian's practical intimacy with the Word which *feeds* and *edifies* him. I will explain this later in more detail, but I want to emphasize this right from the beginning. For quite a few theologians, theology seems to be a goal in itself, and this is not what it should be. Theology's goal is to be subservient to the community of the Christians. That is why Karl Barth called his bulky systematic theology *Church Dogmatics*. One good reason for this is that systematic theology should help the church, the common believers, to better understand what they believe and what they stand for, and why they should do so. The circle is to be closed: from our practical knowledge of the Scriptures we move into theology as a scientific, theoretical enterprise to deepen our insights, and from there we move back to the practical faith of God's children. Intellectual knowledge is a great gift of God. But if intellectual knowledge is not used to deepen our practical *wisdom*, it is of little avail.

There is a great difference between knowledge, especially intellectual knowledge, on the one hand and wisdom on the other hand. In principle, it is possible to acquire a tremendous amount of theological knowledge and expertise without having acquired any wisdom in the biblical sense of the word. This is the wisdom the young King Solomon asks for: "Give your servant therefore an understanding mind (lit., a wise heart) to govern your people, that I may discern between good and evil" (1 Kings 3:9, 12). This corresponds with what the Lord told Job: "Behold, the fear of the Lord, that is wisdom, and to turn away from evil is understanding" (Job 28:28). Such a wisdom does not require any higher education, but spiritual growth: the Epistle to the Hebrews speaks of "the mature," that is, "those who have their powers of discernment trained by constant practice to distinguish good from evil" (Heb. 5:14).

Knowledge is a matter of education and study, whereas wisdom is a matter of growing up spiritually. As Paul says: "[A]mong the mature we do impart wisdom" (1 Cor. 2:6). Theological scholars are *learned* men and women, whereas the "fathers" and "mothers" in Christ (cf. 1 John 2:13-14) are *mature* men and women. These are very different matters. Fortunately, though, men and women can be both. But that is not automatically the case. I suppose I may be called a "learned" man, but whether I am also a "spiritually mature" man is for others to judge.

Wisdom is indeed greater than theology. A Dutch professor in ethics, Harry Kuitert (b. 1924), once wrote: "Everything is ethical, but ethics is not everything." I will make a slight adaptation of his phrase and say, "Everything in this universe has theological aspects, but theology is not everything." Some theologians do seem to make theology *everything*. They speak of Paul the theologian or of John the theologian, without seeing the enormous difference between theology as a form of academic enterprise and the practical wisdom of God as presented by Paul and John.

Ancient "Theologians"

Some time ago I was reminded of this distinction when I spent some time studying a great Greek church father, Symeon the New Theologian, who lived around the year 1000. The word "New" in his honorary title is in reference to two previous church figures who had been given the same title: the Apostle John, who in the

East is sometimes called "John the Theologian," and the fourth-century Cappadocian father Gregory of Nazianzus, who is also known as Gregory the Theologian. Here, the word "Theologian" has its original meaning of someone who "knows God." In this sense, the term has nothing to do with academic theology but refers to someone who knows God through personal intimacy. One of the things Symeon did was to teach *theoria*, which in this case does not mean "theory" but "contemplation," the direct experience of God. "The friendship [or intimacy; lit., secret] of the LORD is for those who fear him, and he makes known to them his covenant" (Psalm 25:14).

Symeon claimed to have had such a direct experience of God. When he was twenty years of age, he supposedly had a great vision of light, which for him signified the encounter with God. In Eastern Christianity this light is referred to as the "Tabor Light," that is, the splendor which Peter, John and James had beheld on the Mount of Transfiguration (Matt. 17:2,5), traditionally Mount Tabor, and which supposedly had also been seen by other Eastern Christians.

Already during Symeon's lifetime, we observe the age-old battle between rationality and feeling. Whereas Symeon put the emphasis on feeling (the experience of God), his greatest opponent, Archbishop Stephen, put the emphasis on a strongly rational theology. Another difference was that Symeon believed that every non-consecrated person who had experienced God should be allowed to preach about this, and to grant the forgiveness of sins to his listeners. Over against this, Stephen strongly pleaded for consecration, and for the official ministries in the church. These are discussions that can be recognized in almost all centuries of church history up to the present time. And as in so many other cases, rationality won and experience lost. In the year 1009, Symeon was sent into exile. In spite of this, he has exerted a lasting influence on Eastern spirituality—more so than Stephen—and has contributed to keeping the balance between the rational-theological and the spiritual aspects of faith. In his writings, both aspects are fairly treated. He might be called a "charismatic theologian," even though this term did not exist at the time.

One of the fascinating aspects of someone like Symeon is that he strongly reminds us of his Jewish namesake, the first-century Simeon bar Yochai, and of so many other charismatic rabbis throughout the centuries, especially the eighteenth-century Baal Shem Tov, father of the Chassidic movement. Like Symeon, these rabbis also gathered pupils around themselves and taught them many profound, wise things from the Scriptures, while at the same time strongly emphasizing a personal intimate relationship with God. But they never taught theology as we know it today. In fact, Judaism has never developed its own theology, or, more precisely, its own dogmatics, and the Jews even seem to be rather proud of this.

This is certainly a striking fact. The study of the Talmud led to the writing of several codes, such as the *Arba'ah Turim* of Jacob ben Asher, the *Mishneh Torah* (or the *Yad haHazaka*) of Maimonides, and the *Shulchan Aruch* of Yosef Karo. In the same way, one might have imagined that this Talmudic study would have led to a formulation of the main Jewish dogmas. Of course, there was no formal Jewish institution comparable to the institutional church which for Christians proclaimed official doctrinal statements. But the consensus among the rabbis was such that later great minds could easily have formulated this doctrinal consensus. But, apart from Maimonides' thirteen articles of faith, this never happened.

I will make two marginal notes here, however. First, this lack of a Jewish dogmatics does not mean that Jews cannot be just as "dogmatic" about their faith as Christians. Second, in modern times we are seeing a tendency among more liberal Jews to adopt the term "theology." As I said, nowadays there are "Jewish theological seminaries," and books appear with the words "Jewish theology" in the title. The American rabbi Jacob Neusner (b. 1932) even uses the term "theology" unreservedly in relation to rabbinic (or Talmudic) Judaism.

Rationalism

Here we observe a phenomenon that has existed among Christians already for centuries, namely, a devaluation of the term "theology," which then simply denotes Jewish or Christian doctrine. The danger of this is that, in practice, "theology" is easily equated with "faith" or with the contents of the Bible. The consequence of this is that attacking someone's theology is often taken as an attack upon Scripture itself. It is no wonder that theologians believe they just "repeat" what the Bible says. Many church divisions have been caused by this fundamental confusion between Scriptural faith on the one hand, and academic theology on the other. We should always be prepared "to contend for the faith that was once for all delivered to the saints" (Jude 3). But I am not prepared to contend in the same way for theological theories, and impose them on common church people, as has been done so often. This is a basic problem in our thoroughly rationalistic Western world. I will come back to this in more detail.

In order to find out for yourself how far you have become a victim of this rationalism in theology, this absolutization of theology as such, let me confront you with some statements by the great British apologist, C.S. Lewis (1898-1963). He said in his book *The Great Divorce*: "There have been men before ... who got so interested in proving the existence of God that they came to care nothing for God himself... as if the good Lord had nothing to do but to exist." God is infinitely more than our theories about Him! Elsewhere in this book, Lewis says: "Every poet and musician and artist, but for Grace, is drawn away from the love of the thing he tells, to the love of the telling till, down in Deep Hell, they cannot be interested in God at all but only in what they say about Him." This applies even more obviously to academic theologians; they may easily be swept away on the tide of their own brilliant thoughts and neglect their intimate relationship with God.

Please do not misunderstand me. What I am emphasizing here is the need for a rational—not rationalistic—theology. Why else would I have become a professor of systematic theology? However, I wish to add that the active intimacy with God and his Word is always more important. The theologian should not only study and interpret Scripture, but—as a good Christian—also *meditate* upon it, which is a very different thing. God's Word should be investigated, but it should also be, if I may be allowed the term, *prayed over*. Being an active member of a lively church community, and, if he is qualified to do so, *preaching* the Word to common believers or sharing that Word with those who do not yet believe will save the theologian from an unsound intellectualism.

WHAT THEN *IS* THEOLOGY?

Let me quote here some theologians from the German-speaking world. The Swiss Reformed theologian Karl Barth (1886-1968) emphasizes the immediate relationship between dogmatics and our practical attitude of faith, and therefore he actually calls dogmatics "an act of penitence and obedience." He feels that it is not possible without the attitude of prayer, and to this end he quotes Augustine, Anselm of Canterbury, and Thomas Aquinas. Barth's Swiss pupil and successor, Heinrich Ott (1929-2013), states that theological knowledge proceeds from the prayer of faith, and that biblical texts are to be read and understood in a state of dialogical openness toward God and while applying oneself to prayer. According to another pupil of Barth, the German theologian Edmund Schlink (1903-1984), the primary form of confession, and thus the primary field of interest for dogmatics, is prayer and praise.

A third pupil of Barth, the German theologian Wolfgang Trillhaas (1903-1995), calls Christianity the religion that is the most thoroughly reflected upon in the whole world. According to him, this implies a loss of the immediacy of faith (think of what I said above about the detached nature of theology). True faith always contains something of the naïveté of childish confidence in God the Father, whereas a critical dogmatics, which is anything but naïve, falls below preaching, below the hymns and prayers of the church congregation, and below faith itself, just as reason falls below the great mysteries of God.

The German theologian Helmut Thielicke (1908-1986) puts it as follows: "He who studies theology, and especially dogmatics, has to observe himself carefully to find out whether he does not think more and more in the third instead of the second person," that is, whether he speaks about God more as "he" and less as "you," or, in other words, whether he prays and praises less and less. Thielicke adds: "He who stops being a spiritual person [cf. 1 Cor. 2:14-16], is automatically working out a false theology, even when this theology in its contents is decent, orthodox and truly Lutheran" (Thielicke uses the word "Lutheran," but you may substitute your own denominational label). I would say, do not fall from praying into probing, neglecting the former and stressing the latter.

AN INTRODUCTION TO THE INTRODUCTION

The Swiss theologian Emil Brunner (1889-1966) contrasts faith, prayer, and testimony on the one hand with theology on the other. He too warns against turning from the second to the third person, from "you" to "he," against the objectification connected with it, so that the personal element, the "heart," is switched off during theological reflection. He points to the danger of being a "good" theologian from an academic point of view, while at the same time being a "bad" Christian when it comes to practically living your faith. Brunner also emphasizes that church doctrine is always the confession or *expression* of faith, not the *object* of faith. That is, Christians do not believe in any confession, nor in theological doctrines, but in God's revelation, in Jesus Christ himself (cf. chapter 5). The revelation of God is about Jesus, *not* about Christology (which is nothing but our humanly flawed "reconstruction" of God's revelation about Jesus). Faith is confrontation, is an encounter with Jesus *himself*, not submitting to a *doctrine* about him. We do not believe in "truths," but in him who is the Truth (John 14:6). We should not just "reason about the truth," but "be of the truth" (John 18:37; 1 John 3:19).

In Summary

What has gone on in this chapter so far? On the one hand, I have emphasized the significance of theology. Any person who is a Christian and who has the gift of critical, detached, analytical, systematic thinking will greatly benefit from the study of theology, and may become a great blessing to others. He or she will learn to have a much broader picture of Christianity, to relativize his or her own specific tradition, to go to the Bible, or any other Christian text with a much more critical and objective mindset, to learn from other Christian (and Jewish) traditions, to acquire profound knowledge both of the Scriptures and of the great Christian (and Jewish) thinkers of the past and present. He or she will learn the hermeneutical rules of interpreting texts, and will learn from the ways in which many other theologians have interpreted the texts. He or she will learn to relativize theology, for instance by realizing that theologians do not establish "truths" but develop theological "theories" which have as much or as little value as the expertise of the theologians responsible (cf. chapter 10).

WHAT THEN *IS* THEOLOGY?

Preachers preach the truth—or so we hope!—whereas *theologians* establish what experts in the field *think* is the truth. Preachers speak with the authority of their Sender—or so we hope!—whereas theologians are more modest; they can speak only with the authority of their scientific reputation. The reason for this, you must understand, is that theological theories are not so much gifts of God as free products of the theologians' minds. I am not denying that the Holy Spirit can also guide the theologians (John 16:13)—of course he can, and often does. But I do deny that theologians could ever *appeal* to this guidance to *prove* the correctness of their theories. Whether their ideas have any truth in them is not established by an appeal to God's providential guidance but by the force of (theo)logical *arguments*. Otherwise, we are dealing not with theology, but with some kind of sectarian dogmatism. Moreover, there are so many theological *paradigms*, all of which might claim to have achieved their theological results by the guidance of the Spirit (cf. chapters 8 and 9). That does not work.

It is *prophets* who say, because they are allowed to do so, "Thus says the Lord" (which occurs more than four hundred times in the Old Testament), and in the New Testament, "Thus says the Holy Spirit" (Acts 21:11). But theologians, in their function as theologians, are *never* allowed to say this. As theologians, the best they can say is: "We think it is so-and-so, but other theologians think differently, and they might be right..." Subsequently they submit their *arguments* to us, so that we can compare them with the arguments of other theologians, and come to our own conclusions.

Final Remarks

Please note carefully that, in saying all this, I am not relativizing the Scriptures! Theologians who tend to equate their theories with the Scriptures might easily think so. These are the theologians who say (as it were), "Thus says the Lord," all the time. They speak as if theologians were prophets. But they are not. On the contrary, God's Word is absolute, *but all our theorizing about it is relative*. In the Bible there is basically nothing that I would ever dare to relativize. But in my own theology, or in that of others, there is nothing that I do not relativize. What God says is absolute and perfect. But what theologians *assert* God is saying is, like all human work, relative and flawed. An earlier title of this book was *Thinking God's Thoughts*. But the perpetual challenge theologians must set themselves is: "Are our theological thoughts really God's thoughts? And are the formulations of these thoughts really adequate?"

Preachers, if they do speak in the name of the Lord and by the power of the Holy Spirit, tell us how things *are*; theologians tell us at best how things *might be*. The Berean Jews had something of the theological mindset. They did not believe Paul because of his apostolic authority, but they were "examining the Scriptures daily to see if these things [that Paul said] were so" (Acts 17:11). Theologians would take this even one step further. They would also like to investigate whether the *way* the Berean Jews "examined the Scriptures" was according to proper hermeneutical rules. And they could go one step further yet, by asking who determines what the *proper* hermeneutical rules are. You see, the *proper* theologian is never satisfied; he or she always continues searching, examining, investigating, scrutinizing. He or she tries to get to the bottom of things, hopefully with the help of the Holy Spirit, because "the Spirit searches everything, even the depths [or, deep things] of God" (1 Cor. 2:10).

Theologians know—or should know—about the relativity of theological theories, about the latter's short-lived character, about the many differences between the various Christian traditions. They know—or should know—about the dangers of sectarianism, of absolutizing one's own "paradigm," of the ways in which theological theories in the past have been enforced upon church people, and consequently have even led to painful church divisions. They may study *dogmatics* (i.e., systematic theology) but they should never be *dogmatic* about any Christian teaching. Every theological subject is constantly open for fresh investigation; hence, no tradition is "sacred."

But that is one side of the story; I began the previous section with the words, "On the one hand." Now, finally, we switch to the other hand. The *good* theologian is a Bible-believing Chris-

WHAT THEN *IS* THEOLOGY?

tian, he or she is a member of a lively church community, an active worshipper, someone who prays and praises, and often a preacher. That is the second thing I emphasized, and I quoted all those theologians to make my point. It is a big step to go from the simple phrase "The Bible says," to the intricacies of academic theology. But it is equally important *to take a step back*. If, in the end, theology does not enlighten the members of the church, if it does not strengthen their faith and their worship, and if it does not further their spiritual growth, it is of little avail. The Christian who is a critical, accurate theologian in his office should constantly ask, about his own ideas and those of other theologians, "Is this correct?" But when he is in the pulpit, he does not stand there as a theologian—God forbid!—but as a preacher, who now and then has the courage to say, as Jesus so often did, "It is written," and therefore it is true (Matt. 4:4,6,7,10; 21:13; 26:24, 31; etc.). This is such an important point that I will come back to it in greater detail.

Terminological Note

When I speak of "theology" in the chapters to come, I usually mean that which I consider to be the heart of theology, i.e. *systematic theology* (often called *dogmatics*), together with Old and New Testament theology (hermeneutics, exegesis, and theology of the Old and the New Testaments, respectively). Taken together, they give us an analysis of biblical texts and a survey of Christian doctrine.

Of course, there are many more disciplines in the theological faculty, but they have a more subordinate character. They include such things as church history, the history of theology, missiology, "practical" theology (liturgy, homiletics, counselling, etc.), canon law, and the study of Hebrew, Aramaic, Greek, and Latin, not to mention the wider sciences of religion, such as the phenomenology of religion, the philosophy of religion, the psychology of religion, etc.

Chapter Two
Theology and Philosophy

In order to understand the character of that which we call theology, it will help us enormously if we delve briefly into the history of theology. There is not only such a thing as church history, but also something called the history of theology. You will easily understand that the two have always gone hand in hand. Theology is not the static thing you might have thought it was. On the contrary, it undergoes constant development and changes continually, along with the changes undergone by the Christian church.

This simple fact may already help us to relativize theology. If you are Anglican, Lutheran, or Reformed, I recommend to you a little experiment. Try to get hold of an Anglican, Lutheran, or Reformed theological handbook of, say, the seventeenth century, and compare it with an (orthodox) Anglican, Lutheran, or Reformed handbook of the late twentieth or twenty-first century. You might be astonished. I dare say that the two books, for instance two Lutheran handbooks that are four centuries apart, differ more from one another than a present-day orthodox Lutheran handbook differs from any present-day orthodox Reformed, Pentecostal, or Baptist (etc.) handbook.

Theology changes all the time, partly because our theological insights change, but particularly because *people* change. You may call yourself a Baptist or a Presbyterian, but what a difference there is between a *pre-modern* Baptist (that is, from before the eighteenth-century Enlightenment), a *modern* Baptist (that is, from after the eighteenth century Enlightenment), and a *post-modern* Baptist (that is, from the last few decades)! Baptists, Presbyterians, Lutherans, Anglicans, and Roman Catholics have all changed much more than they often realize. (I leave out the Pentecostals here because they have been around for only a century, and the Charismatics even less than that.) They all affect the times in which they live, but these times have a far bigger effect on *them*.

WHAT THEN *IS* THEOLOGY?

They are influenced by "the course of this world" (Eph. 2:2), in which the word "course" in the original Greek is *aiôn*, normally translated as "age," or sometimes "world." This word could be rendered beautifully here by the German term *Zeitgeist*, the spirit (gist, mentality) of the present age.

Origin of the Term "Theology"

Perhaps the first thinker to use the term "theology" in a sense similar to the one it has today was the Greek philosopher Xenophanes. In the sixth century B.C., he rejected the traditional Olympian gods, and replaced them with one single deity, who was non-anthropomorphic and unmoving, and who governed the universe. It is not so much the contents of his ideas that interest us right now but rather the way he dealt with the notion of "theology." He broke away from all mythical speculations about the gods, and gave preference to reason. Not mythical traditions but only rational arguments were allowed in his "theology," that is, in his philosophical reasoning about the divine. Here, "theology" is part of philosophy—this fascinating attempt by the ancient Greeks to design an image of the world purely on the basis of logical arguments. In this thinking, true theology, that is, true human knowledge of the divine world, can only be reached through philosophy. Most of the Greek philosophers believed in some god, but only a god that could be defended on the basis of philosophical arguments.

The church fathers clearly saw the enormous danger of Greek philosophy for early Christianity. The Greeks considered their philosophy to be "true theology" because within their philosophy they spoke in a "scientific" way about God (to put it in more modern terms). But for the church fathers this was unacceptable. No human reasoning could be the source for any true knowledge about God, but only *divine revelation*. Nothing could be known about God that God himself had not revealed to mankind. This divine revelation is contained in the Holy Scriptures. Anything we want to know about God, but also about his creation, about Man as God's creature, about nature, culture, or human society from a divine perspective, should be derived from the Scriptures. It seems that, in the early church, the Alexandrian father Origen was the first to use the word *theology* in a Christian sense, perhaps as a challenge to the pagan world around him. To him, theology was indeed the rational-academic doctrine of God, in line with the Greeks, but this time according to God's revelation of himself in the Scriptures.

The great church father Augustine (354-430) turned the view of Xenophanes upside down: according to him, (Christian) theology was the "true philosophy." He even claimed that the true Christian was the true philosopher; in his *De Civitate Dei* he wrote, *Verus philosophus est amator Dei*, "the true philosopher is the one who loves God," and only in this way could he know God. This knowledge of God is theology. Therefore, if philosophy is the study of the true nature of God and creation, and Christians are interested in these matters, they should consult not ancient philosophy but theology. In Christianity, theology had allegedly taken the place of ancient Greco-Roman philosophy. The truth about anything was supplied by divine revelation as we have it in the Scriptures, and the Christian theologian was the interpreter of the Scriptures. If you were interested in philosophical questions, you henceforth turned to theology.

In fact, to this very day many Christians still hold Augustine's position. This is no wonder, because the view is quite attractive. Christians argue that we do not need any specific Christian philosophy because we already have theology. Nevertheless, it is not difficult to demonstrate that this position is mistaken (I have discussed this point extensively in my book *Wisdom for Thinkers*, Volume One of the present series). People forget that theology attempts to answer only *theological* questions. It has no answers for and does not even deal with, typically *philosophical* questions, such as: What is knowledge? What is science? What is nature? What is culture? What is the foundation for, and coherence of, all the special sciences? At best, theology has *theological* things to say about some of these and many other matters, but these are of no concern to the other special sciences.

Theology does not have, nor has it ever had, the task of functioning as a foundational science for all the special sciences, from mathematics to the humanities. In fact, as we will see, theology itself is nothing but one of the many special sciences. As such, it has its own basic philosophical questions (see chapter 1), such as: What is theology? Is it science, and if so, what kind of science? How does it relate to the other special sciences? As a theoretical enterprise, how does it relate to practical faith-knowledge? What are its specific scientific methods? We will explore all these questions in great detail in the following chapters. But it is important to keep in mind already now that these are all *philosophical* questions. Theology is not the true "Christian philosophy"—we need *both* a Christian theology and a Christian philosophy, equally founded upon biblical wisdom.

The Middle Ages

In my humble opinion, both the Greeks and Augustine were mistaken: philosophy is not the true theology, as the Greeks asserted, nor is theology the true philosophy, as Augustine claimed. Unlike the Greeks, Augustine did see, though, that human reason is not autonomous, and this was a tremendous step forward. That is, reason alone cannot find the truth—it needs the enlightenment of divine revelation. This fundamental insight is still valid in any Christian philosophy. Augustine wrote: *Crede, ut intelligas,* "Believe, so that you may understand." Faith precedes, underlies, and preconditions reason, not the other way around. (See my book *Wisdom for Thinkers* for this important matter of the relationship between faith and reason.)

In the thirteenth century, Thomas Aquinas proposed a very different solution: philosophy is not the true theology, nor is theology the true philosophy; no, the two have to be clearly distinguished. Philosophy covers the field of that which can be investigated with the help of our natural reason alone, whereas theology covers the field in which, while not dispensing entirely with reason, we depend completely on divine revelation. There is a thing called *natural theology,* but this is actually more a part of philosophy, and not of *supra-natural* or *sacred theology,* as it was called. Natural theology, working by the light of reason only, has the alleged capacity to logically demonstrate *that* God exists. But after this, supra-natural theology has to intervene to tell us, on the basis of God's revelation, *what* and *who* he is.

24

You see, philosophy and theology are carefully distinguished here. In Thomas's thinking, they are not separated, however. On the contrary, the two are closely linked in that philosophy (including natural theology) leads, or should lead, to theology, that is, supra-natural theology. Philosophy is a *praeambula fidei*, (lit. "forerunner of faith"), as Thomas put it. According to him, only supra-natural theology is sacred; philosophy, and, we may add, all the special sciences that have issued from it, are *profane*. *Sacred* theology is occupied with the soul, with the spiritual, with heaven, with the church, with *special revelation* (in the Bible) and with the supra-natural. *Profane* philosophy, by contrast, is occupied with the body, with the material, with the earth, with the state and society, with *general revelation* (in nature), and with the natural, respectively. This dualism of the profane and the sacred has often been described using the terms *nature* and *grace*, respectively. Thus we speak of the Nature–Grace dualism.

Because of the division I have just described, you may easily understand why Thomas Aquinas was strongly opposed to the notion of a *Christian* philosophy, that is, a philosophy based on a Christian worldview, inspired by Scripture. On the contrary, he claimed that philosophy is an autonomous science. This means that it is a science independent of any foundation outside itself, based exclusively upon human reason *severed from faith*. Theology operates by divine revelation, whereas philosophy (including all the special sciences) operates by (autonomous) human reason. Therefore, as I said, the former was called "sacred," the latter "profane."

You would be amazed to find out how many theologians still accept this scheme, whether consciously or unconsciously. The group includes not only Catholic but also Protestant theologians—and not only traditional Protestants but also modern Evangelicals. We say that this dualistic scheme is *Scholastic* in nature. (Scholasticism, by the way, is the all-encompassing term for Western philosophy in the Middle Ages, from about the ninth century onward.) Thomas's philosophy, usually called *Thomism*, is still the official philosophy of the Roman Catholic Church. But its influence reaches more widely; early Protestants such as the German theologian Philipp Melanchthon (1497-1560) and the French theologian Theodore Beza (1519-1605) introduced this way of thinking into Protestant theology as well. From the sixteenth to the eighteenth century, Protestant theology was thoroughly Scholastic, and in certain circles it remains Scholastic to this very day. This can be seen in the fact that in the Netherlands, Abraham Kuyper (1837-1920) and Herman Bavinck (1854-1921), some of the greatest Reformed theologians at the beginning of the twentieth century, still used the term *sacred theology* (Dutch: *heilige godgeleerdheid*).

But it was only in the course of the twentieth century that some Christian thinkers began to realize that *all* special sciences are, as it were, "sacred" in that they, whether we realize it or not, are all occupied with unravelling God's revelation, be it in nature or in Scripture. And *all* special sciences, including theology, are, as it were, "profane" in that they all operate by the light of human reason.

It should be emphasized that Thomas Aquinas at least made an effort to keep theology and philosophy together. But a later thinker, the British philosopher William of Occam (1285-1349), considered this to be hopeless. He severed theology entirely from philosophy, rejected the notion of *natural theology* with its so-called proofs for the existence of God, and kept divine revelation and human reason entirely separate. With him and his successors, faith and reason were forever put asunder. And from that time onward, faith had nothing more to do with either philosophy or science. William of Occam even adopted a slogan that, in a somewhat different form, had been attributed to the church father Tertullian (ca. 160-ca. 225): *Credo quia absurdum*, "I believe because it is absurd." That is, Tertullian and Occam both thought their beliefs to be fully outside the domain of reason. In my terminology, Occam considered faith to be non-rational, or even irrational, instead of supra-rational (see again my book *Wisdom for Thinkers*).

Summary of the Four Options

So far, we have found four solutions to the puzzle of the relationship between theology and philosophy:

(a) *Philosophy is the true theology* (Xenophanes): This solution is false because it leaves out the need for any divine revelation. By natural reason alone we can never acquire any true knowledge about divine things.

(b) *Theology is the true philosophy* (Augustine): This is false because there are many specifically philosophical questions that must be answered by philosophy alone, questions which never turn up in theology as such. If Augustine had thought a *Christian* philosophy were at all possible, he would not have made such a statement, I suppose. Theology and philosophy have very different callings and objectives, as do Christian psychology, Christian sociology, Christian ethics, etc.

(c) *Theology and philosophy are to be distinguished but kept together* (Thomas Aquinas): This implies a profane philosophy, leading up to sacred theology. This is false because both philosophy and theology, as I have just said, are occupied with divine revelation (in nature and Scripture)—whether they acknowledge this or not—and both operate by the light of human reason (preferably guided by the Holy Spirit). Moreover, philosophy is a *totality science*, whereas theology, as we will see, is *only* one of the many special sciences. And last but not least, philosophy should be *of one piece* with theology in that it is never neutral but should be rooted in the same *religious ground-motive* as theology. This is why, in my book *Wisdom for Thinkers*, I have extensively argued for a *Christian* philosophy.

(d) *Theology and philosophy are to be separated* (William of Occam): In its most extreme form, this means that, henceforth, theology has nothing more to do with human reason, or even with common sense; allegedly, it is only occupied with the mysterious, "the absurd." As for philosophy (including all the special sciences), it has nothing to do with divine revelation, but can operate by natural reason alone. I utterly reject both ideas. First, as a science, theology is a thoroughly rational enterprise. Second, in my opinion, for a Bible-believing Christian only a *Christian* philosophy is to be considered.

A Fifth Option?

If we reject all four of these options, we may wonder whether there is a fifth one. In its briefest form, it involves, first, the notion of a

WHAT THEN *IS* THEOLOGY?

Christian philosophy, as I just emphasized, and second, the notion of a theology that is *only* one of many special sciences, rooted in this Christian philosophy. In my view, the two are closely linked in that, on the one hand, theology, as a special science, has its own ground-questions, which by definition are of a philosophical nature (questions like the ones mentioned earlier: What is theology? Is it a science, and if so, on what grounds? How does theology relate to non-scientific Bible study? What are the criteria for, and methods of, academically outstanding theology? What is its academic purpose? How are theological theories formed? What is their status? How do they relate to church dogmas and confessions? And so on). On the other hand, any Christian philosophy can hardly do without theology because almost all its basic Christian notions have been theologically investigated.

It is unthinkable to write an introduction to Christian philosophy without referring to theology, and, vice versa, to write an introduction to theology without any reference to philosophy, that is, *Christian* philosophy. This is particularly the case because we are linked to a historical tradition in which theology has often claimed to be *the* representation of Christian faith, as if it neither had nor needed any philosophical *prolegomena*. The word *prolegomena* literally means "things that have to be said before," i.e., before we start with theology as such. These basic questions that *precede* theology are by definition of a philosophical nature (I refer you again to *Wisdom for Thinkers*). No special science can do without such *philosophical* prolegomena, and since theology is one of the special sciences, it is no exception to this rule. But I admit that this is not at all self-evident to many theologians! Throughout the centuries, they have learned to mistrust philosophy, and understandably so, after it has so often been infiltrated and marred by paganism.

Both Christian philosophy and Christian theology are sciences, in the broad sense in which I have earlier defined this term, i.e., forms of academic scholarship. But, as I have just indicated, the relationships between philosophy and theology have always been rather strained, to say the least. In a famous lecture first published in 1798, the German philosopher Immanuel Kant (1724-1804) spoke of *The Conflict of the Faculties*, especially the conflict between the theological and the philosophical faculties. In my opinion, both theologians and philosophers were guilty of this conflict because of their "highbrow" attitude towards one another. Liberal Christians tended to give the priority to philosophy as the ultimate source of truth, whereas traditional Christians tended to give the primacy to theology as the ultimate source of truth. In my humble opinion, both were—and are—wrong.

Guilt of the Theologians

The theologians were guilty of the conflict between the two because:

(a) Theologians have often claimed that theology was the true Christian "philosophy," as I have explained above. They did not see the necessity of a philosophy for Christians at all, and, as far as they were concerned, the notion of a "Christian" philosophy was absurd.

(b) Theologians routinely asserted that they worked by the light of divine revelation, whereas philosophy, according to them, possessed only the light of human reason. In this way, such theologians persist, right up to our own day, in the old Scholastic error of the Nature–Grace dualism, splitting up God's creation in an unbiblical way. As I said, *all* sciences are occupied with divine revelation—although they may not recognize it—because God reveals himself not only in Scripture but also in nature, especially in the law-order for nature, which is his own spoken command for nature. God reveals himself even in cultural products because they too always presuppose the divine law-order. Science can be defined as the attempt to unveil the law-order that applies to reality, and in this law order God reveals himself. Moreover, *all* sciences, including theology, work necessarily by the light of human reason because science is a logically qualified human activity. Even though many theologians claim to have a supra-natural *starting point*, theological work as such is of an analytical-theoretical, that is, fully rational nature.

(c) Theologians have sometimes boasted that theology is "special" because it "receives" its data from God, whereas philosophy and the common sciences have to search for the required data through observation and experiment. This is another mistake. Theology is as *empirical* a science as any other. It cannot undertake an academic investigation of God as such, in spite of its name, "theology," that is "science of God" (German: *Gottgelehrtheit*; Dutch: *godgeleerdheid*, "learnedness about God"). Strictly speaking, theology can only study what people have said and written about God (see chapter 3). Theologians study certain written sources, namely, the Bible and thousands of Jewish and Christian writings. Literary scientists do the same with other pieces of literature, and historians do the same with historical sources that are relevant to them. As we have seen, theology has sometimes been called a "literary science," a set of theories concerning a specific type of literature, namely, Jewish and Christian literature and the Bible in particular. God cannot be laid on the dissection table of theological science, but writings about God can, and thus theology is an empirical science; its sense data are what it reads.

(d) Theologians have often boasted that theology is capable of working out its own premises, and neither has nor needs any philosophical premises. This was understandable insofar as Christian theology can indeed do without the help of any *secular* philosophy. But these theologians were not aware of the possibility, let alone the necessity of a *Christian* philosophy to work out the philosophical prolegomena of theology. The truth is that *all* science, including theology, has not only internal but also external, that is, philosophical, *prolegomena*. For instance: (1) Defining whether theology is a science depends on philosophical considerations concerning the differences between scientific and non-scientific knowledge. (2) The comparison between theology and other special sciences is founded on a philosophical totality view of cosmic reality. (3) Defining the study object of theology again presupposes a philosophical totality view of cosmic reality, in which this study object is delineated with respect to the study objects of other special sciences (see chapter 3). (4) Defining the proper methodology of theology presupposes general criteria for scientific methodology, a topic that belongs to the subject matter of philosophy.

(e) Theologians have often confused theological (theoretical) knowledge and practical faith-knowledge, or elevated the former above the latter. I have heard theologians say that, whether you speak of Christian beliefs or of theology, in the end it comes down to precisely the same thing. I hope the rest of this book will make it clear why this is a basic mistake (although I have already touched on this subject in chapter 1).

(f) Theologians often submitted all the special sciences to theology because of their claim that theology alone represented divine revelation. When the Free University in Amsterdam was founded in 1880 by Abraham Kuyper and others, the statutes prescribed that every faculty of the new university was to be based on "Reformed principles" (*gereformeerde beginselen*), which had to be worked out, not by the philosophical faculty, but by the theological faculty. One of the reasons why Christian principles were never worked out for the various new faculties was that theology was totally unequipped for the fulfillment of this task. And when, starting in the 1930s, a Christian philosophy *was* worked out, it was too late to prevent the university's shift from a Scholastic to a liberal course (which was a jumping out of the frying pan into the fire).

(g) Theologians sometimes seemed to be ashamed of a "Christian" theology. They were so anxious to maintain the position of theological faculties at public universities that they began to claim that theology, in order to be "scientific," ought to be neutral and unprejudiced. They forgot that a Christian theology is not *a priori* less scientific than a liberal, socialist, Darwinist, materialistic, or atheist theology. There is no such thing as a neutral, objective, unprejudiced science, be it philosophy, theology, or whatever other science you could think of. Only *specialists,* i.e., people who oversee only a very small part of their own science, are able to live with the illusion of some neutral, objective science because they hardly ever touch upon the basics of their science. People with a much broader perspective will, I trust, better understand what I mean.

The philosophers too were guilty of the centuries-old conflict I have mentioned. This is not my main topic now, but let me briefly mention some points. Philosophers claimed (a) that philosophy, that is, purely rational knowledge of reality, was the true "theology" (knowledge of God, or the gods, or the transcendent in general). (b) They claimed that working by the (alleged) light of divine revelation robbed theology of a truly scientific character, because only empirical observation and reason were to be accepted as sources of true knowledge. (c) They claimed that the notion of a "Christian philosophy" was in conflict with the scientific demand for autonomy, neutrality, and objectivity, and the rejection of all prejudices. Again I must refer you to my book *Wisdom for Thinkers* for these matters.

Necessity of Philosophical Premises for Theology

Many of the philosophical errors that theologians have made in the past are the consequence of refusing to critically investigate the philosophical premises of their own science. From a historical point of view, this is quite understandable when you consider the many harmful influences of *secular* philosophy, whether ancient or modern, within theology. However, the desire to get rid of all secular philosophy usually implies getting rid of philosophy altogether. The consequence is a lack of philosophical reflection upon the external prolegomena of theology. And inevitably, this leads theology straight into the very snare it was so anxious to avoid, that is, secular philosophy.

The reason is simple: theology cannot work without philosophical prolegomena. If it rejects the notion of a Christian philosophy, it will face a hard choice. The first option is landing in the arms of Scholasticism, that is, the semi-pagan philosophy of the Middle Ages and of early Protestantism. The second option is landing in one of the modern or postmodern humanistic schools: (neo-) positivism, existentialism, analytical philosophy, postmodernism, etc. The third option is landing in biblicist fundamentalism, itself a strange mixture of Scholasticism and (neo-)positivism, a fact of which fundamentalists remain unaware. Remarkably enough, both those who plead for a separation between theology and (Christian or secular) philosophy, and those who plead for a kind of "interaction" between theology and (secular!) philosophy, usually land in one of these three snares.

In everyday practice, it turns out to be extremely hard to con-vey these things to the minds of the majority of theologians. I know this from experience because I am both a philosopher and a theologian myself. Great twentieth-century theologians, such as the Swiss theologian Heinrich Ott (whom I have mentioned earlier), and the German theologian Otto Weber (1902-1966) still spoke of theology and philosophy in terms of the relationship between revelation and reason—a false contrast, which I have exposed above. And the German-Swiss theologian Gerhard Ebeling (1912-2001) said that "the orientation upon Jesus Christ" and the notion of sin are foreign to philosophy. Apparently, he was referring to *secular* philosophy alone, without even thinking of the possibility of a *Christian* philosophy. The semantic problems in the "conflict between the faculties" are deeply rooted!

Of course, Christian philosophy does give a place to sin, to redemption, to Christ. And it can do this without ever becoming "theology." The reason, you should remember, is that theology does not have a monopoly of talking about God and the Bible. For Christian philosophy, as well as every Christian *special philosophy* (*Fachphilosophie*) underlying one of the various special sciences, talks about God and the Bible as well. And they do so because, from a Christian point of view, each and every one of the special sciences is founded in a Christian worldview that refers to God and His Word.

The great Dutch Christian philosopher Herman Dooyeweerd (1894-1977) wrote in his book *In the Twilight of Western Thought*: "[I]f the possibility of a Christian philosophy is denied, one should also deny the possibility of a Christian theology in the sense of a science of the biblical doctrine. . . . Luther called natural reason a harlot which is blind, deaf, and dumb with respect to the truths revealed in the Word of God. But, if this prostitute can become a saint by its subjection to the Word of God, it is hardly to be understood why this wonder would only occur within the sphere of theological dogmatics. Why may not philosophical thought as well be ruled by the central motive of Holy Scripture?"

Not only did Dooyeweerd ask this question but he also answered it by laying the foundations, together with his brother-in-law, Dirk Vollenhoven (1892-1978), for a Christian philosophy. Until recently, however, there is unfortunately only a small group of orthodox theologians who seem to have some idea of what such a philosophy might involve, and what its possible meaning might be for Christian theology. I refer to a philosophy that is no speculation, but based on the solid ground of the divine revelation. Already in 1955, the systematic theologian just mentioned, Otto Weber, acknowledged the significance that a Christian notion of science would have also for theology. He stated that such a Christian approach in fact existed, and referred to attempts to develop it which had been made in the Netherlands not long before. He quoted several works by Vollenhoven and Dooyeweerd. Other theologians in the twentieth century, while not actually referring to this philosophical school, independently developed closely related ideas. I mention in particular Emil Brunner, Paul Tillich, and Gustav Aulén, and to a lesser extent Paul Althaus, Helmut Thielicke, and Wolfgang Trillhaas.

Conversely, the Dutch philosopher and theologian, Andree Troost (1916-2008), saw that adopting the theological view that philosophy is mere "speculation" would put theology on the fast track to positivistic decline. A theology that wishes to be based on "solid facts" will in the end destroy itself because solid facts do not exist; there are only "facts for people." As I have said before, a theology that rejects Christian philosophy will inevitably find itself enmeshed in some secular philosophy—often without realizing it—and that will be disastrous.

Rationalism vs. Irrationalism

Let me give you a revealing example of what will happen if you refuse a Christian philosophical basis for your theology. This example involves the relationship between rationalism and irrationalism. Let me first point out that these are not theological terms but philosophical ones, and that they involve a strictly philosophical problem. No theological investigation as such can ever teach you what rationalism or irrationalism is, or the difference between the two. Knowledge of such terms, and of their problems, belongs to your philosophical baggage, whether you realize it or not. If you are a theologian who refuses to study some necessary philosophy, you can hardly be aware of all the theoretical intricacies surrounding the terms rationalism and irrationalism. As a consequence, you can easily get confused.

In Christian philosophy, the terms rational and irrational are carefully balanced against the terms non-rational and supra-rational. Without this, the only alternatives you can see for the rational and rationalism are the irrational and irrationalism.

An example of this is the theologian Millard J. Erickson (b. 1932). When his rather ingenious attempts to reconcile some hard Scriptures are dismissed by opponents as forms of rationalism, Erickson counters that such criticisms are a consequence of the usual existentialist emphasis on the paradoxical nature of reality, and the absurdity of the universe. Can you see what is happening here? Erickson has been accused—whether rightly or wrongly is not the issue now—of rationalism, and the only way he is able to defend himself is by accusing his opponents in turn of *ir*rationalism. Apparently, he is not aware of the third and fourth options, i.e., the non-rational and the supra-rational. Other theologians knew that Christian philosophy dealt with the supra-rational, but rejected this as vague mysticism or metaphysical speculation.

In this way, traditional theology remains entangled in rationalism because it knows no alternative, and the reason it does not is that it has no philosophical framework within which the rational and the irrational, as well as the non-rational and the supra-rational, can find their appropriate places. As I have said earlier, as long as theology has to operate without a Christian philosophy that is concomitant with it, it will fall into one of three possible snares: rationalism (whether of the Scholastic or the Enlightenment variety), irrationalist mysticism, or biblicism.

Let me give you an example of the third option. First, many theologians are well aware of the snares of rationalist theology but think they are safe from them. For instance, such a theologian, when warned of the dangers he is facing, may reply, "Scripture will help me in this point also," without realizing that Scripture as such does not supply us with instructions or defensive weapons to help us avoid both rationalism and irrationalism. Scripture does not even teach us how to do scientific theology in the first place.

Second, our theologian may say, "I am simply drawing my doctrines straight from Scripture, so nothing can go wrong," without realizing that Scripture as such does not offer any systematic treatise on any particular Christian doctrine. The theories of systematic theology are not "drawn" from Scripture but always designed by systematic theologians themselves. If carried out properly, theory-making is done so as to account for Scriptural data. But that does not alter the fact that the theories as such are the mental products of theologians. The Bible does not contain any theories, so you cannot draw theories from it. It does not even contain instant doctrines that are merely waiting to be dug out by the theologian. The fact is that theology never simply repeats what Scripture says, but it is the product of human theological reflection upon Scripture. There are many beauties connected with such an undertaking, but also all kinds of perils, especially if you are not exactly aware of what you are doing.

Third, our theologian may say, "The Holy Spirit will help me, and keep me from snares." Now, of course, this guidance of the Spirit is of eminent importance; as Jesus said, "The Spirit of truth... will guide you into all the truth" (John 16:13). This holds for all believers, not just for theologians. But the theologian who claims to do exegesis in a "scientific" way has to realize that if he does not account for his exegetical methodology, he will quickly deceive himself. Such a theologian can easily confuse his own ideas with the work of the Spirit. And even if they were, as an academician he could never appeal to it, because in a theological debate that does not carry any weight. He must always come with *arguments*, not with an appeal to divine inspiration.

No Theology without Philosophy

I hope I have shown at the very least that the problems involved are, by definition, *philosophical* problems, such as the relationship between the rational and the irrational, or between faith-knowledge and theological knowledge, or between heart and reason. In later chapters we will discuss problems such as the so-called study object of theology (chapter 3); the presuppositions of theological hermeneutics (the science of interpretation); theological methodology, in relation to, and in possible contrast with, the methodology of other special sciences (chapters 6 and 7); the foundations of anthropology; the problems of time and eternity, of immanence and transcendence, etc. The fact that, just as in other special sciences, these are *philosophical* problems implies that theology needs its own philosophical prolegomena, rooted in a coherent Christian cosmology and epistemology.

Of course, in many cases theologians in the past *did* realize the importance of philosophical prolegomena for theology. But most of the time they did not realize the importance of a *Christian* philosophy, that is, of philosophical prolegomena that are rooted in the same biblical ground-motive as theology itself. Usually, theologians who do see the importance of philosophy speak about it as if it were some *neutral* instrument, not unlike the neutral tools of the carpenter or the physician. Such theologians freely quote either from Scholasticism, or from modern pragmatism, existentialism, analytical philosophy, process philosophy, phenomenology, etc., without any qualms of conscience. But at the same time, they often remain staunchly opposed to the notion of a "Christian" philosophy. This is quite a mystery, unless one begins to realize the enormous power of Scholastic thinking, with its separation of theology and philosophy, of "divine" and "natural" thinking, and its denial of even the possibility of a truly "Christian" philosophy.

How can a truly Christian theology have such bad bedfellows, or drink from such polluted waters? That is also quite a mystery. Of course, I know very well that not everything in such secular philosophies is wrong. But where does the theologian find the *philosophical* guidance to know what he can safely adopt from these secular philosophies, and what he cannot? Does he rely on what his "Christian intuition" tells him? He would be wiser to beware of it! "Do not lean on your own understanding" (Prov. 3:5b). Does he find it within his own theology? But theology was never equipped to answer philosophical problems. What he needs is a philosophy that has the same foundation as his Christian theology. But why is the most obvious solution so unacceptable to him and so many like him?

The Origin of Theology's Philosophical Premises

Nowadays, many theologians have begun to realize that they cannot do without philosophical presuppositions. The only re-maining question is, *from where do they get them*? I can see three possible options:

(a) *These philosophical prolegomena are derived from the Bible.* An example of this is the American theologian Norman L. Geisler (b. 1932). He actually accepts a philosophical foundation for his hermeneutics, and finds it in theism, supernaturalism, and meta-physical realism. According to him, these "-isms" are taught, or at least presupposed, by Scripture. Despite Geisler's good intentions, what he offers is an unacceptable "theoreticalizing" of Scripture, as if it could teach, or even presuppose, any scientific or philosophical theory. Scripture neither contains nor presupposes theories or "-isms." But Geisler does not seem to recognize the fundamental difference between the non-theoretical faith language of Scripture and the theoretical language of philosophy and theology. That is because he apparently lacks a Christian philosophy in which such distinctions are analyzed.

(b) *The necessary philosophical prolegomena are found in current philosophical tradition.* But what is this tradition? It is either medieval Scholasticism, still very much alive in the bosom of traditional Roman Catholic and Protestant theology, or, during the last five hundred years or so, the humanistic tradition with its many ramifications. The correspondence between the two is that Scholasticism ties in with *ancient* (Greco-Roman) paganism, while humanism ties in with *modern* paganism. But both of these are foreign to a theology that is rooted in the self-testimony of Scripture.

I repeat that this certainly does not mean that humanistic philosophy is of no value to Christian theology. First, every scientific enterprise, no matter how deeply rooted in an apostate ultimate commitment, contains important truth elements. The perspicuity, the obstinacy of the truth shines even through the darkest philosophies. However, such truth elements are no excuse for also adopting the humanistic framework in which they are contained. Only a Christian philosophy can help us to safely filter the truth elements from the rest of such philosophies.

Second, theology is never done on an island. It is always done over against, and in dialogue and interaction with, the culture to which it belongs, and thus also with the philosophical schools of its time. In that respect, the specific form of a certain philosophy or theology always has a limited significance, bound to the time in which it is designed. Philosophy and theology keep their relevance only if they are capable of answering, not only the questions of the time in which they were designed, but also the questions of later times. Such questions are often raised by secular philosophers (or by artists). A Christian philosophy that is not relevant for a certain time period, including its secular philosophies, is useless.

(c) The only option left is a philosophy that is *rooted in the same biblical ground-motive as theology itself,* and not in some Scholastic or humanistic philosophy. In the words of the American Reformed theologian, Gordon J. Spykman (1926-1993): "Prolegomena must be of one piece with dogmatics proper. . . . Such integration is possible only if philosophical prolegomena and dogmatic theology are viewed as sharing a common footing. Though differentiated in function, prolegomena and dogmatics must be perspectivally unified. The major thesis at this point is therefore that the most fitting prolegomena to a Reformed dogmatics is a Christian philosophy. The noetic point of departure for both is Scripture. It provides the revelational pointers, the guidelines, the 'control beliefs' (Nicholas Wolterstorff) for shaping a biblically directed philosophy as well as a Christian theology."

Not so long ago, the American philosopher John D. Caputo (b. 1940) argued that philosophy and theology, though different, are "companion ways" to nurture the "passion of life." This is that which elevates Man above the boring stream of indifference and mediocrity, and gives us something superlative to love more than we love ourselves. Though Caputo writes in a much more poetic way, it seems to me this is not very different from what Dooyeweerd has called the ground-motive, and what others have called the ultimate commitment of thinking Man.

Of course, the choice of a certain Christian philosophy, or more specifically the Christian philosophy of Dooyeweerd and Vollenhoven and their South African and North American companions, does not imply that only *after* this choice is a Christian theology possible. A radically Christian theology, and a Christian philosophy for that matter, is possible as soon as the central ground-motive of the divine Word revelation is really taken seriously— even though this ground-motive as such is neither philosophical nor theological. Time and time again, theology has to rediscover its starting-point in this ground-motive, and not in Greco-Roman, Scholastic or humanistic thought. If it does so, it will *automatically* (cf. *automatè,* "by itself," in Mark 4:28) move along Scriptural lines, and implicitly apply philosophical insights inspired by this ground-motive.

At the same time, it is obvious that theology will *profit* enormously from an explicit, coherent Christian philosophy that can serve as a foundation for theology. Such a philosophy will constantly ensure that the motives which are introduced are in fact biblical, rather than Scholastic or humanistic, and that theology will develop along the lines of the biblical ground-motive. The design of a Christian philosophy for theology will turn it from a naïve theology into a full-fledged scientific one.

The Hermeneutical Circle

A consistent *humanistic* philosophy rejects both a Christian philosophy and a Christian theology, at least if such a theology aims to be truly scientific. A consistent *Scholastic* philosophy makes, as we have seen, a fundamental distinction between a neutral, objective, unprejudiced—and therefore certainly not "Christian"— philosophy on the one hand, and "sacred theology" on the other. A philosophy rooted in the biblical ground-motive accepts both the possibility of a Christian philosophy and that of a scientific and yet truly Christian theology. If a Christian philosophy is not possible, then neither is a Christian theology. But if a Christian theology is possible, then so is a Christian philosophy. In short, humanists reject both, whereas Scholastic thinkers reject Christian philosophy while still accepting Christian theology. As for us, we accept both, and go so far as to claim that we cannot have the one without the other.

Here we have arrived at an interesting state of affairs. All Christian arguments in favor of the possibility of a theology founded in the biblical ground-motive are *a priori* to be explained from the biblical ground-motive of this Christian theology. And all the arguments opposed to the possibility of a Christian theology are ultimately rooted in the Scholastic or humanistic ground-motives of the opposition. We are dealing here with what is called a *hermeneutical circle* from which no thinker can escape. The theoretical question concerning the possibility or necessity of a Christian theology is *a priori* determined by one's *pre-theoretical* ground-motive, which is either Christian or humanistic, or a mixture of both. To put it in simpler terms, whether you believe in a (scientific) Christian theology depends on how radical a Christian you are.

Do you realize what this means? In my view, the question whether you believe that all human thinking is rooted in a religious ground-motive depends on your own religious ground-motive. There is no way I could ever escape from this conclusion. This is precisely what I meant when I spoke of the "hermeneutical circle." If you do *not* believe that all human thinking is rooted in a religious ground-motive, I cannot help being convinced that that is because of your own religious ground-motive. To put it a bit bluntly, your religious ground-motive prevents you from believing that human thought is always rooted in a certain religious ground-motive!

Let me try to illustrate this. Suppose you are a rationalist, that is, you believe that human reason is the highest explanatory principle you know of. You believe that everything you believe must be based on logical arguments. My question to you is: how do you know this? How can you demonstrate—that is, with the help of logic—that logic is the highest principle? In order to demonstrate this, you would need some "higher" mental position—which the American philosopher Hilary Putnam (b. 1926) has called a "God's Eye point of view"—from which you can judge whether it is logical to be logical. If it were even possible for you to find such a position, it would be *beyond* logic, and thus you would refute your own viewpoint, because what is *beyond* logic cannot itself be logical. The thesis, "It is scientific to assume that all fruitful ideas must be logical," is itself not logical, and thus apparently not scientific! So the thesis refutes itself.

If you cannot find such a "higher" position, such a "God's Eye point of view," this means that you cannot logically demonstrate your position, and in that case, your standpoint would also be lost. Apparently, it is not possible to be a consistent rationalist without refuting your own position. In other words, you too find yourself in a hermeneutical circle. In order to believe in the value of rationalism as a good ("logical") position, you must first be a rationalist.

As I have argued before, your choice of rationalism is in itself

WHAT THEN *IS* THEOLOGY?

necessarily a *supra-rational* choice. In my terminology, it is a choice of the heart, and therefore in the end a decision of a religious nature because it arises from your *ultimate commitment*, the Last Ground in which you put your confidence. So even if you, being a rationalist, reject the notion of religious ground-motives, I think I can easily prove not only that your position is untenable but that your own thinking is rooted in a religious ground-motive. I even claim that in the end there are only two *ultimate commitments*, one that is congenial with the Word of God, and one that is not.

Chapter Three
The Study Object of Theology

We now come to the question that touches the heart of the matter: What actually is theology? Let us consider several traditional descriptions of theology which I think are not very satisfactory, and then try to find a more appropriate approach.

"Theology is the Study of God"

This is the most ancient and familiar, as well as the most obvious, definition of theology, because it is directly related to the original meaning of Greek *theologia*, "study (or doctrine) of God." The church father Augustine (354-430) gives us an early description of theology as *de divinitate ratio sive sermo*, that is, "rational knowledge or preaching concerning the Deity."

The Dutch theologian Abraham Kuyper (1837-1920) insisted that "God" is the object of theology. He asserted that theology is "the knowledge of God," just as natural science is "the knowledge of nature." This is a rather strange comparison, for, while natural scientists have empirical access to nature, theologians do not have empirical access to God, so that there can be no "scientific observation" of him. The problem with Kuyper, as with so many other Scholastically oriented theologians, was that he did not clearly differentiate between the heart's *faith*-knowledge and rational-*scientific* knowledge of the Bible. As a science, theology has no empirical access to God; it has empirical access to *writings about God*, especially the Bible, which is a very different matter.

The great Dutch systematic theologian Herman Bavinck (1854-1921) described theology as "a scientific system of the knowledge of God" as far as this knowledge has been revealed. He considered the knowledge of God within systematic theology as an "imprint" of the knowledge that God has revealed about himself in his Word; the theologian has the task to *thinkingly reproduce* revealed truth.

WHAT THEN *IS* THEOLOGY?

Until the end of his life, Bavinck defined theology as the *scientia de Deo*, "the science about God." To this very day, several leading Protestant theologians have followed this line of thought. The German theologian Wolfhart Pannenberg (b. 1928) claims that theology is a "systematic doctrine of God and nothing else." The American theologian Millard J. Erickson (b. 1932) tells us that theology is "the study or science of God." And the German philosopher Lorenz B. Puntel (b. 1935) asserts that theology has a "concrete object," namely, God.

A good exception to such ill-considered definitions is that of the South African Reformed theologian Johan A. Heyns (1928-1994), who emphasized that theology, like all special sciences (German: *Fachwissenschaften*; Dutch: *vakwetenschappen*), is oriented toward cosmic, that is, empirical, reality. While God does not belong to this empirical reality, the Bible does. The Dutch theologian and philosopher Andree Troost (1916-2008) suggested that any attempt to "analyze" God, as if he were an empirical "given" like his own creatures, is basically blasphemous. Theology can never deal with God as a "object of cognition" in any direct way; it can deal only with what God has revealed about himself in the Scriptures. So Troost too, in his own way, underscored the fact that theology is an empirical science.

Moreover, Troost emphasized that our theological doctrine of God is not an imprint or copy of the divine revelation—as if this doctrine were just as perfect as God's original revelation—but an abstract image of God, which theologians have creatively designed themselves. God cannot be put on the theologians' dissecting table; he is no object for human analysis, no study field. The *only* object of human analysis is *human statements about God*, as we have them in Scripture, and in Jewish and Christian commentaries on Scripture. *Orthodox* theology analyzes these texts on the basis of the pre-scientific faith conviction that biblical statements about God are founded upon God's own self-revelation. This conviction can be rationally accounted for by theology, but it is itself not a result of theological investigation.

By the way, images of God are dangerous things. God himself warns his people against making "carved images" (Exod. 20:4). Included here are not only carved images of false gods, but even images purporting to represent God himself (cf. Exod. 32:4-5). We cannot help forming an image of God in our minds, but we should beware of "bowing down" to it (Exod. 20:5). This is a great snare for theologians, who may begin admiring more and more the image of God that they themselves, or others, have designed. We should never make our image of God more important than God himself. Theological images may be a means to get better acquainted with who God is, but nothing more. If a theological image, or theology itself, becomes an object of veneration, then we must "break it in pieces" (cf. 2 Kings 18:4).

"Theology is the Study of God's Word"

Besides the definition we have just discussed, none seems to be more obvious and appropriate than this one: theology studies the Word of God. Nothing seems to be more self-evident. The German theologian Hanfried Müller (1925-2009) claims that the object of theology is the "living Word of God." The Dutch theologian Jan van Genderen (1923-2004) defined dogmatics (systematic theology) as a theological science that systematically speaks about what God has revealed in his Word. And I could quote many other Christian theologians as well. But is this definition tenable?

If by the term "Word of God" we mean simply the Bible as we have it in our hands, there can be no doubt that theologians do indeed study the Bible. But acknowledging the Bible *as the Word of God* is something that transcends and precedes all scientific analysis, theology included. *Knowing* both God and his Word is a matter of faith, an existential matter of the regenerated heart of Man. "This is eternal life, that they *know* you, the only true God" (John 17:3). This kind of *transcendent faith*-knowledge is not directly related to theology as such, since theology is a strictly *immanent* theoretical enterprise. The transcendent knowledge of God and his Word which the believer has in his heart is not the *object* of theology. Rather, it is that which precedes, pre-conditions and underlies truly biblical theology. To the theologians of his time, who had made the Scriptures the object of their continual investigation, Jesus had this to say: "You do not know me or my Father" (John 8:19; cf. vs. 55). Of the *believers* it was written: "The word of God abides in you" (1 John 2:14). But this does not necessarily apply to every theologian. (For the terms "transcendent," "immanent," "existential," "heart" as contrasted with "reason," etc., I again refer the reader to my book *Wisdom for Thinkers*.)

The British theologian William H. G. Thomas (1861-1924), the Dutch theologian Gerrit C. Berkouwer (1903-1996), the American theologian Carl F. H. Henry (1913-2003) and others relate the study object of theology to the (written) "revelation of God." Of course, at this point we could put forward objections similar to the ones we had against the idea of theology as the study of the "Word of God." The good intentions behind such definitions are obvious, but we need to make a careful distinction here. The study object of theology is a book called the Bible, and Bible-believing theologians study it on the basis of the pre-conceived *transcendent faith* conviction that this Bible is *the revealed Word of God*. Strictly speaking, neither God, nor the Word of God, nor the revelation of God can be placed on the theologian's dissecting table. It is the *Bible* he studies, analyzes, and investigates. And if he is a Bible-believing theologian, it is his believing *heart* that *a priori* recognizes in the Scriptures the revealed Word of God.

The idea that the Bible is the revealed Word of God can never be the objective *outcome* of any theological analysis. Rather it is the *transcendent faith conviction* of the Bible-believing theologian which *precedes* and *conditions* his theological analyses. The certainty that Scripture involves divine revelation is not a scientific certainty, but a faith certainty, worked in the heart through God's Word itself and through the Holy Spirit. This does not mean that, *a posteriori*, we cannot or should not put forward powerful logical arguments for our transcendent faith conviction concerning the Bible. Of course we can. A transcendent, supra-rational conviction is not a mystical, irrational conviction! On the contrary, we believe we *do* have strong (rational) arguments why we believe the Bible to be the revealed Word of God. But these arguments are never the outcome of some neutral, objective theological investigation; rather, they are determined by the *a priori* faith conviction of the regenerated heart.

"Theology is the Study of Man's Religious Consciousness"

Other Christian thinkers have tried to give very different answers to the question as to what is theology. They do not have God or his Word as their starting point, but the study and investigation of Man. This is, so to speak, not a *theistic* approach but an *anthropological* approach, according to which theology is the science that investigates Man's religious consciousness. Theology cannot start with God or his Word, as if these were *objective givens*. Rather, it ought to start with religious man and his beliefs, or so it says. In the end, what theologians do is not the objective description of God or his Word but only their subjective description of their beliefs about God and his Word. They can never rise beyond their own beliefs. If there were anything beyond that, such a conviction would be nothing more than another of Man's "beliefs."

This view of theology has been linked to Friedrich Schleiermacher (1768-1834), who has been called the greatest theologian of the nineteenth century. But, although Schleiermacher himself warned against subjectivism and "psychologism," to a large extent he reduced faith to pious self-consciousness. The emphasis is not upon God's "objective" revelation—though that in itself is a dangerous expression—but at best upon Man's religious response to it, and in an even vaguer sense, upon religious feelings in general. As Schleiermacher wrote, "Christian faith theorems are ideas of the Christian's pious moods, presented within reason."

Please note that starting from Man's religious consciousness—as a clearly *immanent-empirical* given—is something very different from the conviction that faith, in its *transcendent-religious meaning*, necessarily precedes and conditions all theology. In his discussion of systematic theology, Karl Barth (1886-1968) suggests that in itself it is not so much an *act of faith*, as something which *presupposes* an act of faith. In other words, the way a theologian practices theology is *a priori* determined by the way he views his study object, whether or not belief is involved. There is no practical or theoretical knowledge about anything without some prior faith or belief (as I have discussed in *Wisdom for Thinkers*).

47

WHAT THEN *IS* THEOLOGY?

To call theology an act of faith shows some good intention; after all, what would theology be without faith? Nevertheless, the statement is evidence of a lack of distinction between practical faith knowledge and theoretical-scientific theology. Unfortunately, even today the Scholastic confusion of the two is widespread in theology. It is still extremely common to hear the unexamined claim that every good Christian is also "a bit of a theologian," or that common faith and theology only differ in the degree of reflection involved, or that even when we pray we make "theological statements," etc. All this is said with the best intentions, but these comments all suffer from category mistakes.

All such statements neglect the fundamental difference between practical, supra-rational, transcendent faith and theoretical, rational, immanent theology. Outside the sphere of Christian philosophy as defined by the likes of Dooyeweerd and Vollenhoven, one of those who in my opinion have best grasped this distinction was the Swedish theologian Gustav Aulén (1879-1977). He saw theology not as a scientific study of God and his Word (see above), but as a scientific analysis of Christian beliefs. He also saw clearly the distinction between scientific theology and the faith of believing individuals or church confessions.

"Theology is the Study of the Christian *depositum fidei*"

The *depositum fidei* is the whole of Christian beliefs (in fact the word *depositum* occurs in the Vulgate, the ancient Latin translation of the Bible; see for example 2 Tim. 1:14: *"Bonum depositum custo-di..."*). This totality of everything a Christian believes is a very *prac-tical* matter. However, (systematic) theology is a *theoretical* enter-prise whose purpose is to analyze and systematize this *depositum*. There is no continuum between the practical and the theoretical, as many theologians have suggested, because believing doctrines and analyzing them are different things; the difference is one of essence rather than degree. It is, to use the analogy from chapter 1, the difference between eating bread and chemically analyzing it. How could there be a continuum between the two activities? As the German theologian Hans Waldenfels (b. 1931) puts it: "Faith discourse and theological discourse, faith and theology, are as un-identical as a subject and the reflection upon that subject."

It is crucial to get a clear picture of this. What believers do is believe. What theologians do (whether or not they themselves believe) is theoretically analyze these beliefs. Or, in the words of German theologian Paul Althaus (1888-1966), theology is the scientific self-reflection of the Christian faith. Other theologians, such as Fritz Buri, Karl Barth, Paul Tillich, Heinrich Ott, Wolfgang Trillhaas, John Macquarrie, and many more have said similar things.

In order to correctly understand this, we must now analyze the terms *faith* and *belief(s)* a little further. The Greek word *pistis* refers, first of all, to that which *arouses* faith and confidence—that which is faithful, reliable, and trustworthy—and, secondly, *pistis* refers to this faith itself and to confidence as such. This faith is:

(1a) (*actively*) the act of believing, that is, having faith in God, or in Christ;

(1b) (*actively*) faith, irrespective of its object, in the sense of (faith) confidence (Latin: *fides qua creditur*), or faith by which people believe;

(2) (*passively*) that which is believed (Latin: *fides quae creditur*), or faith that people believe; also *ea quae credenda sunt*, or the things that are to be believed, i.e., the *depositum fidei*, the deposit or doctrine of faith.

All these various meanings are found in the New Testament, and of course they belong together. Every real *faith*, (i.e., *fides qua*) implies certain beliefs, (i.e., *fides quae*). Conversely, there cannot be any genuine *fides quae* without some form of *fides qua*, no matter how poor and weak.

It will be helpful for us to define *faith* as the existential, supra-rational, transcendent condition of the human heart, and *beliefs* as the rational, immanent views in which this faith expresses itself. Faith is the transcendent focal point of all our immanent beliefs, and our beliefs are the immanent ramifications of our transcendent faith. Believers are those to whom the Holy Spirit has granted this supra-rational faith of the heart (Eph. 2:8), which then expresses itself in rational beliefs. Or, to put it a little differently: the gospel preacher has translated his *fides qua* into *fides quae*, that is, he has expressed his transcendent-supra-rational faith into immanent-rational formulations. Subsequently, he preaches these beliefs ("this is what I believe") to his hearers. These hearers accept this *fides quae* (immanent-rational beliefs)—we hope—and in their hearts the Holy Spirit translates it into a *fides qua* (a transcendent-supra-rational faith).

This is the pathway: from heart A (*faith*) to mouth A (*beliefs*), from mouth A to ear B (*beliefs*), and from ear B to heart B (*faith*). *Fides qua* (faith) and *fides quae* (beliefs) are never to be equated; but they are never to be severed either. There is no faith without beliefs, and there are no beliefs without faith. The simplest way we can express this is that theology investigates Christian *beliefs*, although theologians are also interested in the *faith* that underlies these beliefs. Theology can logically analyze beliefs and formulate them in a linguistic form, but it can only tentatively approximate faith. In the deepest sense, however, faith is a mystery that theology cannot conceptualize (squeeze into rational forms). At best it can form a (rational) *idea* of it (see chapter 6 on the distinction between concept and idea).

Practical vs. Theoretical Thinking Attitude

Because the difference between faith and theology is so important, let us examine this subject in a little more detail. Remember that, in his practical dealing with Scripture the believer uses it as his daily source of spiritual food, comfort, edification, and encouragement. This practical thinking attitude, as compared with the theoretical thinking attitude, has the following characteristics:

1. *Integrality versus abstraction.* The practical thinking attitude toward Scripture is of an integral nature as far as the Bible reader himself is concerned. At no time will he ever switch off his logical thinking function. However, this function is only one of many different functions, which in his Bible reading are all active at the same time (see *Wisdom for Thinkers* on this concept of *functions*). There is the perceptive function (how else could he read or hear the Word?), the sensitive function (how could he take in the Word without being moved by it?), the logical function (how can he understand the Bible if he does not make necessary distinctions, such as the ones between apostles and angels, Jews and Gentiles, believing and seeing, grace and responsibility, lost and saved, etc.?), the lingual function (how can he receive the Word if he hears it in a language he does not un-

derstand?), the formative function (how can he read the Word without being struck by the very different cultural-historical situations he encounters in it, and without trying to "translate" it to his own time?), the aesthetic function (how can he read Scripture without being touched by the literary form in which it comes to him?), etc.

In the act of Bible reading, none of these aspects is ever (consciously) abstracted from the others. All of these various functions always present themselves *integrally* to the reader, without him being conscious of them. However, abstraction is the very thing that takes place in theoretical thought: the theologian is no linguist or historian. Moreover, as a good scholar he has to leave his affections and emotions aside, concentrating solely on the *logical distinctions* present in the faith contents of Scripture. In short, when he adopts the theoretical thinking attitude, his logical thinking function is abstracted from his other modal functions.

2. *Immediacy versus distance.* The practical thinking attitude toward Scripture is of an *immediate* nature, in the sense of a direct intimacy with God's Word, without the *distance* that is so characteristic of the theoretical thinking attitude. The Word is directly *received* from the Lord. It is not *approximated,* as it is by the theologian, for the notion of approximation presupposes the theoretical distance, in which the logical function of the scholar places itself in opposition to the one modal aspect—in this case, the *pistical* aspect—of his study object.

Seen from the strictly *formal* standpoint of the philosophy of science, there can be no such thing as a continuum between ordinary Bible reading and studying on the one hand, and theological investigation on the other, but only a sharp distinction. *In practice,* this distinction may not always be very clear, but this does not affect the formal distinction as such. The differences between (theoretical) theology and practical Bible reading are at least three:

(a) *Modal abstraction.* From the whole of the biblical faith contents only one modal aspect is abstracted, in this case the pistical one. Even though there are historical, linguistic, emotional, and aesthetic aspects in the text (to name only some), the theologian sees them all from the perspective of faith, not as ends in themselves. For other scientists this is different. For instance, biologists might be interested in the biblical food laws for purely biological reasons. Historians might be interested in biblical history as such, that is, for purely historiographical reasons. And economists might be interested in the economic relationships in ancient Israel. Every science looks at the Bible contents from a certain modal angle; as for the theologian, he looks at it from the pistical angle.

What all these special scientists have in common is that they are interested in the *logical* distinctions in their various fields of investigation. Thus, for a scientist two modal aspects always stand out: the logical aspect within the investigator, and the pistical (or biotic, or historical-formative, or economic, etc.) aspect within his field of investigation.

(b) *Modal universality.* Within the framework of the pistical aspect, which forms the field of investigation for the theologian, he endeavors to acquire a universal (general) insight. This means that he searches for general patterns, principles, rules, laws, and norms. In other words: he is hardly ever interested in one particular religious phenomenon, but in the general features that are valid for all the similar religious phenomena under investigation. Even if the theologian looks at one event, for instance a unique salvational event such as the crucifixion of Jesus, he will begin to understand this event if he views it as fitting—though in a unique and exceptional way—into a long series of propitiatory and reconciliatory sacrificial events prescribed by God, from early human history onward, and especially in connection with the sacrificial worship of ancient Israel.

(c) *Theoretical concepts.* Just as any other science, theology is characterized by specific concepts that have the nature of *theoretical entities.* These are used to explain certain states of affairs within the field of investigation, and are in principle absent in the practical thinking attitude. I say "in principle," because in the Western world, where science is highly venerated, many theoretical concepts have penetrated the everyday language of non-scientists. The same holds true for the language and thinking of many non-theological believers: they use terms such as "Trinity," "substitution," "covenant of works," and "covenant of grace," "eternal reprobation," "believer's baptism," "dispensation," "millennium," "second blessing," the "two kingdoms," "state church," "satisfaction" (a term taken from soteriology), etc. But none of these expressions are found in the text of Scripture itself. They are all products —whether successful or otherwise—of theological reflection.

THE STUDY OBJECT OF THEOLOGY

The Modal Aspect of Faith

In the last few paragraphs I introduced to you the pistical modality of cosmic reality. If you have studied my book *Wisdom for Thinkers*, you are already familiar with the notion of modal aspects in general and with the pistical modality in particular. In that case, you will also know what my answer is to the question concerning the topic of the present chapter, i.e., the study object of theology. In the view of theologians working within the framework of radical Christian philosophy, theology is only one of many special sciences. These are sciences that look at cosmic reality from one specific modal *angle*. Arithmetic looks at it from the arithmetical angle, biology from the biotic angle, linguistics from the lingual angle, ethics from the moral angle, to mention just a few examples.

As I explained in *Wisdom for Thinkers*, I believe that it is very imprecise to say that special sciences study various "parts" or "domains" of cosmic reality. In fact, the opposite is true: *all* special sciences study the *whole* of cosmic reality rather than particular parts or domains, but each of them does so from one specific modal viewpoint. Now you will understand why I would never say that the Bible is the study object of theology. Theologians study *the whole of cosmic reality*, but only from the pistical perspective, just as other sciences study that same cosmic reality from the energetic, perceptive, social, or aesthetic perspective, etc. I will come back to this in more detail later in this chapter.

I have explained how, within the theoretical thinking attitude, a double abstraction takes place. First, within the investigator the *logical* modality is abstracted from the other modalities for the duration of the investigation. That is, his personal aspects, such as the sensitive, cultural, social, economic, aesthetic, etc., have to be put aside for a time. They are not allowed to interfere with the scientific investigation that he is carrying out. Second, in his field of investigation, there is also one single modality that is abstracted from all the other aspects during this period. As I said, in theology this is the pistical aspect of cosmic reality. Theologians are occupied with people, but mainly or exclusively with the pistical subject-functions of these people. And even when they are occupied with animals, plants, or inanimate things, they are only concerned with the pistical object-functions of these things.

Again, I want to emphasize that in the *practical* thinking attitude these two abstractions—in the observer and in the thing observed—never take place. *All* the spiritive functions of the person are active at once. And that person looks at cosmic reality in the coherence of all modal aspects of that reality, even without being conscious of all these various modal aspects. In the theoretical thinking attitude, two modalities are singled out, as I have just explained. In theology, these are the logical modality of the investigator and the pistical modality of his study object. In simple terms, theologians attempt to come to grips with the faith side of reality in a logical-analytical way.

A Closer Look

I have to admit that the pistical modality of cosmic reality, as presented by Herman Dooyeweerd, seems to be rather complicated! Even some of Dooyeweerd's early followers, such as the Dutch theologian Johannes M. Spier (1902-1971), and the Dutch philosopher Klaas J. Popma (1903-1986) eventually rejected the notion of a pistical aspect altogether. The most fundamental misunderstandings concerning the pistical modality, as I see it, are the following:

1. The pistical aspect of the *immanent*-functional reality is confused with faith in its *transcendent*-religious meaning. Some-times it is already complicated enough to explain the difference between *fides quae* (that which you believe) and *fides qua* (that through which you believe; see above). But at least there is something tangible about these two expressions. With the notion of the pistical modality it is different; it demands a much higher degree of abstract thinking. Let me say right away that the pistical modality has nothing to do with either the *fides qua* or with the *fides quae*. It is neither the believing faith of the heart, nor the whole of all the things believed. The pistical lies in an altogether different dimension, as it were. It refers to a *side*, a *mode*, an *aspect* of cosmic reality; it is one among a whole group of sides (or modes, or aspects). These include the arithmetical, the spatial, the kinematic, the energetic, the biotic,

the perceptive, the sensitive, the logical, the formative, the lingual, the social, the economic, the aesthetic, the juridical, the ethical and the pistical. If you are not already familiar with them, I strongly recommend that you consult the chapters of *Wisdom for Thinkers* in which they are explained in greater detail.

The pistical aspect refers to that *kernel* which *all* forms of human religiousness, true or false (even religious humanism, which recognizes no God or gods), have in common. A few practical examples will help. In *Wisdom for Thinkers* I have explained that there are logical things (e.g., scientific handbooks), lingual things (e.g., traffic signs), social things (e.g., park benches), economic things (e.g., bank notes), aesthetic things (e.g., paintings), ethical things (e.g., birthday gifts). In a similar sense, there are pistical things, for instance church buildings, pulpits, baptismal fonts, synagogues, mosques, temples, altars, as well as pistical communities, such as church denominations and synagogue congregations; but there are also ideological communities (e.g., a political party or a humanist association). All these things function in all modal aspects, but each is specifically qualified (typified, characterized) by one of these aspects. Thus, there are also things, such as those I have just mentioned, that are qualified by the pistical aspect. By the way, this illustrates nicely how the pistical aspect is just one among many other aspects.

2. The law-side of the pistical aspect—including criteria for true and false belief—is confused with the subject-side, where we can distinguish matters like the subjective faith activities and faith content ("beliefs").

3. Concrete entities, such as a particular belief or creed, are confused with the modal aspects in which these entities function. Remember, creeds have a *thing-like* or entitary character, which means that they function in all nine spiritive aspects, whereas the pistical *aspect* is only one of these nine. Critics observe all these more or less concrete faith matters, and argue that faith cannot be an aspect. But then, they could argue in precisely the same way with respect to other modal aspects: looking at all living or non-living things, they will argue that life or matter cannot be aspects.

4. A philosophical idea such as the pistical aspect is confused with concrete Scriptural statements—or in this case, the lack

thereof—so that people argue, "Scripture does not recognize a pistical aspect." Of course it does not; and it does not recognize any other modal aspect either. The Bible does not contain or teach philosophical ideas; it does not recognize any modalities of cosmic reality. The idea of the pistical aspect is a product of Christian philosophical reflection.

5. The pistical modality is confused with some general "belief" that all humans allegedly have in common, or some "faith capacity," or "faith possibility" that all humans are supposed to possess. This again is evidence of a confusion between the modal and the entitary dimension of cosmic reality.

6. *Parts* or *domains* of reality are confused with *aspects* of reality. Theology does not study certain parts or domains of reality. On the contrary, *every* part of reality may come to the attention of the theologian as soon as he is struck by the pistical *aspect*, or the pistical *object-function*, of that part of reality. As I have shown before in *Wisdom for Thinkers*, object-functions are a vital element in cosmic reality. We can say that theology, like every other special science, is interested in the whole of cosmic reality, viewed—in this case—from the pistical angle: all of reality is composed of pistical subjects (humans and human communities) and pistical objects. King Solomon was speaking more like a theologian than like a biologist when he "spoke about plant life from the cedar of Lebanon to the hyssop that grows out of walls" and about "animals and birds, reptiles and fish" (1 Kings 4:33). He could speak about these matters in a "theological" way because all these organisms had pistical object-functions (although they were not necessarily *qualified* by the pistical aspect, in contrast with Solomon's temple and its equipment, which were).

Perhaps the common element of all these six misunderstandings is the inability to state and solve a certain *philosophical* problem—in this case, to abstract one's own thinking from concrete faith events and faith contents, and to grasp the *kernel element* that all pistical subjects and objects have in common.

"Theology is the Study of the *Fides qua*"

I can now state that we can assign at least four different meanings to the word "faith": (a) faith as the act of believing; (b) faith as the *fides qua creditur*; (c) faith as the *fides quae creditur* (or the *depositum fidei*); and (d) faith as the kernel that all pistical subjects and objects have in common. I should now add that theology can in no way be the study of the *fides qua*, i.e., the study of faith as the existential-transcendent condition of the human heart. Man's transcendent-religious relation with God, or even Man's heart in its transcendent-religious sense, cannot be the object of theoretical analysis.

There is nothing mystical or irrational about this statement. The transcendent faith relationship is not irrational but supra-rational; the difference between these two terms, although not often understood or appreciated, is tremendous. The *fides qua creditur* is that which precedes, underlies and surpasses all theoretical analysis, but this analysis is strictly limited to the empirical, immanent world.

From the fullness of the transcendent-religious relationship between the believer and God, theology can only abstract the immanent-modal-functional *fides quae*. This abstracted, theoretically isolated knowledge element can, to a certain extent, be worked out, articulated, and systematized in theology. The whole task of (systematic) theology could even be defined as mapping out the logical-rational distinctions within the Christian *depositum fidei* (Andree Troost). Only within the framework of a Christian-philosophical cosmology can the theologian hope to avoid both the traditional snare of equating or confusing the immanent *fides quae* and the transcendent *fides qua*, and well as the snare of dualistically separating the two.

"Theology is the Study of the Bible"

The American theologian Charles Hodge (1797-1878) once said that systematic theology has as its study object "systematizing the facts of the Bible." What could be more familiar and self-evident? But we have now arrived at the point where we can try to analyze why this is not an adequate definition. To say that the Bible is the theologian's field of investigation is a claim that is on the one hand too broad, and on the other hand too narrow.

On the one hand, it is too broad because, strictly speaking, scientists are not occupied with certain objects or collections of objects, but only with a certain modal aspect of objects. Thus, the theologian studies the Bible only from a pistical angle. On the other hand, he studies not only the Bible but, in principle, *all* objects in the universe from a pistical viewpoint. Given this fact, the claim we mentioned above is too narrow. For the whole universe is the field of study of the theologian, as well as of every scientist, even though in every special science it is considered from just one modal angle. For the theologian, this is, I repeat, the pistical angle.

In the case of botanists, they do not study plants in their creaturely fullness, because the cultural-historical, the social, the economic, the aesthetic, the juridical, and the ethical object functions of plants hardly come to their attention. In principle, botany is limited to the biotic aspect of plants. Plants can be of interest for *every* possible special science, but each of these sciences limits its attention to just one single modal aspect of plants.

In the same way, the Bible is not the field of study of the theologian alone. As I said above, the historian may be interested in what the Bible has to say about ancient history, whether that be Assyrian, Babylonian or Persian. The biologist may be interested in the Bible's distinction between clean and unclean animals (Lev. 11; Deut. 14), and the biological, medical, hygienic, or sanitary significance thereof. Or he may be interested in the descriptions given of the animal world in Job 38-41. The psychologist may pay attention to what the Bible has to say about heart, soul, and spirit, and their interrelationships. The economist may examine the economic relationships in ancient Israel (e.g., Lev. 25), or in the early church (Acts 2-5). The legal scientist may look at elementary juridical principles in the law of Moses, such as retribution, legal accountability, the relationship between crime and punishment, etc. The astronomer may be interested in the biblical picture of the universe (especially passages which suggest a flat earth, a global earth, or a vault over the earth). (See chapter 4 for more examples.)

In all this, we must remember that the Bible's goal is never to teach historical, biotic, psychical, or astronomic matters as such. It always sees history, living organisms, soul, and spirit, economic relationships, its picture of the cosmos, etc., *from the viewpoint of faith*. That is why we can assert that, as a thoroughly religious book, the Bible is primarily the field of interest of the theologian.

Creation is not divided in a number of objects, parts, or domains, which are each assigned to some special science. I repeat that, strictly speaking, it is not correct to say that each science, including theology, has its own object or field of study (although I myself use such terms in this book). Rather, each science has its own modal viewpoint, from which it can look at all possible objects, parts, domains, and fields in the universe. This is why the theologian's area of interest is so much wider than the Bible, and why disciplines such as church history, missiology, practical theology (i.e., liturgy, homiletics, counselling, etc.), and canon law could develop. None of them concerns the study of the Bible as such, but they do belong to the scope of theology.

Let us take a concrete example. The whole functioning of a church denomination or a local congregation is of interest for the systematic theologian, but in its pistical aspect. Since the church is *qualified* (typified, characterized) by this aspect, it is of *special* interest to the theologian. However, in its immanent form this church functions in *all* modal aspects of cosmic reality. It has a sensitive aspect, which is of interest for (social) psychology. It has a cultural-historical aspect, which comes to the attention of the (church) historian. It has a social aspect, which is important for sociology (of religion). It has a budgetary aspect, which is of interest for the economist. It has a juridical aspect—think of canon law—that concerns the legal sciences. The importance of all these aspects has not been widely appreciated. Outside the circle of radical Christian philosophy, the German-American theologian Paul Tillich (1886-1965) is one of the few who have clearly grasped this state of affairs.

Feedback

As I have explained above, in the theoretical attitude we create an artificial distance from reality, so that we can more explicitly distinguish the various modal aspects. But these abstract aspects are never to be absolutized. They are to be fed back into our everyday faith knowledge, there to be viewed in their *universal* coherence within cosmic reality. This universal coherence itself depends on the *fullness* of the Truth, which is in Christ and as such transcends the whole of cosmic reality.

Let us look again at the examples given above. The full truth about the laws of Moses, or about the immanent church, is not given to any of the special sciences (not even theology), or to the totality of all special sciences, or to philosophy. Only in the practical-existential-transcendent faith attitude is the church grasped in its integral concreteness and its transcendent orientation toward the Creator and Re-Creator. This feedback to the practical, *believing* thinking attitude is of tremendous importance. The modal abstraction of the theoretical-theological thinking attitude can never be an end in itself but is artificial and temporary. Theological concepts and theories are thought instruments, logical artefacts, which stand *between* knowing subjects and known objects. The word "between" serves to emphasize yet again the distance that separates theoretical thought and cosmic reality. This distance is useful and necessary in order to obtain ecclesiological knowledge. But no ecclesiology can ever tell my *heart* what the church is. This is something I know only on the existent, transcendent "level" through the practical experience that I have of the church.

Scientism is the philosophical ideal that makes scientific knowledge independent of practical knowledge and absolute with respect to it. One must be a strong adherent of such scientism to earnestly believe that a scientific—in this case, theological—picture of reality yields purer and higher knowledge than a direct, concrete encounter of the heart with reality—in this case, with the Bible. It is like believing that a scientific (biological, psychological, social, economic, aesthetic, etc.) picture of my wife would yield purer and higher knowledge of her than a direct, concrete encounter with her.

Similarly, no ecclesiology as such can give to the believer the true believing consciousness of what "being church" in practice means to him, and, I would add, to God. The truth elements in our theological theories come to full disclosure only in the feedback to our integral, practical life experience. No true understanding of the church and its true significance is possible apart from the ultimate commitment of our heart, and the orientation of these truth elements toward Christ, who *is* the Truth in its fullness and unity. A theoretical study of ecclesiology may certainly *deepen* and *enrich* the Christian's practical faith, but it can never replace it.

In Summary

Looking back at all the suggested definitions of theology that we have reviewed so far, to what conclusions can we come? What are the circumscriptions or definitions that, to my mind, seem most acceptable? I mention two definitions that seem to express best what I have been trying to say:

1. *Theology is the special science that investigates the whole of cosmic reality from a pistical viewpoint.*

This definition emphasizes (a) that theology is just one of the many special sciences, and (b) that, just like all other special sciences, theology investigates the whole of cosmic reality, albeit from just one modal viewpoint, in this case the pistical modality. Note the extension (the *whole* cosmos) as well as the limitation (only one modal aspect) in this definition.

Please note what the definition does *not* say:

(a) It does not assert that theology is of an extraordinary (sacred) character because of its lofty subject, which would make it essentially different from all common (profane) sciences.

(b) It does not claim that theology investigates some *transcendent* reality. It does not, and cannot do this, because as a science, it has no access to it. Like all special sciences, theology is an empirical science; it can investigate only what it can empirically observe. The most important thing it observes is *texts*, especially biblical texts, and ancient and modern texts about the Bible. It is these texts that speak of a real transcendent reality, and in the (pre-scientific) conviction of his heart, the believing theologian takes this very seriously. But it is the texts themselves that he analyzes, not the transcendent reality to which they refer.

(2) *Theology is the special science that investigates the logical-analytical distinctions that it encounters in the depositum fidei.*

This differs from the previous definition in that here a more concrete study object is indicated, i.e., the *depositum fidei*, or the totality of what (orthodox) Christians believe, the sum of (orthodox) Christian beliefs. To be sure, in principle anything in

WHAT THEN *IS* THEOLOGY?

the empirical world can come under the scrutiny of the theologian because all entities are either pistical subjects (humans as well as human communities) or pistical objects (things, plants, animals, events, states of affairs all have a pistical object function). However, it will be obvious that it is primarily things (inanimate things, plants, animals, events, states of affairs) *qualified* by the pistical modality that will attract the theologian's special attention. Think of the key events in salvational history, or salvational states of affairs, the Kingdom of God, the Church (with a capital C), or the key figures in salvational history, the most important of all being Jesus Christ. Think of what (orthodox) Christians confess about all these matters.

It is the theologian who, so to speak, places his own logical-analytical faculty in opposition to this set of Christian beliefs. In modal language we would say that the theologian's logical modality stands here in opposition to the pistical modality of cosmic reality. In simpler terms: it is the theologian who endeavors to map out, in a logical-analytical way, what it is that Christians believe. There is a limitation involved here: the theologian usually puts aside the sensitive, or social, or aesthetic, or moral aspects of his own examination of these Christian beliefs. He leaves out what these beliefs mean to the *hearts* of the believers. But this limitation is a means to an end: by clarifying the Christians' (immanent) beliefs in a logical-analytical way, in the end he may deepen and strengthen the (transcendent) faith of the believers.

Chapter Four

THEOLOGY AND THE OTHER SCIENCES

It is really no wonder that Christians have always felt that theology takes up a very special place among the various sciences. Theology is about God and his Word, it was argued, whereas the other sciences had to do with more profane subjects such as mathematics, nature, history, literature, society, economy, the arts, and law. These are all very mundane subjects, at any rate not on the same footing with the lofty Word of God. One has only to look at the history of our universities to notice the special place of theology. The earliest universities (Bologna, 1088; Paris, c. 1150; Oxford, 1167, etc.) always saw in theology the mother of the whole academic community.

Even in my youth, in the listing of faculties at the State Universities in the Netherlands, theology was always ranked number one. Today, it is very different at my first *alma mater*, the University of Utrecht (Netherlands): the natural sciences are mentioned first, and theology has been eliminated altogether. At my second *alma mater*, the Free University of Amsterdam (Netherlands), theology stands at number nine, but the reason for this is that the various faculties are listed in alphabetical order. At my third *alma mater*, the University of the Free State at Bloemfontein (South Africa), theology is mentioned seventh and last. Things have changed . . . .

Is Theology Special?

The great Swiss theologian Karl Barth (1886-1968) once had a famous discussion with the German theologian, Georg Wobbermin (1869-1943), about the status of theology. Wobbermin argued that, whatever differences we may see between theology and the other sciences, at least they have in common the fact that they are all *sciences*. As such, they are concerned with empirical reality and with logical thinking. Karl Barth retorted, "What *good* theology would ever count as its object the 'reality accessible to us'?" In other words, theology's object—God and his Word—surpasses empirical reality. To give Barth his due, he did place theology as a science among the other sciences, and affirmed its "solidarity" with the others as human quests for truth. But in Barth's view, as far as theology's *object* is concerned, it is special (see chapter 3). No other study object of any other science whatsoever can be compared to "God and his Word."

Along the same lines, the Swiss theologian Emil Brunner (1889-1966) in his inaugural address (1924), answered the question as to why theology has a place in the *universitas scientiarum* ("the whole [or the community] of the sciences"). He argued that this is to help the university have a "good conscience" by answering the deepest and ultimate questions that other sciences cannot solve. These other sciences are limited to the empirical world and to the laws of reason, and it is only with the help of reason that they can break through the limitations of reason. Beyond reason, there is only theology, which is able to move on this level because it penetrates the profound source of revelation. Thus, only theology has the answers to the deepest questions, for only theology can speak about God. Therefore, Brunner considers dogmatics (i.e. systematic theology) to be the mediator between "secular" science and the "supra-secular" testimony of faith.

Of course, we understand what these great Swiss theologians, Barth and Brunner, wanted to say. What is the loftiest subject one could think of? God, of course! And what scientist (scholar) would you ask if you wanted to know anything about God? The theologian, of course! And if the science that deals with the loftiest subject is the loftiest science, then this can only be theology. So far, so good. But notice that, if you look at the question this way, it could be simply a matter of degree: we are asking only which science is loftier than the others? If you look at it this way, this question does not even touch upon the character of theology as a science in comparison to other sciences. Barth and Brunner, however, suggest that the difference between theology and the other sciences is not one of degree but of essence. Theology is different in essence, not just in degree from all common special sciences. By arguing in this way, theologians such as Barth and Brunner move entirely along Scholastic lines, as so many still did in those days. That is, their views presuppose the medieval Nature–Grace dualism.

There is something funny about this situation. If I am right about Barth and Brunner, they must have been rather old-fashioned theologians because they still stuck to certain basic views that went straight back to medieval thinking. Had nothing happened in the meantime? Had there been no Renaissance, no Reformation, no Enlightenment? Were Barth and Brunner basically Scholastic thinkers? I seriously believe that, to a certain extent, they were. Now the striking thing is that quite a few orthodox—or, if you prefer, traditional—theologians do consider Barth and Brunner to be products of the Enlightenment, at least to a certain extent. They think they can spot all kinds of "liberal" elements in their views.

If this is correct, it is apparently possible to find both traditional—even outdated—elements and modernist elements in someone's thinking! Humans are certainly complex beings, and theologians are no exception: they can be very old-fashioned in some respects, and very modern(ist) in others.

The Scholastic View

The Scholastic view that I just pointed out in the views of Barth and Brunner is the one we have already encountered in chapter 2. According to this view, *sacred* or *supernatural* theology has the privilege of working by the light of God's Word and Spirit, whereas the other (*profane*) sciences have to be satisfied with the light of natural reason. The implication is that theology far surpasses the other sciences, not only because of its lofty subject but because of its sources of knowledge: the divine Word-revelation and the Holy Spirit. Not only is this a long-established and persistent view, flourishing far and wide among Christian communities from Catholics to Charismatics, it is also wrong. In the briefest formulation, the refutation of it goes as follows:

(a) *Both* theology and the other special sciences are capable of operating by the light of God's Word and Spirit, if they so choose. In my book, *Wisdom for Thinkers*, I have argued that all sciences are necessarily rooted in a certain philosophical view of reality, which in its turn is rooted in a pre-scientific worldview. For Christians, this is obviously a Christian view of the world, which is ultimately based on the Bible. For a Christian scientist, it should therefore be self-evident that he works by the light of Word and Spirit, even if, during his scientific work, he will not open his Bible nearly as often as the theologian does. But that does not change the principle: his work must be rooted in a Christian worldview, and for a good Christian worldview we look to God's Word and his Spirit.

That is why, in the previous volume in this series (*Power in Service*), I spoke of *Christian* political thought, and in the upcoming volumes, I plan to speak of *Christian* psychology, *Christian* biology, and *Christian* historical science. This is political thought, psychology, biology, or historical science that is rooted in the Christian ground-motive. In this respect, there is no principial difference at all between these sciences and Christian theology.

(b) *Both* theology and the other special sciences are theoretical activities, characterized by logical analysis. As such, they both work by the light of natural reason. There is nothing wrong with natural reason in itself. However, as soon as we say that the other (non-theological) sciences work by the light of natural reason *only*, we commit a basic error. There *is* no such thing as "natural reason only," the idea that rational activity should be, and can be, neutral, objective and unprejudiced. In my book on Christian philosophy (*Wisdom for Thinkers*) I have extensively argued that all functions, including the logical function, arise from the heart, the existential-transcendent center of human existence, and therefore can never be neutral and objective. Therefore, human reason is always governed by the condition of the heart, that is, either by apostatic ideas, or enlightened by Word and Spirit, or by a mixture of both apostatic and anastatic ideas.

In this respect again, there is no principial difference what-so-ever between theology and the other special sciences. Both work by the light of natural reason, which is always reason as governed by the (anastatic or apostatic) heart.

(c) *Both* theology and the other special sciences investigate exactly the same immanent-empirical reality. We cannot say that there is some "higher" realm studied by theology, and a "lower" realm studied by the other sciences. If some insist on speaking of some "higher" realm—the realm of God—then I state as emphatically as possible that *no science has access to it*. As an empirical science, theology too is limited to the "lower" realm of cosmic reality. The reason that theology (but in principle any other science as well), *can* and *does* say something about God is that *he has revealed himself within the "lower realm*," so to speak. God has revealed himself in nature and in Scripture, and these are accessible to the sciences.

I repeat, theology is just as much an immanent-empirical science as all the others. The difference does not lie here at all. The *only* difference that really matters is the different modal viewpoints of all the special sciences. On this point, theology does not differ from the other special sciences taken together. On the contrary, all the special sciences, including theology, differ from one another only in that each has its own modal viewpoint.

Theological Help

The medieval and Scholastic idea of the two "realms" (Grace and Nature), and its consequence for the place of theology in the midst of the other sciences dominated the Free University in Amsterdam in its early years (from 1880 onward). As I said in chapter 2, when this University was founded, the statutes prescribed that every faculty was to be based on "Reformed principles" (*gereformeerde beginselen*), which had to be worked out, not by the philosophical faculty but by the *theological* faculty. The reason for this was that only theology had God's Word-revelation at its disposal. Please try to imagine the situation: a *Christian* university was founded in good faith; however, *all* its faculties had to satisfy themselves with the light of natural reason only, with the single exception of the theological faculty. But if this was so, what was so Christian about all these other faculties? This is where theology had to come to the rescue by serving the other faculties with its "Reformed principles."

Of course, theology was woefully ill-equipped for the fulfillment of this task; as a consequence, this whole ideal never got off the ground. The good intentions with which this Christian university was founded yielded tragic results. Nevertheless, even today this Scholastic approach is still very much alive in all parts of Christendom, whether it be Catholic, Reformed, Lutheran, or Evangelical circles. Even today, it seems to be self-evident for many believing scientists to ask the *theologians* if they wish to shed some "Scriptural light" on what they, in their science, are doing. It seems so obvious that Scripture is the theologians' business. (Whose else would it be?)

For years, I have been teaching—with the greatest pleasure— at the Potchefstroom University for Christian Higher Education in South Africa from July to September. As a philosopher, I have visited almost all the faculties and departments at this staunchly Reformed University. (At least, it was Reformed at the time, but unfortunately, in the "new South Africa" it was forced to become "neutral.") During my visits, I noticed something very curious, which was that when the (sub)faculty of art history, or of economics, or of the education sciences, wanted to ease its conscience again for a while by convincing itself that it was still in line with the Christian character of the University, it would invite a *theologian* to supply it with the "Christian principles" for art history, economics, education sciences, etc. In this sense, the people in these departments were exactly like the Free University in its early years. (By the way, the great German philosopher G. W. F. Hegel once said that we learn from history that we learn nothing from history!)

The theologian in question would happily agree to do this but, of course, as a theologian he did not know anything about art history, economics, education sciences, etc. He could not be held responsible for this, of course, but it did mean that he could not possibly meet the expectations of his hosts. So what he did was—and I speak here from experience—to give a lecture on the beautiful temple of Solomon and its music (for the art historians), or on the Mosaic laws (for the economists), or on education in the book of Proverbs (for the education scientists). I am not saying that these lectures were not interesting. Quite the contrary, in fact. But they were not relevant to the (sub)faculties concerned and did nothing to help them develop a Christian-philosophical perspective on their respective fields of study, because the theologian was not equipped to do that. And what was even worse: *neither side seemed to be aware of the problem*, nor did they seem to be concerned about it.

Actually, I must admit that a Christian philosopher from the same University could not have helped these various faculties any better. No philosopher as such can be expected to have the necessary expertise for all these faculties. What is needed in practice is academically educated art historians, economists, education scientists, etc., who are prepared to gain further academic qualification in Christian philosophy. *Then* we may expect them to have something substantial to say about the Christian-philosophical foundations of their respective sciences, and help these (sub)faculties to become truly Christian in nature.

In a sense, one could pity the poor theologian who, throughout the centuries, has had to dwell in such Scholastic environments. "Woe to me, that I sojourn in Meshech, that I dwell among the tents of Kedar!" (Ps. 120:5). Probably it was the Italian theologian, Petrus Damiani (d. 1072), who first used the Latin expression *Philosophia ancilla theologiae*, "Philosophy [including all the special sciences that split off from it at later stages!] is the maidservant of theology." Just imagine that all the common sciences were there to serve theology! How could poor theology handle this tremendous but overwhelming honor? How could it ever live up to the status of a "mistress"? It could not—and thus it got demoted in due time, falling from a high pedestal.

This is a thing, Solomon says, under which the earth trembles: "a maidservant" who "displaces her mistress" (Prov. 30:23b). Particularly at the time of the Enlightenment, philosophy, so to speak, took to itself the place of the "mistress," and poor theology was relegated to the humble place among the ashes of Cinderella (German: *Aschenputtel*). The very greatness theology had possessed in earlier days now became its shame. That is, it was considered to be even *lower* than the common special sciences because it appealed to something which the other, "genuine" sciences would never consider: some divine revelation, which is beyond common science and cannot stand up to academic scrutiny. The theologians could truly say, in imitation of Paul, "We think that God has exhibited us theologians as last of all…" (cf. 1 Cor. 4:9).

By the way, interestingly enough, this treatment shows that, even during the Enlightenment, the same sacred–profane dualism was still presupposed. The great difference was that the epithet "sacred" no longer placed theology at the *top* of the pyramid of sciences, but at the *bottom*. The dualism, however, was still taken for granted. It seems to be extremely difficult to get rid of this scheme, even in cases where scholars are interested in doing so. As far as I can see, only radical Christian philosophy such as that of Dooyeweerd and Vollenhoven, and many of their followers, has managed to do this with any success.

"Natural" Theology

As long as the theology of Scholastic Roman Catholicism and Protestantism still remains the queen, mother, or mistress, whose duty it is to take care of all the other faculties, the true relationship between theology and the other sciences can never be properly grasped. To explain this in more detail, I will first point out the Scholastic distinction between a *natural theology* and a *supernatural one*. A natural theology is supposedly one that can be scientifically demonstrated to every thinking person. Thus, it appeals to Man's *nature*, which, in this situation, is defined as his (allegedly autonomous) reason, without presupposing any (*supernatural*) faith. *Natural theology* speaks about matters of faith—otherwise it would not be theology—but only on the basis of neutral, objective-logical arguments, without the need of some preceding *fides qua*. For instance, this theology believes it can demonstrate the existence of God with the help of purely rational arguments. These days, you must be staunchly Scholastic, rationalistic, or scientistic, if you still believe this.

Natural theology is fully intertwined with the Scholastic distinction between Nature and Grace (or Supernature), and has found its most powerful advocate in the theological giant, the Italian theologian and philosopher Thomas Aquinas (1225-1274). According to him, as I said, human reason possesses a relative autonomy in the domain of *nature*, so that it is capable of deducing the natural truths from creational reality with the help of its own light. However, Aquinas believed that human reason is incapable of demonstrating the *super*natural truths, such as the nature of God, the Trinity, resurrection, redemption, the last judgment, the end of the world. At best, reason is able to refute arguments *against* these truths. In the domain of *grace,* reason is not entirely switched off; supernatural grace does not annul nature. On the contrary, *gratia non tollit, sed perficit naturam,* "Grace does not annul nature, but perfects [or completes] it." In this higher realm, reason is entirely dependent on the divine revelation in Scripture, and on (supernatural) faith. In Aquinas's view, faith is a God-given *donum superadditum* (a "gift" added "on top of" human nature); therefore, being supernatural, faith is necessary in the investigation of the supernatural sphere of grace.

Generally speaking, it goes without saying that the question of the relationship between human reason and divine truth has been highly interesting and relevant throughout the ages, and I suppose it will always remain so. In the Middle Ages, there were three solutions to this problem which stood out above the rest:

(a) *The solution of Thomas Aquinas*: Aquinas argued that reason can only trace and demonstrate the natural truths; it can help us to understand the supernatural truths, but here, Man is fundamentally dependent on divine revelation.

(b) *The solution of Peter Abelard* (1079-1142): Abelard implicitly rejected the distinction between natural and supernatural truths because he believed that *all* divine truths can fundamentally be traced and demonstrated by human reason. Divine revelation is there to support our knowledge of the truth, but even without revelation we could give rational proofs to show why God must *necessarily* be Three-In-One, and why resurrection must necessarily follow upon death, etc.

(c) *The solution of William of Occam* (c. 1287-1347): Occam implicitly rejected the distinction between natural and supernatural truths because he believed that *none* of the divine truths can fundamentally be traced and demonstrated by human reason. Although they are contrary to reason—they are basically *absurd*—we believe them as divine mysteries, on the basis of divine revelation.

How would we formulate our own answer to the same question, in comparison with the three just given? I suppose that it could be briefly summarized as follows :

1. For *all* divine truths we ultimately depend on divine revelation (cf. what Occam said, *contra* the two others).

2. *All* divine truths can be appropriated to a certain extent by theoretical reason (cf. what Abelard, and even what Aquinas said, *contra* Occam).

3. However, the second point is only possible as far as the immanent, modal aspects of these truths are concerned (*contra* all three).

It is important to remember that theology is an empirical and rational science, just like all the other special sciences. That which is supra-empirical and supra-rational can—as far as it has been revealed—only be *believed*. With the help of theology, it can be "approximated" but not conceptualized (rationally enclosed in concepts; see chapter 6 below, on conceptualization). The greatness of its subject should not make theology arrogant but, on the contrary, very humble. No special science should realize more profoundly that there is much to observe and to analyze in theology, but that it has to come to a halt before the great mysteries of God. *What it cannot dissect anymore it should worship.* "Oh, the depth of the riches and wisdom and knowledge of God! How unsearchable are his judgments and how inscrutable his ways! . . . For from him and through him and to him are all things. To him be glory forever. Amen" (Rom. 11:33, 36).

Aquinas and Theological Science

It is interesting to see why Aquinas calls not only "natural" theology but also "supernatural" theology a "science." According to him, there are two kinds of "science." Some sciences start with axioms, which in the natural light of reason are self-evident, for instance, arithmetic, geometry. (This is a fascinating viewpoint, because in modern mathematics *no single* axiom is self-evident, and thus sacrosanct, anymore.) In Aquinas's view, other sciences start with axioms that are self-evident because of some higher science; and this, for instance, is the relationship of musicology with respect to the higher science of arithmetic. Aquinas relegates theology to the lower level because it starts with axioms that are self-evident because of a higher science, which in this case is the knowledge of God (as well as the beatified souls, adds Aquinas). Just as musicology accepts the axioms that are communicated to it from above by arithmetic, theology accepts the axioms that are communicated to it from above by God. To my mind, this is a rather appalling equation of, or confusion between, scientific knowledge and the faith knowledge revealed by God.

Radical Christian thinking rejects this dualism of nature and supernature, and thus also of reason and faith, of philosophy (plus the other special sciences) and theology, as totally against the spirit of Scripture. In opposition to this, it states that, from a *structural* point of view, human reason is not autonomous at all but dependent on the spiritual attitude of the transcendent, existential heart. It is from this apostatic or anastatic heart that all immanent human functions, including the logical thinking function, come forth, as we have seen. In consequence, all human thinking is basically apostatic or anastatic (or an unfortunate mixture of the two). The laws of logic as such have not changed, but Christians and non-Christians apply these laws in an anastatic or an apostatic way.

This does not mean that human reason is so corrupt that fallen Man is no longer able to think logically. There is nothing wrong with the intelligence of fallen Man. However, as far as its *direction* is concerned, human reason in *natural Man* (Greek: *psychikos anthrôpos*, 1 Cor. 2:14) is totally corrupt because of his corrupted heart (cf. Gen. 6:5; Prov. 6:14; Jer. 17:9; Matt. 15:18-19; Eph. 4:17). Horizontally speaking, Man's thinking is fine, as it remains logically accurate. Vertically speaking, however, Man's thinking may be totally rotten because of rotten starting points.

Aquinas's denial of the total depravity of natural reason implies, as far as the *direction* of the heart is concerned, a denial of the radical nature of the fall into sin. I have argued before that it was not the *structures* themselves which were corrupted—because sin cannot affect God's law-order as such—but the *direction* of the human heart. Sin has totally corrupted Man's "natural" functioning under the God-given structures. Human reason, darkened by sin, is, apart from the *fides qua* in the regenerated heart, incapable of demonstrating, with purely rational arguments, God's existence from creational reality (*contra* Aquinas), or any divine truth for that matter (*contra* Abelard).

Unfortunately, the Scholastic dualism lives on, not only in traditional Roman Catholic theology, but also in traditional Protestant theology, within Lutheran, Reformed, Evangelical, and other faith communities. For instance, there is still a Christian apologetics that really seems to believe that people can be convinced of the truth of Christianity through purely rational arguments. The American theologian and philosopher Francis A. Schaeffer (1912-1984) was a great advocate of this rational—not to say rationalistic—approach. In consequence of a lack of explicit reflection upon its philosophical prolegomena, this kind of theology has proved incapable of extricating itself from the effects of Scholastic dualism, although Schaeffer in particular managed to expose the errors of the Nature–Grace dualism.

Thus, Protestant theology has often made room for some "natural theology." The Dutch systematic theologian Herman Bavinck (1854-1921) even claimed that all Reformed theologians from the outset have maintained natural theology in its truth and value. This amounts to saying that all Reformed theologians share the same un-Reformed Scholastic roots! Perhaps, to a certain extent this was still the case in Bavinck's day, a century ago, but it is certainly no longer true in our own. The twentieth century has been of crucial importance for an investigation of theology from the viewpoint of the philosophy of science (I refer the reader once again to my *Wisdom for Thinkers*).

Supernatural Theology

Just as traditional Protestant theology accepts the idea of a *natural theology*, it also accepts the idea of a *supernatural* one—and, as the Dutch theologian and philosopher Andree Troost (1918-2008) has put it, both are equally *un*natural. Usually, Scholastic theology does not use the term *supernatural* when speaking of theology, preferring rather the term *sacred*—but it amounts to the same thing. The notion of *sacred* theology goes back to the *sacra theologia*, or *sacra doctrina*, of medieval thought. One has only to think, for instance, of the ancient title *sanctae theologiae doctor* ("doctor in sacred theology"). The expression "sacred theology" is found in the title of Herman Bavinck's inaugural address (1883), and in that of Abraham Kuyper's *Encyclopaedie der Heilige Godgeleerdheid* ("Encyclopedia of Sacred Theology," 1894). Of course, we also find it in the titles of

THEOLOGY AND THE OTHER SCIENCES

many older Reformed works, such as the *Theses de sancta theologia* of Paul Madrat and Abraham Ramburtius (1661), or the *Katechismus der heilige godgeleerdheid* ("Catechism of Sacred Theology") of Samuel van Emdre (1781-82).

Kuyper fully accepted the idea of a *theologia naturalis* ("natural theology"), as well as the idea of its opposite, *theologia revelata* ("revealed theology"). The latter term is quite misleading because it suggests that the contents of theology have been revealed by God. Such an idea can easily arise when the contents of Scripture and that of theology are more or less equated. According to Kuyper, the theorem of theology was traditionally this: *Principium theologiae est Sacra Scriptura* ("The principle [or starting point] of theology is Holy Scripture"). Just before making this pronouncement, he defended the idea of a "sacred" theology at great length. Elsewhere in his work, we encounter the traditional distinction between a *principium speciale* ("special principle") and a *principium naturale* ("natural principle")— yet another of the many after-effects of the Nature–Grace dualism.

The theologian Lewis Sperry Chafer (1871-1952) is an American example of a similar line of thinking. He called systematic theology "the greatest of the sciences," and even applied the notion that theology is "super" to the theologian himself by saying, "The worthy student of Systematic Theology, were he not qualified for the higher and more inclusive title of *theologian*, would be entitled to recognition as a *superscientist*, which he is." Interestingly, this is the very opposite of the idea that is current in secular thinking, namely, that theology actually should not be called a science at all anymore. By the way, the term "superscientist" is rather misleading, because it focuses more on the theologian (by suggesting that he is a "superman") rather than on his theology.

The idea of a *supernatural* or *sacred theology*, which implies an unbiblical overestimation of theology, has the same unacceptable background as *natural* theology. This background is the hoary Nature–Grace dualism, and the equation (more or less) of theology and Scripture. It is therefore just as objectionable. God is sacred (or holy; Isa. 6:3), his Word is sacred (or holy; Ps. 105:42), and his people are sacred (holy; 1 Pet. 2:9). But, as a Reformed thinker once told me—and rightly so—theology, as a fallible, defective piece of human work, is no more or less sacred than economy or chemistry. One could also say that biology or psychology, done by serious Christians, starting from a Christian-philosophical view of cosmic reality, is just as sacred as theology. We could even add that a linguistic or a social science that is rooted in the biblical ground-motive is more sacred than a theology rooted in an apostate ground-motive.

This notion of a sacred or supernatural theology is closely related to ideas concerning the alleged study object of theology (see chapter 3). Even if it were correct to say that Holy Scripture is this study object, this would not make theology as such any more sacred. But, as I tried to point out in chapter 3, this idea of the Bible being theology's study object is itself a Scholastic notion. Theology is then considered to be the science of the higher domain of grace, to which Scripture is supposed to belong. The other sciences, including philosophy, are assigned to the lower domain of nature, to which natural (autonomous) reason is also supposed to belong.

One of the bizarre consequences of this two-storey thinking is that it has sometimes been asserted that theology is a *deductive* science, since it is rooted in revelation and faith, whereas philosophy and the other sciences would be *inductive* sciences, moving from empirical observations to general hypotheses. In opposition to this, I argue that *all* sciences are rooted in certain worldviews, and thus in faith, though it would be wrong to say that scientific statements are "deduced" from such a faith. On the contrary, theology, because it is searching for general patterns on the basis of its empirical "data," is just as inductive as the other sciences (except for the truly deductive sciences such as mathematics and logic, which are basically *not* empirical sciences).

We have studied in great detail the fact that, strictly speaking, the special sciences do not investigate *objects*, but the *whole* of empirical reality, although every special science looks at reality from its own specific modal viewpoint. Thus, theology does not investigate Scripture as such, but the whole cosmic reality from the single viewpoint of the pistical modality. (We may add that Scripture plays a very special role in this investigation because it is pistically *qualified*.) In exactly the same way, the other special sciences also investigate the whole of cosmic reality, but each does so from its own modal viewpoint.

In other words, theology and the other special sciences do not study certain parts of cosmic reality; this means that the whole distinction between *supernature* (the realm allegedly investigated by theology) and *nature* (the realm allegedly investigated by the other special sciences) is a priori untenable because different sciences do not investigate different realms (domains or parts of reality). All these sciences investigate one and the same cosmic reality, albeit from different modal angles. We can also say that all special sciences study one and the same revelation of God, because God's revelation in nature and his revelation in Scripture are not dualistically opposed, but they are basically one single revelation of God, of which Scripture is the center (Andree Troost).

Overlap with the Special Sciences

To put this as clearly as possible, *anything* in cosmic reality can come to the attention of the theologian, as well as things in nature, although they are always seen from the viewpoint of faith, that is, from a pistical angle. Conversely, *anything* in Scripture can come to the attention of *any* non-theological scientist, although each scientist will consider such a point from his own specific modal perspective. I gave some examples for this in chapter 3; let me now give a more complete list:

(a) *Arithmetic*: At what points in the Old Testament does the Hebrew word *êleph* mean "thousand," and where does it mean "clan" or "squad"? What is the consequence of this for the allegedly exaggerated numbers of Israelites in Numbers 1?

(b) *Geometry*: How can it be said that the "sea of cast metal" in the temple of Solomon measured ten cubits from rim to rim, and that its circumference was thirty cubits (instead of 31.4 cubits, according to the value of π) (1 Kings 7:23)? Did Jews at that time use a value of 3 for π (which is hardly imaginable), or was the diameter measured from the outside of the rim of the "sea", and the circumference from the inside of the rim?

(c, d) *Physics (kinematics and energetics)*: The astronomer may be interested in the biblical cosmography, or picture of the universe, as compared with cosmographies from other cultures and other time periods. Does the biblical cosmography presuppose a flat earth, or a global earth? What is the meaning of the "vault" over the earth, which we find many times, from Genesis 1 onward, a vault "in" which are the celestial bodies, and "beyond" which are waters?

(e) *Biology*: What is the possible biological, medical, hygienic, or sanitary significance of the distinction between the "clean" and "unclean" animals in the Bible (Lev. 11; Deut. 14)? What do the descriptions of the animal world in Job 38-41 tell us about biological knowledge at the time? And just how accurate was this knowledge?

(f, g) *Perception and sensitive psychology*: The psychologist may pay attention to what the Bible has to say about the heart, the soul, and the spirit, the many meanings of these terms, and their inter-relationships.

(h) *Logic*: How do logical arguments function in the Bible, for instance, in the Letters to the Romans or the Hebrews? What syllogisms could we isolate in the reasoning found there? Could we, with our present-day ideas about logic, identify logical flaws in the Bible?

(i) *Historiography*: The historian may be interested in what the Bible has to say about ancient history. For instance, can he identify the rather mysterious figure of Darius the Mede in Daniel 6? Or how does the "feast" lasting 180 days in Esther 1:4 relate to what we know of Persian history at the time?

(j) *Linguistics*: What is the precise linguistic meaning of what happened at the confusion of languages in Babel (Gen. 11:1-9), and the apparent lifting of this confusion in Acts 2? What is the linguistic significance of glossolalia (or speaking in tongues) in general?

(k) *Sociology*: When and how did the tribal community of Israel develop into a true nation, and when did it become a true nation state? In what way, if any, were the typical tribal characteristics of Israel maintained, especially after the Babylonian exile and during the New Testament period?

(l) *Economics*: The economist may be interested in the economic relationships in ancient Israel (e.g., Lev. 25), which made both (extreme) capitalism (landlordism) and communism impossible, or those in the early church (Acts 2-5, with possible economic consequences among later Messianic Jews in Palestine; cf. Rom. 15:26).

(m) *Aesthetics*: It is striking that the notion of *beauty* in the Old Testament is most strongly linked with feminine beauty. What sense of beauty does the Bible recognize apart from the beauty of human beings?

(n) *Legal sciences*: The legal scientist may focus on elementary juridical principles in the law of Moses, such as retribution, legal accountability, the relationship between crime and punishment, etc.

(o) *Ethics*: Is there any progress in moral values from the earliest to the latest parts of the Old Testament, for instance when it comes to marriage? What, if any, are the ethical differences between the Old and the New Testament?

Some Concluding Remarks

To be sure, in most of the cases just mentioned the problems we have listed will hardly be studied by other special scientists, but rather by theologians. The reason for this is that, in Scripture, all these matters are viewed from the angle of faith (the pistical viewpoint). But that does not change the fact that the matters mentioned are of a particular nature, whether that be arithmetical, geometrical, or of some other kind.

Every believing scientist—and of course this is what *every* scientist should be—will be able to make fruitful use of biblical insights and principles without making his field of study "sacred," "supernatural," or "theological." And theology can study the whole of creational reality—always strictly from a pistical viewpoint—without ever "profaning" itself. Scripture is not the exclusive domain of theology, just as nature and culture are not the exclusive domains of the natural and the cultural sciences, respectively. There is no single element in this world about which Scripture does not make some fundamental statement, and at the same time there is no subject in reality about which theology speaks as the *only* one (Johan A. Heyns).

There is still one view that I would like to discuss briefly here, namely the view of the South African philosopher Hendrik

WHAT THEN *IS* THEOLOGY?

G. Stoker (1899-1993). Stoker is of special interest because, after Dooyeweerd and Vollenhoven, he may be called the third founding father of the Christian philosophy that I have described in *Wisdom for Thinkers*. Stoker makes an interesting distinction between theology, philosophy, and the special sciences. The latter each investigate a certain aspect of cosmic reality. Philosophy studies the totality of cosmic reality, and Stoker therefore calls it a *universal* science. Theology supplies every special science with fundamental truths, and for this reason it is called a *foundational* science.

As far as I can see, the basic mistake that has been made here is that these "fundamental truths" underlying all special sciences are not supplied by theology. They come from Scripture. This is not a mere quibble; Scripture and theology are not identical. Scripture underlies our Christian pre-theoretical worldview, which in turn forms the basis for our Christian (theoretical-philosophical) cosmology. This cosmology is the foundation for our entire scientific enterprise. Neither theology, nor philosophy, can or should take the place of this biblical worldview, which forms the foundation for all sciences alike. Theology is just as dependent on this Scriptural worldview as any other special science. No science can be truly foundational in the sense in which only Scripture can be. Here again, we encounter the danger of putting Scripture and theology on the same level, or, so to speak, in the same "theological space" (Karl Barth), in the same (Scholastic) "upper storey" of grace (or supernature).

However, in one respect we can follow Stoker to some extent. Theology definitely plays a useful and important role in the *formation* of a truly Christian view of the world and of life by helping to understand the Scriptures on all the relevant points it covers. We could not very well imagine a "Christian worldview" of whatever nature without any influence of Christian theology. We might even be suspicious of such a worldview, because it is probably biblicistic! But we continue to remember that such a worldview is not theological in nature (nor, for that matter, is it philosophical).

Moreover, the contribution of theology should be modest; it should *influence* the formation of the Christian worldview, not *re-*

place it. Andree Troost, himself Reformed, mentions that Herman Dooyeweerd several times expresses his *confessional* prolegomena, which evidently had undergone the strong theological influence of the great Reformed theologians of his youth, Abraham Kuyper and Herman Bavinck. If we desire a *Christian* worldview to underlie all scientific activity, it should be of an ecumenical character. That is, it should exhibit as few particulars as possible that are Catholic, Lutheran, Reformed, Evangelical, Pentecostal, etc., but it should instead go back to the great central truths that all orthodox Christians throughout the centuries have held in common.

Chapter Five

THEOLOGY AND CONFESSION

When we speak of the relationship between practical faith knowledge and theoretical-theological knowledge, we have to realize that church creeds, confessions, and catechisms are important forms in which that practical faith knowledge throughout the ages has expressed itself. It is therefore important to take a closer look at the relationship between theology on the one hand and confessions, creeds and catechisms on the other.

One of the reasons this question is relevant is that traditional Roman Catholics and Protestants have often claimed that theology is a "function" of the church, and therefore ought to be bound to a church confession. Evangelical Christians in the stricter sense, i.e., those who prefer free churches and claim to be non-confessional, generally do not like such an idea at all. Nevertheless, they too should be interested in this question because of the underlying problem concerning the identity of theology. Is it an (academically) *free* science, or a *church* (ecclesial) science? Or is it both, or neither?

Dogmatics and the Church

For clarification, let me make the following distinctions right away: (a) *faith* is practical-concrete; (b) the *confession* (or the doctrine, the dogma, the creed, the catechism) is systematic-concrete; and (c) *theology* (the theoretical science of the Christian faith) is systematic-abstract. In other words, faith and confession both belong to practical Christian life, whereas theology is of a theoretical nature. Confession and theology are both of a systematic nature (though systematic in a different way), whereas faith—in the sense of the transcendent *fides qua*—is not systematic, although it may be cast in the immanent form of a *fides quae*, the *depositum fidei*.

I add to these points the following considerations: (a) faith is primarily an *individual* matter; (b) the confession is an *ecclesial* (or, church) matter; and (c) theology is an *academic* matter. Whereas faith is individual, confession and theology each belong to societal communities, namely the church and the academy respectively. It is to be emphasized from the outset that church and academy are definitely not the same.

When Karl Barth wrote his systematic theology he opted single-mindedly for the title *Church Dogmatics*. He saw his work as a *kerygmatic* dogmatics, because it ties in with the preaching (Greek *kèrygma*) by "the church." Therefore Barth begins by saying that dogmatics is a theological discipline, but that theology is a function as well as a measuring-rod of "the church," and is subservient to church preaching.

Barth quotes the well-known German Lutheran theologian Johann Gerhard (1582-1637) who described theology as (a) *fides et religio Christiana* ("Christian faith and religion"), (b) *functio ministerii Ecclesiastici* ("a function of church ministry"), and (c) *accuratior divinorum mysteriorum cognitio* ("a more accurate knowledge of the divine mysteries"). My comments on these points are as follows: (a) Theology is not faith as such but the study of Christian beliefs. (b) "The church" as a denomination or a local congregation is confused here with the community of faith in the transcendent sense, a community that expresses itself in *many different* societal relationships. (See below for a more in-depth discussion.) (c) A "more accurate" knowledge than what? Than the true faith of the heart? An immanent-logical analysis of these "divine mysteries" lags far behind the transcendent-existential knowledge that the believing heart has of these mysteries.

The idea that theology belongs to the church, or, as Friedrich Schleiermacher (1768-1834) said, to the church leaders, is widespread. I could quote many German, Dutch, and North American theologians who are of the same opinion. Abraham Kuyper points to the fact that the traditional name for systematic theology, *dogmatics*, clearly indicates its ecclesial character, for a dogma is a decree of "the church." Another indication is the fact that many church denominations have their own explicitly denominational theological academies or faculties, which are intended to serve these denominations. Thus, the Theological University in Apeldoorn serves the Christian Reformed Churches in the Netherlands, and Calvin Theological Seminary in

Grand Rapids, Michigan, serves the Christian Reformed Churche in
North America.

Academic Freedom

This is exactly where the problem lies. Is a theological faculty a
center of scholarly theological investigation, or is it a training center for certain (ecclesial) offices? Can the two be combined in one
school in a reasonable way, without one or even both of them suf-
fering as a result of this arrangement? Can you tell the students
what they later will have to teach to the members of their particular denomination, while at the same time guaranteeing them academic freedom? Is true academic freedom even possible at such
an institution, given the fact that the school and the professors
and lecturers are subsidized by the denomination concerned, and
are under the surveillance of its representatives?

My critical question is in no way to be confused with the secular idea of the autonomy of reason. I do not believe in this idea at
all. My suspicion flows forth from a very different consideration,
namely, *sphere-sovereignty* (see the two previous volumes in this
series for a detailed discussion). Sphere-sovereignty is Abraham
Kuyper's term for the relative sovereignty of the various *spheres*
(societal relationships), in this case, a church denomination and
an academic institution. There is no question whatsoever of in-
dependence or autonomy because *both* the church and the academy *must be rooted in the biblical ground-motive*. But they should not
meddle in each other's affairs. On the one hand, theologians in
their quality as theologians should not rule over the faith of the
church by dictating its creeds (which then will inevitably have a
theological color; see further down for examples). Church confessions must be determined by *churches*, not by academics.

On the other hand, the church should not dominate the scientific
activities of the theologians by subjecting them to constant surveillance. The simple reason is that the church *as such* is ill-equipped to
judge theological theories; only the academic community is qualified to do so. This is not to deny that the believing theologian is
bound to a biblical ground-motive, but only that churches have the
capacity to evaluate academic work. The church is the church, and

the academy is the academy. The church does not judge, still less rule over, the academy, and the academy does not judge, still less rule over, the church. *That* is what sphere-sovereignty is all about: the one is not to meddle in the affairs of the other.

This is purely a matter of principle. The Christian theologian is strictly bound to the authority of Scripture, and also to academic rules for doing science, *not* to rules of "the church," that is, a specific church denomination. The only exception is the case of flagrant heresy, that is, false doctrine that undermines the foundations of Christianity itself. In such a case, the theologian would fall under church discipline, just like any other church member. Even then, as a matter or principle, he is not academically judged as a theologian, but ecclesiastically judged as a heretic.

As the Reformed theologian and philosopher from the Netherlands Andree Troost (1916-2008) puts it: "Theology *as such* is *not* (!) a priori to comply with the church confessions, for these are not of a theological nature, and have no scientific-theological authority whatsoever. They are confessions of a living *faith!* Whoever treats the biblical and the more systematic church 'doctrine' of the *confessions* as *theology*, plants a time bomb under the unity of his church denomination. ... As an institutional organization, the church of Christ is not rooted in *theology*, but in a common *faith*. ... And a genuine theological education must declare that it agrees to be bound to a confession, that this binding is the norm *for the theologians' faith*, but *not for their theology*."

The Meaning of "Dogma"

We can learn from history how the idea arose that dogmatics is subservient to the church. The term *dogmatics* literally means the study of dogmas, and these are by definition *church* dogmas. In the New Testament, the Greek word *dogma* means "decree," whether that be an imperial decree (Luke 2:1), an apostolic decree (Acts 16:4), or a decree in the Mosaic law (Eph. 2:15). A second meaning of *dogma* is "tenet, canon, doctrine," which we find in several early Christian writings. The early church began using this term for divine tenets and ordinances, revealed in Christ and in Scripture, and afterwards laid down in church decrees.

In its strict church historical sense, *dogma* is an authoritative doctrinal statement made by the church. The most important of these statements were about (a) the deity of Christ, who is of the same being as the Father (Council of Nicea, 325), (b) the "eternal generation" of the Son by the Father (Council of Constantinople, 381), (c) the deity of the Holy Spirit (which completed the doctrine of the Trinity) (Constantinople, 381), (d) Christ as one person, and therefore Mary as the Mother of God because Jesus is God (Ephesus, 431), (e) the two natures of Christ, who is true God and true Man in one person (Chalcedon, 451).

In the most fundamental sense, the early Church knew only two dogmas: the Trinitarian dogma (about the three persons in the one Godhead) and the Christological dogma (about the divine and the human nature of Christ). This means that Eastern Orthodox Christians, Roman Catholics, and traditional Protestants (at least formally, if not always in practice) stand on the common ground of the Nicene Creed (325/381) and the decrees of Chalcedon (451). Many "free" churches do not recognize these dogmas formally, but they do substantially. All these Christians together form by far the greatest part of Christendom.

In a wider sense, we can take *dogmas* to mean *all* doctrinal statements made by the church, including Protestant ones. Thus, the Canons of Dort (about predestination and human responsibility), established in the Netherlands by the Synod of Dordrecht (1618-1619), could be called a church *dogma*, despite the fact that it is limited to Reformed Christians. Some theologians, such as Emil Brunner, are of the opinion that, strictly speaking, Protestant churches acknowledge no dogmas, only confessions.

Yet, interestingly, the term *dogmatics*, derived from "dogma," arose in Protestantism. Early Lutheran theologians distinguished between a *dogmatic*, that is, a doctrinal, and a *historical* content of Scripture. In the seventeenth century, several Protestant theologians began to use the term *dogmatic theology*, which actually was not limited to the literal church dogmas but simply meant "doctrinal theology," the theology of church doctrines in the widest sense. However, some emphasis on authoritative church tenets remained: Christian doctrine was considered to be that which is invested with the church's authority. In this sense, we

WHAT THEN *IS* THEOLOGY?

have some fresh insight into what Karl Barth meant when he called his systematic theology a *church* dogmatics (see above): dogmatics is the study of doctrines maintained and authorized by the church. However, this still leaves us with a problem: is it fundamentally correct to force academic theology to subscribe to authoritative church canons, without sacrificing its academic freedom?

We can relativize this problem a little by relativizing the meaning of dogmas a little:

(a) The *immanent* aspect. Today, not many will accept the statement made by Athenagoras in the second century that dogmas "do not stem from people but have been spoken and taught by God." Many theologians will recognize that dogmas are immanent, humanly fallible formulations of faith contents which themselves are basically transcendent and infallible. In the latter, supra-rational sense, the biblical truth is beyond all criticism. But the immanent, humanly fallible, and defective formulation of it is not. God's Word is absolute, whereas all tenets, canons, and dogmas humanly derived from it are relative. Dogmas are *not* "taken" or "deduced" from Scripture, for Scripture does not "contain" dogmas. At best, dogmas are "inspired" or "evoked" by Scripture. Therefore, strictly speaking, Christians are not bound to dogmas but to Scripture—although they may believe that certain dogmas are the best human expressions available of certain biblical truths.

(b) The *historical* aspect. Dogmas never really stay the same. The wording may remain unchanged, but words take on different connotations in different ages; our "context" differs greatly from that of our ancestors. Most Christians still believe that the Son is of the same "substance" as the Father; but for us, the word "substance" has become misleading. It can mean many things to us, but we hardly think of the meaning that terms like Greek *hypostasis* or *homo-ousios* (from *ousia*, "being") had for fourth-century Christians. We still believe that we are justified by faith—but are we speaking of forensic, imputative, or ethical justification? *Confessing* your faith is one thing—but usually at that point the theological analysis of the matter has not even *started*. We may accept the Belgic Confession—but we can be sure that the phrase "true church" (Art. 29) sounds very differently today than it did in the sixteenth century. The term "accursed idolatry" used in the Heidelberg Catechism (see Answer 80) has come to sound as questionable in our ears as it was acceptable in sixteenth-century Protestant ears.

Dogmas change, even if their wording does not. It has sometimes been said that if someone wants to say the *same* things as in earlier centuries, he often has to say them *di erently* today.

The Place of the Confession

Protestants have always underscored the rule *Sola Scriptura* ("by Scripture alone") of the Reformation, but dogmas are not identical with Scripture. Church dogmas and theological doctrines are not "revelational truths," but humanly fallible attempts to *approximate* the truth. The utterances of both the church, that is, dogmas, and those of the academy, that is, theories, always remain subject to the Word of God. This is why even the most cherished confessions *in principle* always remain open to critical testing, although this should be done by church members, not by theologians. Think of the right of *gravamen* ("objection") in the Reformed churches with respect to confessions and church doctrines. The Word always has the last word over all *our* words. Of course, this Word has to be expounded; our understanding of it depends on correct exegesis, but also our exegesis is always to be checked against the Word it-self. We can never escape from this "hermeneutical circle" (see my *Wisdom for Thinkers* for this important expression).

Strictly speaking, the term *Sola Scriptura* logically contradicts itself, for it cannot be derived from Scripture. Nor—as Karl Barth emphasized—can it be scientifically demonstrated to be better than alternative views. In its primacy as our ultimate normative authority, Scripture cannot be deduced or derived from any other authority—it has to be received in faith. Barth saw in this viewpoint the only answer to both modernism, which rejects authority, and Roman Catholicism, which factually transfers this authority to the church. He says that dogmatics is not the science of dogmas, but of *the* dogma, that is, the agreement of the *kèrygma* ("preaching, message") with God's revelation. According to him, we are here *in statu confessionis* ("in the position of confessing"): we can only confess here our "ultimate commitment," whilst "proofs" are excluded, even if we are always obliged to give an *a posteriori* account for this ultimate commitment.

Many Evangelical denominations have difficulties with doctrines that have been formally established by churches on the basis of some alleged ecclesiastical authority. Sometimes they even see in this a relic of Catholic "leaven," and mistrust every form of formal church "authority." Other Christians have condemned this view as "biblicistic," especially if they see an ahistorical or even an anti-historical element in it. Behind this difference of opinion, there is an ecclesiological difference, in particular with respect to church structure, whether this structure be of the Episcopalian, Presbyterian, or Congregational variety. What is "the church"? Is it any random denomination? Where is the body within a church (whether it consist of bishops, elders, or synods) that can *formally* claim the authority to establish the doctrine of "the church," and to impose this on its members, as it does in creeds, confessions, and catechisms?

It is hardly relevant to refer here to the apostolic meeting in Acts 15, even if the *ius dogmatum cudendorum* ("right to establish dogmas") has always been based on this chapter. First, this gathering was not a "synod" or a "council" at all, but was explicitly the meeting of the *local* church of Jerusalem (vv. 4, 22). Second, its decree was binding for the churches, not because the *church* decided anything but, because the decree was invested with *apostolic*—not "synodical"—authority. Third, in fact no dogmas in the sense of doctrinal canons were involved here, but only regulations for the practical dealings between Jewish and Gentile believers.

Not only Evangelical but also Lutheran and Reformed theologians have expressed their doubts with regard to the whole matter of the church authoritatively stating doctrines. Emil Brunner saw in it a dangerous overestimation of the community, more specifically of church organizations, as a guarantee for the truth. He points to the important fact that, in *all* creeds and confessions that have appeared so far, we have afterwards discovered elements that turned out to be doubtful. With *unconditional* authority, Brunner says, canons were issued that in certain points were afterwards viewed as *untenable*. Think of Greek-philosophical concepts in the ancient creeds (*homo-ousia, physis*), and the Latin *anima rationalis* ("rational soul") of Jesus in the Athanasian Creed. These are terms that are not only unscientific but also foreign to the spirit of the New Testament. Nevertheless, the Athanasian Creed tells us that those who do not accept its tenets cannot be saved!

Binding to a Confession

In our discussion so far we can easily distinguish two extremes. On the one hand, there is a church that formally and compulsorily prescribes to its members, in great detail, what they are to believe. Such a denomination could easily fall into the snare of confessionalism: factually placing the confession on the same level as Scripture itself, if not above Scripture, and demanding a formal common agreement on many theological issues that do not touch the salvific foundations of our faith. Compare the well-known maxim, *in necessariis unitas, in dubiis libertas, in omnibus caritas* ("In essentials unity, in doubtful things liberty, in all things charity"). That is, denominations should limit themselves to imposing only the "essetial" things.

On the other hand, an (often biblicistic and ahistorical) resistance to any form of confession or creed can lead to a dangerous individualism and solipsism. No church denomination or local congregation can get around the demand of having some common opinion, or consensus, as to what basic canons of faith they accept. If they think they can do without this agreement, you will see that, as soon as a doctrinal conflict arises, they are either totally confused and fall apart, or you will discover that they possess some unwritten "creed," supplied by the leaders, which expresses what the church believes. This situation is usually typical for sectarian groups with a strong central leadership.

Keep in mind that the theologian is usually a church member, a believer like all the others, and as such, he may be expected to share in the consensus about the main tenets of the Christian truth. Of course, if (systematic) theology wishes to be truly academic, it cannot be bound to the confessions of a certain denomination. However, as a common believer the theologian is bound to the main lines of the consensus in his faith community. If it were otherwise, no church discipline with regard to heresy would be possible (cf.

Rom. 16:17; Gal. 5:7-10; 1 Tim. 1:3; 4:6-7; 6:3-6, 20; Titus 1:9-11; 3:9-11; 2 John 9-11; Rev. 2:14-16). As a *theologian*, the believer is academically free; as a believer, the theologian is bound to the consensus of his church.

Confession and Theology

In the Netherlands, the Reformed philosopher Klaas J. Popma (1903-1986) has formulated the relationship between confession and theology as follows:

(a) *Agreement*. There is an indirect, but clear and important relationship between confession and theology, in the sense that *both* are (or must be) *rooted in the same biblical ground-motive*. As I have explained earlier, such a ground-motive is of a transcendent, existential, supralingual, and supra-rational nature (that is, surpassing lingual and rational formulations), and is therefore never to be confused with a confession, which is of an immanent, lingual, and rational nature.

(b) *Distinction*. A confession of faith is a *church* matter, while a (systematic) theology is an *academic* matter. The two societal communities involved, namely the church and the academy, are never to be confused. Where this still happens, two dangers can arise. The one is that the church begins to rule over theology, or at least over its foundations. However, church organizations are neither equipped, nor formally qualified, for the task of supervising theologians. For instance, the catechism is a *church* matter, not a form of "theological" instruction. Teaching a congregation is essentially different from teaching a class of theology students; the former is for the practical building up of faith, the latter is for the increase of theoretical-theological knowledge.

The other danger is that theologians begin to rule over their denomination, or at least over its confessions. Their power may become so great that "the church" does not dare to confess its faith anymore without the regulations and the authority of science. It is easy to understand why church denominations require their church leaders and preachers to be academically trained. But it is easily forgotten that theologians are first and foremost academicians, and *not* necessarily church leaders or preachers. The two categories can easily be confused. If we compare other fields of society, we will find similar situations. Political scientists would not necessarily make good politicians, and vice versa. Medical researchers would not necessarily make good physicians, and vice versa. Researchers within the legal sciences would not necessarily make good judges, and vice versa. The ideal church would not necessarily be one made up of theologians who, in this capacity, had a decisive say in matters of doctrine, liturgy, church government, etc. Theology can be a great help, but the church is made up of its *members*, not of theologians.

The confusion between church and academy has disturbing consequences. It leads either to *churchism* (overestimation of the church with respect to theology), or *scientism* (overestimation of theology with respect to the church), or both. Because of an insufficient recognition of *sphere sovereignty*, people came to the idea that dogmatics had to be *church dogmatics* (see above) because the church, according to the Scholastic way of thinking, encompassed the whole of the Christian life of faith. Of course, theology was to be subservient to the whole of the Christian community—but strictly speaking, *the church* is only one of the societal relationships within this Christian commonwealth. Christians are not just church members, they are also marriage partners, parents and children, teachers and students, state authorities and subjects, employers and employees, etc. (this is discussed in great detail in Volume 2 of this series, *Power in Service*).

If you allow me to exaggerate a little, dogmatics could just as easily—or rather, just as incorrectly—be called "marriage dogmatics," or "family dogmatics," or "school dogmatics," or "company dogmatics." This is because Christian couples, families, schools, companies, etc., are rooted in exactly the same Christian ground-motive as a church denomination or local congregation on the one hand, and the Christian theological academy on the other. The Christian commonwealth, that is, the Kingdom of God (see my *Power in Service*), consists not only of Christian churches but also of Christian marriages, Christian families, Christian schools, Christian companies, Christian associations, Christian political parties, etc. Perhaps, instead of speaking of church dogmatics, we would do better to speak of Kingdom dogmatics.

The Swiss Reformed theologian Heinrich Ott (1929-2013) has summarized this view in a way that comes very close to what I have presented here:

WHAT THEN *IS* THEOLOGY?

(a) The theologian must not allow any church authority or confession to put immovable fences around him. He must remain free. In cases of doubt he must appeal to Scripture alone, and nothing else. (This last point is important; in my terminology, the theologian is never free from his transcendent-religious faith, which is either anastatic or apostatic. He is never free from his conscience, or from his duty to submit to God's Word and the guidance of the Holy Spirit.)

(b) The previous point implies that the theologian has to relativize not only all extant church authorities and confessions, but also himself. He should never view his "formulations" as ultimate truth "formulas." His work is nothing more or less than a contribution to the encompassing dialogue of the church. (I would like to add this distinction: as an *academic,* the theologian contributes to the dialogue of the *scientific* community of theologians, whereas, as a *believer,* he contributes to the ongoing dialogue of the *church* community.)

(c) The theologian not only has a (passive) "receptive" but also an (active) "formative" bond with the church. That is, he not only receives faith impulses from the community of faith, but also feeds something back to the church with his theological theories. (Again I would like to make here the distinction between theoretical theology and practical faith and church life: the church does not *need* theories, but they *can* help to sharpen its Scriptural teaching and preaching.)

Church—Academy—Faith Community

We have seen that, in his theological activity, a believing theologian realizes that he is bound to Scripture as well as to every confession which, as far as he knows, was really composed in the spirit of Scripture. That is not the issue. The issue is that theology is a *theoretical* activity, whereas neither Scripture, nor any confession, explicitly deals with *theological* problems as such. The confession simply moves on a different plane than the theologians' theoretical-analytical activities.

The difference between theology and confession is *not* that dogmatics is more "systematic" than any confession, as some have suggested. In fact, creeds, confessions, catechisms, and the like, are usually constructed in a very systematic way. That is not the point. The point is that theology and confession differ in *nature*. A confession is the testimony, given in faith, with respect to what God has revealed to people in Scripture. Neither this speaking by God, nor the believing response given by humans, is of a theoretical, detached, analytical nature. A confession is basically a matter of practical intimacy between God and Man.

This intimacy is never to be theoreticalized, that is, to be "degraded" to theology or philosophy. The practical faith attitude is immediate, encompassing, concrete, a matter of the transcendent-religious *heart*. The theoretical attitude, however, is detached, one-sided—only one modal aspect is considered—analytical-abstract, a matter of immanent *reason*. The former leads to the joy of intimacy with God, while the latter leads to the joy of a better logical understanding of the truth. The two are *related* in the sense that intimacy with God can be a fantastic impulse for every believing theologian, and, conversely, a deepened theological understanding can help the theologian to develop a closer communion with God. But faith and theology are never identical.

As I have noted earlier, although a church confession cannot belong to the prolegomena of theology, this does not mean that a believing theologian could not feel very attached, not only to Scripture but also to one or more Christian confessions. On the contrary, this will be a natural consequence of the fact that he is rooted in the biblical ground-motive. This places him in a *faith community*, where he interrelates with others who are committed to the same faith.

Again, we must distinguish here between the community of *the church* (a concrete church denomination or local congregation) and the scientific community of *theologians*. The one commonwealth of *faith*—the Kingdom of God—underlies both the church community and the academic community. A certain believer takes part in the former as a church member, and in the latter as a theologian (a faculty member). But in both cases he is first and foremost a believer, connected with all other believers on this earth. The same thing applies, by the way, for him as husband, parent, teacher or student, employer or employee, state citizen, party member, etc. In *this* commonwealth of faith in its widest sense, believers are not bound by whatever special (functional-modal, rational, lingual, pistical) creed or confession.

WHAT THEN *IS* THEOLOGY?

What does bind them is one and the same (supra-functional, supra-modal, supra-rational, supra-lingual, supra-pistical) transcendent-religious biblical ground-motive, which drives the hearts of all believers, no matter how divided they may be on many secondary and tertiary issues.

Confessions not Theological

Again, we have encountered here the essential difference between practical faith statements, such as creeds, confessions, and catechisms, and theoretical (theological) statements. Creeds, confessions, and catechisms were never intended to be theological declarations, like utterances of the academy, like theories that have been, or must be, checked by other theologians. They could not have been published as scientific articles in theological journals. They would not have been accepted by such journals because of the *lack* of any theological features. They exhibit all manner of theological imprecision that presents no problem at all in a confession, which speaks the everyday language of common believers. However, they *are* unacceptable in a theological treatise.

Take, for instance, the statement that, at the resurrection, body and soul are "reunited" (Heidelberg Catechism Q&A 57). This betrays some influence of Greek-dualistic thinking about soul and body, and would be inappropriate in any theological publication on the subject. But in everyday language it is much less of a problem. It is actually very difficult to express the miracle of resurrection in any other terms that would be just as easily accounted for theologically, and which would be equally simple. The example also shows that, although the catechism is not theological in nature, theological and philosophical influences can easily creep into it, because the latter have become part of our everyday Christian thinking. This phenomenon does not affect the basic character of the confession or catechism, however. It is a testimony of *faith*, of people's most inward, existential, transcendent convictions, even though it is expressed in immanent, everyday language.

It would be foolish to suggest that the language of theology is on a "higher" level than a plain testimony of faith. Take as an example the words used by the man and the woman in the Song of Solomon to describe each other's beauty (e.g., Song 4:1-15; 5:10-16). This language is warmer, loftier and more touching than any scientific analysis of human beauty could ever be. It is everyday language, used by people who are in love with each other. Imagine what might happen if someone were to analyze these descriptions of beauty in order to get a "higher" degree of scientific precision. Imagine that he argued that human beauty is rather ridiculous when you realize that 60 percent or more of the human body is made up of H_2O (i.e., water). Have we now arrived at a higher level of scientific accuracy? A scientific analysis could never form a continuum with a declaration of love; the idea would be preposterous. A judgment by aesthetic science is *essentially* different from—and never "higher" than—the deeply admiring voice of love. And this, in a sense, is what a creed or a confession is: a passionate declaration of love, not a cool statement of theological science.

Imagine that someone analyzes Matt. 5:45 ("God makes his sun rise"), only to find in it a double flaw. First, he would say, it is not God who makes the sun rise, but the natural laws he instituted in the beginning. And second, he would add, the sun does not *rise* at all; it is the earth that revolves. What heartfelt thanks we would give him for these corrections! Do we, with their help, now possess a better Bible, or a better understanding of the Bible? I could give you many more examples of this kind. But we need to ask ourselves whether a scientifically "corrected" Bible, or a "theologicalized" confession for that matter, gives us an improved product? We may stumble over the way in which the verse I have just quoted expresses a certain truth, and at the same time miss out on this truth altogether. In such a case, we strain out a gnat but swallow the camel (Matt. 23:24). We deal with the verse as if it were an astronomic statement, and criticize it as such, but we pass over the real intention of the verse as a believing statement about the faithfulness of God. There can never be continuums between astronomic statements and faith statements, because they differ in the most fundamental possible way. Theologians only begin to speak of a continuum after they have first *theologicalized* the everyday language of faith, or of confessions of faith.

Soteriology says, "The biblical doctrine of salvation is as follows . . ." The confession says, "I belong unto *my* faithful Savior Jesus Christ, who . . . delivered me" (Heidelberg Catechism, Q&A 1). The former is a theoretical treatise, while the latter is a very personal proclamation of faith. What continuum could one possibly find here?

Christology says, "The biblical doctrine of Christ is as follows . . ." The Bible says, "*My* lover is radiant and ruddy" (Song 5:10). Christology says, "The Lordship of Christ entails . . ." Thomas says, "*My* Lord and *my* God" (John 20:28; cf. Phil. 3:8). There is absolutely *nothing* personal about (scientific) Christology; on the contrary, its objective, detached character is essential to it. As for the confession, however, there is absolutely nothing *im*personal about it. Christology argues about whether Christ can be called "Lord" and "God." Thomas simply does it, in a very personal way.

Theology proper (i.e., the doctrine of God) speaks about God, but never in a personal way. But the apostle Paul, as a "common believer," can say, "*My* God will meet all your needs . . ." (Phil. 4:19). Almost the first words of the Canons of Dort are: "*Our* Lord and Savior Jesus Christ."

Soteriology tries to explain what divine forgiveness is in an impersonal way. To be sure, even the creeds sometimes speak in a somewhat impersonal way as well. The Apostles' Creed states simply: "I believe in the forgiveness of sins." However, such a confession is worthless if it is not expressed as a testimony of one's personally being forgiven (cf. Ps. 32:1). It would be dreadful to confess one's belief in the divine forgiveness of sins without having the assurance of having received forgiveness for one's own sins. The believer may exclaim with delight, "I am forgiven!" However, in cool, detached, analytical soteriology, things are very different. Unfortunately, it is not too hard to imagine a theologian who is very clever, academically speaking, but who, on a personal level, has no interest whatsoever in the forgiveness of his or her sins.

Theology and Church Divisions

One cause for the confusion between theology and practical faith language is that people began to look for assurance of their faith within theology. Certain denominations do not have this problem to the same degree because they look elsewhere for assurance. Roman Catholic Christians look to the hierarchy of their church (from their priests and bishops all the way to their pope).

Charismatic believers also look to their leaders, who allegedly have the fullness of the Spirit. It can only be hoped that Catholic and Charismatic leaders are men of God.

Now, I realize, of course, that theologians also may be men (and women) of God. But this is not the main reason why common church members look to them: it is because of their respect for science, which has become an integral part of our entire modern Western culture. Usually there is a scientist at your bedside when you are born and another one in attendance when you die. Almost every domain of society, including politics and even the arts, is governed by scientists. So it is really no wonder that modern churches are dominated by scientists too. In some Reformed denominations, elders are not allowed to administer the sacraments or pronounce the blessing over the congregation because they are not scientifically trained theologians. You have to be a scientific theologian to be able to bless, baptize, or break the bread.

Besides—or even instead of—believing in Christ, so many Christians began to believe in theology. Or they turned things upside down by beginning to believe in their creeds instead of accepting them as an expression of their beliefs. What was even worse was that they began to elevate theological differences of opinion to the level of confessional questions, and from there to vital faith differences. This is one of the saddest consequences of all the confusion: theological differences were treated as *faith* problems and, as such, imposed on common church people, who were thus forced to take sides in nasty church divisions. This is a shame, since *purely* theological differences should never be allowed to divide God's people. In my opinion, not even confessional differences should be allowed to cause a church division unless the very foundations of Christianity are at stake.

The rule of thumb is as follows: if you really believe the other party could not possibly be called Christians anymore because of its heresies, you are entitled to separate from them. As the apostle John says, "Everyone who goes on ahead and does not abide in the teaching of Christ, does not have God. Whoever abides in the teaching has both the Father and the Son. If anyone comes to you and does not bring this teaching, do not receive him into your house or give him any greeting, for whoever greets him takes part in his wicked works" (2 John 9-11).

WHAT THEN *IS* THEOLOGY?

It may be an open question whether the "teaching of Christ" means here "the teaching by Christ" (subjective genitive), or "the teaching *concerning* Christ" (objective genitive). Whatever it is, the teaching *by* Christ is never to be confused with the teaching by theologians, and the teaching *concerning* Christ is never to be confused with theological Christology. In the latter, many problems are dealt with that should never become points of division among the saints. For example, think of theories about the "eternal generation" of the Son (a matter never explicitly dealt with in Scripture!), about the precise nature of Christ's *kenosis* (his "emptying himself"; cf. Phil. 2:7), about his having one will (monothelitism), or two wills which were divine and human (dyothelitism). This controversy involved the two natures of Christ, his divine and his human nature, and the relationship between them.

In the past, the problem of the one will or the two wills was imposed on the whole church (at the Third Council of Constantinople, 680-681), and even led to divisions between monothelitists and dyothelitists. Today, many theologians would be at a loss if they were forced to choose between these two sides! Monothelitists run the danger of monophysitism (not distinguishing enough between the divine and the human nature of Christ), whereas dyothelitists run the danger of Nestorianism (creating too sharp a separation between the two natures of Christ). Here, fools can easily rush in where angels fear to tread!

Theologians should sometimes be ashamed of themselves. Of course, speculating on matters that Scripture is altogether silent about, is to a certain extent allowed; we should not hinder academics from speculating! But preaching these speculations as divine truth, and enforcing them on common Christians, and in this way even creating church divisions, is pure *hybris* (arrogance towards God). It is like the sin of "looking into the ark of the LORD," for which the men of Beth-Shemesh were heavily struck (1 Sam. 6:19 ASV, NIV, NKJV). "As for a person who stirs up division, after warning him once and then twice, have nothing more to do with him" (Titus 3:10). "I appeal to you, brothers, to watch out for those who cause divisions and create obstacles contrary to the doctrine that you have been taught; avoid them" (Rom. 16:17).

The Extra-Calvinisticum

Sometimes you see that even within the confessions the Christians who put them together (inevitably theologians) could not resist the temptation to include a typically theological issue that was hotly disputed in their day, thus burdening common Christians with it. A striking example of this is a point on which Calvinists differed from Lutherans. This little piece of polemics managed to get a place in the Heidelberg Catechism. Luther claimed that Jesus after his resurrection was omnipresent not only as far as his divine nature, but also as far as his human nature was concerned. Reformed theologians did not agree; they claimed that, as far as his human nature was concerned, Jesus was not omnipresent, even after his resurrection (Q&A 47).

At this point the Catechism continues with the question: "But if his human nature is not present wherever his Godhead is, are not then these two natures in Christ separated from one another?" And it provides the following answer: "Not at all, for since the Godhead is illimitable and omnipresent, it must necessarily follow that the same is beyond the limits of the human nature he assumed, and yet is nevertheless in this human nature, and remains personally united to it" (Q&A 48).

One is astonished to find this piece of purely theological reasoning in what is intended as a textbook for young believers! The Lutherans called it the *extra-calvinisticum*, that is, the Calvinist idea that Christ's deity reaches "beyond" (*extra*) his human nature in that the glorified Christ was, by reason of his deity, still on the earth (because, being divine, he is omnipresent), but not by reason of his humanity. Thus, if Jesus promises to be in the midst of those who gather in his name (Matt. 18:20), it is the Son of God who is there, but not the Man Jesus Christ. This raises once again the ancient problem of the relationship between the two natures of Christ. The American theologian Donald G. Bloesch (1928-2010) put it this way: Lutherans risk being entangled in monophysitism and docetism (mixing the two natures too much), Calvinists risk being enmeshed in Nestorianism (splitting the two natures too much). There are no alternatives! You may go wrong in either of these two directions.

WHAT THEN *IS* THEOLOGY?

The discussion was important in the theological debate about the Lord's Supper. According to Zwingli and Calvin, Christ cannot personally be present as a Man under the symbols of bread and wine, which represent his body and blood, for as a Man he can be in only one place, and today that is at the right hand of God. According to Luther, however, the deity of Christ pervades his humanity in such a way that his humanity too can be everywhere, so that he can be *bodily* present in the Lord's Supper under the symbols of bread and wine. Among other things, it was this doctrine that has kept Lutherans and Calvinists apart since the sixteenth century! Today, this is hard to imagine.

It may be of some comfort to both parties to realize that the tension exists in the New Testament as well. At one point, Jesus says to his disciples, "You will not always have me [with you]" (Matt. 26:11; John 12:8) while he reassures them later with the words, "I am with you always" (Matt. 28:20; cf. John 14:18). Perhaps both parties in the Christological debates should have brought in the Holy Spirit: Christ is "with us"—also at the Lord's Supper—as the Spirit of Christ (Rom. 8:9; Phil. 1:19; 1 Pet. 1:11; cf. Acts 16:7; Gal. 4:6). This is not the divine nature of Christ, but the third person in the Trinity. I am not aware of anyone who has ever suggested this solution, which could have reconciled Lutherans and Calvinists at the time they were fighting over this issue.

However, the real question that concerns us now is this: Who would have the audacity to assert that anyone subscribing to the belief that Christ in his human nature is omnipresent—or is *not* omnipresent, for that matter—*could not be saved*? In what sense are the fundamentals of Christianity at stake here? Both parties believe that Christ is truly God and truly Man, and that his two natures are neither to be mixed too strongly, nor to be severed too sharply. The rest is fodder for theologians; they *thrive* on questions like this. It's in their nature. *But the church people should not be bothered with these issues,* and young Christians certainly should not be plagued with them in a textbook for beginners. They should be taught the essentials of the Christian faith. But they should not be badgered with theological problems that in themselves are interesting enough but do *not* belong to these essentials. And we should absolutely never divide God's people over them. *If* you want to divide them at all, then it should be *only over questions for which you yourself are prepared to give your life.*

Worth Dying For?

When contemplating his execution, the great Greek philosopher Socrates (469-399 B.C.) is said to have stated, "The one purpose of those who practice philosophy in the right way is to prepare themselves for dying and death." Almost two thousand years later, the French philosopher Michel de Montaigne (1533-1592) remarked, "All the wisdom and reasoning in the world eventually amounts to this: to teach us not to be afraid to die." Assuming that their respective philosophies helped them to die, one may wonder if they would have been prepared to die for these philosophies as such. Have there ever been great thinkers, including theologians, who would have been prepared to die for their own theories? Did Socrates die for his philosophy? He was executed on the charges of corrupting Athens' youth and refusing to honor the gods. That does not mean that he died for his philosophical theories, but for the Truth as he saw it.

The wise have always known that "the Truth" is far greater than even the best of our theories. Did Guido de Brès die in 1567 for the Belgic Confession he had written? Or did he die for his faith? He died neither for his confession, nor even for the "truths" contained in it, but for the Truth, or, even better, for him who is the Truth. What Calvinist would be willing to die for the *extra-calvinisticum*? And what Lutheran would be willing to die for the opposite view?

When Christians one day look death in the eye, they do not die for certain theological views they have held, no matter how much they may have cherished them. Strictly speaking, no one will even die for a certain confession, no matter how strongly he may believe that this confession is an accurate expression of his beliefs. Christians die for their *faith* in the sense of the *fides qua*. Of course, this can never be separated from certain *formulations* of that faith, for instance as we find them in certain confessions. But these immanent formulations are always as imperfect as faith itself (on the transcendent level) is perfect.

It is said that in our time more than one hundred thousand

WHAT THEN *IS* THEOLOGY?

Christians every year lose their lives as a consequence of their faith. We may be assured that, at the point of dying, all belief in one's own confessions and one's own theological theories pales. What remains is faith in its most elementary existential form, a form that transcends all that is rational. Or, to put it a better way, what remains is not *faith*, but the One towards whom that faith was oriented throughout life. Shortly before his martyrdom, Paul wrote, "I know whom I have believed" (2 Tim. 1:12). What do confessionalism and traditionalism, all philosophy and theology, all things that have bothered people so much in their lives, mean in the face of death? In the end, are not all confessions and all theologies simply ways of speaking about things that are not only greater than our understanding, but also greater than our hearts, things whose value never comes to light more clearly than in the hour of our death?

Six years after the writing of the Belgic Confession and shortly before his martyrdom, Guido de Brès wrote to his wife, Catherine Ramon, "At present, I put into practice that which I have preached so much to others. However, I must confess that, as I was preaching, I spoke about things that I am only now experiencing, just as a blind person speaks of colors. Since I was made prisoner I have made more progress and have learned more than during all the rest of my life. I am in a very good school. The Holy Spirit inspires me continually, and teaches me how to use the weapons in this battle."

Guido de Brès did not die for the Belgic Confession, but for the faith he had tried to express in it. In many details, its formulations are questionable; all these points have been fodder for theologians during the centuries since its composition. Therefore, it would be foolish for anyone to want to die for the sake of these formulations. It is equally foolish to make of these formulations an unassailable foundation for whole denominations, as well as a cause for divisions within these denominations. It is equally inappropriate to force academic theologians to submit *a priori* to these formulations. But it is worth living as well as dying for the *faith* that is confessed in the Belgic Confession. Christians are never to believe in the Belgic Confession for its own sake. Rather, they should believe in Christ as he, in an admittedly fallible way, is confessed in it, as well as in many other creeds, confessions, and catechisms. If this is true for Christians in general, it is certainly true for (believing) theologians.

Chapter Six

THEOLOGICAL ABSTRACTIONS, CONCEPTS & IDEAS

In my book *Wisdom for Thinkers* I dealt with several kinds of *abstraction* that play a role in scientific thinking. Among these were:

(a) The abstraction of the *universal*, i.e., disregarding the unique character of a phenomenon and searching for that which all such phenomena have in common. In this way, general principles (laws, norms) are formulated.

(b) The abstraction of the *objective*, i.e., disregarding personal feelings and prejudices in such a way that, under equal circumstances, another investigator would have obtained the same results.

(c) *Modal abstraction*: this is the abstraction of a certain modal aspect of cosmic reality. That is, a certain modality is abstracted from an entity, an event, or a state of affairs, which is the same as saying that that entity, event, or state of affairs is viewed from one modal viewpoint. Modal abstraction is the gateway to scientific analysis and theory building. It is this abstraction that is characteristic of the theoretical knowing-relationship. I have argued extensively that theology is the special science that investigates empirical reality from the pistical viewpoint (see chapter 3).

Let us now consider two *wrong* ways in which abstraction can be used in theology. This will help us to better understand proper ways to use it.

Pietism

In *Wisdom for Thinkers* I have argued that the danger of absolutizing one of the modalities is always looming. For instance, think of the following "-isms" (each one of which corresponds to a modality that is being absolutized): materialism (energetic aspect), evolutionism (biotic aspect), psychologism or psychical monism (sensitive aspect), rationalism (logical aspect), historicism (formative aspect), socialism (social aspect), Marxism (economic aspect), and Romanticism (aesthetic aspect).

The common mistake in all these "-isms" is what we call "nothing-but-ism": the idea that "basically everything is . . ." (insert here the modal aspect being absolutized). In the same way, people also overestimate the corresponding sciences (physics, biology, psychology, etc.). Is it possible to absolutize, in a similar way, the pistical aspect with its corresponding science, theology? Unfortunately, this is quite conceivable.

In order to understand this, I must remind you of the ambiguous meaning of the word *religious*. Let me try to distinguish between them by consistently calling the one the *transcendent-religious* (Dutch: *religieus*), and the other the *immanent-religious* (Dutch: *godsdienstig*), which is the same as pistical. To start with the latter, everyday life has many aspects. There are logical acts (thoughts, reasoning), formative acts (historic actions, technical accomplishments), lingual acts (acts of communication), social acts (traffic, meetings), economic acts (buying and selling), aesthetic acts (producing or enjoying art), juridical acts (passing verdicts), ethical acts (pardoning), and immanent-religious (or pistical) acts (praying, singing, chanting, praising, preaching, Bible study, etc.).

You see, immanent-religious (or pistical) acts are just a few among numerous other types of human actions that are *not* pistical. *But in all these activities Man is always a transcendent-religious being.* That is, whether he argues, communicates, drives a car, buys and sells, plays music, or sends a birthday gift, in all these actions Man stands as a responsible person before God, dependent on him, called upon to account to him, and to honor him. That is what the term transcendent-religious tries to express. But none of the actions just mentioned are immanent-religious (or pistical). Of course, when someone acts pistically, he is responsible to God. But when he acts logically, or socially, or aesthetically, etc., he is equally responsible to God. Only *some* of his actions are pistically qualified, but *all* his actions are, so to speak, transcendent-religiously qualified.

Now, here is where the error of pietism comes in. I use *pietism* here as a broad term, including extreme forms of Puritans, Mennonites, the "Dutch Second Reformation" (Dutch *Nadere Reformatie*; sometimes called paleo-Calvinism, *oud-gereformeerd*), German Pietism, as well as certain mystical forms of Evangelicalism. Besides this, one could think of ultra-orthodox Judaism. For instance, the Hebrew word *chassid* ("pious"), from which we get the name for the religious movement of Chassidism, means basically the same as the Latin *pius*, from which "pious" and "pietism" are derived.

There is an ascetic element in these various forms of pietism that absolutizes the pistical side of life, while neglecting, or even despising, other facets of cultural and societal life. The cause of this is generally a confusion between the transcendent-religious and the immanent-religious (or pistical); we might call it a kind of pisticalism. Pistical acts are considered to be the real thing in life, the specialty of monks or pious Jews who only worship and study the holy books. With a variation on Eccles. 3:1-8, I would answer that there is a time to pray, but also a time to work. There is a time to sing, but also a time to buy and sell. There is a time to read the Bible, but also a time to read great literature. There is a time to preach, but also a time to paint. There is time to seek God's face, but also a time to socialize with other people. There is a time to be in one's inner room, but also a time to be out on the street. The one is not better than the other, as long as one does the right thing at the right time, and particularly, as long as one does it *coram Deo* ("before God"), to honor and glorify him.

Pietism, or pisticalism, is a tremendous impoverishment of the Kingdom of God, as if activity in this Kingdom were limited to pistical actions; that is, as if praying, praising, and preaching is more Kingdom-like than socializing, selling, and sculpting. Paul says, "[W]hether you eat or drink, *or whatever you do*, do all to the glory of God" (1 Cor. 10:31, italics added; cf. Col. 3:17). It would be a pitiful mistake to suppose that being a pastor, a worship leader, or a counselor is more "spiritual" than being a baker, a taxi driver, a shopkeeper, or a lawyer. This, again, is a confusion of structure and direction. It is not *what* you are that makes you spiritual, but *how* you go about being it. It is not *what* you do that makes you spiritual, but *how* you do it. The "spiritual person" has the "mind of the Lord," whatever work he does (1 Cor. 2:15-16). This is, by the way, why being a slave gives you a very special opportunity of "adorning" in everything "the doctrine of God our Savior" because it demands more spiritual strength to be a slave than to be a free man (Titus 2:10).

Pisticalism was one of the reasons why theology was often placed above, or even in opposition to, the other sciences (think again of the Nature–Grace dualism). The reason was that pistical acts were placed above acts that have a different modal qualification. But this approach is a serious mistake! The real question is not how many minutes or hours you spend in your "quiet time" (in your "inner chamber," Matt. 6:6 ASV), but whether you have learned to "pray without ceasing" (1 Thess. 5:17; cf. Luke 18:1; Rom. 12:12; Eph. 6:18; Col. 4:2), that is, to live in the attitude of prayer, *also when you are eating, communicating, baking bread, teaching, driving your car, selling your products, making music, etc.*

When the Apostle Paul says that "the kingdom of God is not a matter of eating and drinking" (Rom. 14:17), the context makes clear that he refers to *arguing* over what to eat and drink, and what not. The Kingdom of God is not a place to bicker. From another point of view, however, the Kingdom of God is precisely this: "Blessed is everyone who will eat bread in the Kingdom of God" (Luke 14:15). The Kingdom of God is "eating and drinking" in the sense of practical fellowship with one another, spiritually socializing *as God's people*, laughing and rejoicing together *in the Lord*, not only in singing but also in working together, thinking and studying together, teaching one another, buying and selling among one another, making beautiful things together, playing music together, seeking righteousness, peace and joy together.

Substantialism

We must also discuss a very different way in which certain abstracted aspects of cosmic reality can be wrongly absolutized. This is called *substantialism*. It is a doctrine found in ancient Greek philosophy and later in Scholasticism, based on the idea of *substantia*, i.e., some essence, existing on its own, independent of other things, and unchangeable. Substantialism has been such a mighty thought system that from Scholastic thinking it easily penetrated into Protestant theology where it has remained up to this very day. But long ago John Calvin argued—in quite a modern way—that creation is not a system consisting of substantial forms, but that it is made up of phenomena and laws.

The original notion of substance was based on the undeniable constancy of things, in spite of the exchange of their parts and the changes in their empirical forms. In order to explain this observation, substantialism in antiquity introduced a sharp distinction between the (unchangeable) *essence* of things, and their (changeable) *accidentia* or secondary properties. This distinction was based on *theoretical abstraction*, by which the changeable properties were abstracted from the unchangeable essence. It is important to note that this abstraction existed only in the mind of the *logical subject*, that is, the person logically thinking about cosmic reality.

So far so good. Subsequently, however, substantialism projected this theoretical abstraction upon reality, as if this abstraction—this distinction between *substantia* and *accidentia*—did not exist in the mind alone *but also in cosmic reality as such*. Essences were abstracted from the full, immanent relationships and coherences in which the Creator had placed all things, and were subsequently declared to be true reality. Substances were considered to be such convenient ideas in the mind that people could not believe that they would not exist "out there" as well.

The main source of this harmful substantialism was the great Greek philosopher Aristotle (384-322 B.C.). He assigned to the realm of the substances all living entities as well as the five *elements* of antiquity (fire, earth, air, and water, plus the quintessence [lit. "fifth essence"], the so-called ether). Within Christian thinking, Aristotle's substantialism penetrated in particular into Roman Catholic and Protestant philosophical and theological anthropology, so that Man was seen as a *dichotomy* (a two-part thing), consisting of a soul substance and a body substance (see the next volume in this series, *Searching the Soul*). In (systematic) theology, this false idea was not only widespread but had enormous consequences as well, such as in:

(a) *Hamartiology* (the doctrine of sin): If Man is a sum of two substances, soul and body, how does sin affect both the soul and the body? How can we maintain the *radical* significance of the fall into sin, which corrupted the whole human nature right down to the very *radix* ("root")? If God—as so many have asserted—creates a new

WHAT THEN *IS* THEOLOGY?

soul every time a human being is conceived (*psychocreationism*), how can we avoid the conclusion that God either creates a corrupted soul, or that the fall concerned only the body (which means a denial of the radical corruptedness of natural Man)?

(b) *Soteriology* (the doctrine of salvation): If Man is a sum of two substances, soul and body, how does redemption affect both the soul and the body? How can we maintain the *radical* significance of redemption if human nature is not concentrated in a transcendent-religious root (the "heart"), from where all immanent functions are determined in their spiritual direction, so that redemption is just as radical as the fall? However, the idea of the transcendent centrality of the heart fundamentally conflicts with substantalist soul–body dualism.

(c) *Christology* (the doctrine of the Christ): According to Scholastic theology—traces of which can still be found in almost all parts of traditional Protestant and Evangelical theology—Jesus would only have assumed a material body plus a "rational soul" (cf. the Athanasian Creed!), the two standing in some substantial relationship with one another. However, such a view cannot do justice to the radical unity of Christ's humanity.

Some early Protestant natural scientists, such as the French Reformed Sébastien Basson (c. 1573-after 1625) and the British Anglican Robert Boyle (1621-1691), were aware of the dangers of substantialism. They rightly saw in the notion of independent substances (lit., "things standing on their own") a threat to God's absolute power and sovereignty caused by the deification of certain aspects of cosmic reality. If things are said to work "according to their own being" in a sense, no matter how much they are viewed as being in subjection to God, they inevitably take on the character of an independently acting being, such as a deity. Insofar as people wish to speak of the *essence* of something, this essence is not to be located in ideas *above* concrete things (as in Platonic idealism), nor in forms that are supposed to exist *within* them (as in nominalism). We reject these pagan notions in favor of the idea that *essences* only exist within the power of God in Christ, who "upholds the universe by the word of his power" (Heb. 1:3) and in whom "all things hold together" (Col. 1:17).

None of the great thinkers of antiquity could ever have caught even a glimpse of this insight because they lacked God's self-revelation. If they could not conceive of the idea of a *creatio ex nihilo* ("creation out of nothing"), how much less could they grasp the idea of a Creator as such, and of a relationship of dependence between this Creator and his creation, including Man.

What is far worse is that, in spite of these biblical insights, and notwithstanding the fact that modern natural science has fully refuted the notion of "substance," substantialism lives on in the thinking of some traditional, "orthodox" theologians. They simply do not seem to be able to free themselves of these Scholastic bonds. Only a radical Christian philosophical view of reality and knowledge, as I tried to describe it in *Wisdom for Thinkers*, can hope to break with this pernicious substantialism. For theology, this could yield the following advantages: (a) a clearer insight into the nature and significance of abstraction in theological theory building (see further in chapter 10), and (b) the unmasking of many "substances" (i.e., mental abstractions turned into ontic essences) in systematic theology.

Abstraction as a Theological Method

We have considered two wrong ways in which abstraction can be used in theology. Let us now look at a proper way to use it. As an example, let us consider the church in its abstracted form as we speak of it in ecclesiology (a part of systematic theology).

In its *concrete* form, all believers, and only believers, know with all their hearts what the Church is in the fullest sense of the word. They *are* the Church. This existential "knowing" never excludes the activity of reason because there can be no knowledge of the Church if we have no idea of what it is. Yet, in our everyday knowledge of the Church, it is not the logical but the pistical aspect that qualifies (typifies, characterizes) this knowledge. What the Church is reveals itself as something the believer *experiences* when he meets with God's people to pray, to worship, and to hear God's Word. He experiences it when he celebrates the Lord's Supper at his table because, among other things, it is the expression of the unity and fellowship of the body of Christ (1 Cor. 10:16-17).

The believer experiences what the Church is in the mutual bond, the fellowship of the saints, the brotherly love, the belongingness, the spiritual solidarity in the power of the Holy Spirit, the pastoral care for one another, the words of encouragement and comfort shared between members. To the common believer, that which is "the Church" consists of the faith assurance of the Church's union with its heavenly head (Eph. 1:22; 4:15-16; 5:23; Col. 1:18; 2:19), and of the expectation of the Bridegroom who will come soon to his bride, the Church (Rev. 22:17, 20), etc. All the relevant Scriptures on the subject of the Church speak to the common believer in their full transcendent-religious riches and diversity. Of course, in this process, the believer never puts his *reason* aside, but reason here is just one of many aspects of his mind.

Let us now look at the theologian. Even if he never puts his *heart* aside, from all the Scriptures concerned he *abstracts* those elements that are relevant for a conceptual understanding of the Church in order to arrive at a theological ecclesiology (a scholarly doctrine of the Church). Other elements, for instance those of an admonishing, comforting, prophetic, or doxological nature, which in particular address the heart of the common Bible reader, are also left out of consideration. To be sure, very often the theologian must also be such a "common Bible reader." However, as a *scientific investigator* he leaves these other elements out of consideration in the course of his study, unless they actually become objects of his investigation.

It is very important to grasp this correctly. From the full, concrete riches of Scripture, the theologian abstracts those logically objectified elements that he needs for his study. As a common believer, he likes to be encouraged; as a theologian he studies the phenomenon of encouragement. As a common believer, he enjoys being part of a church; as a theologian he studies ecclesiology. As a common believer, he remembers the Lord in his death at the Lord's Supper; as a theologian he studies the doctrine of the Lord's Supper. As a common believer, he belongs to a local faith community; as a theologian, he is detached from any kind of belongingness. I ask again, where is there any room for a *continuum* here?

In such a study concerning the *doctrine* of the Church (that is, ecclesiology) the theologian is not primarily occupied with his "experience" of the Church, with his faith assurance concerning her, with his expectation of the second coming of her Bridegroom.

Of course, these things are *always* present at the back of his mind and, since they are related to his religious ground-motive, they govern his study from beginning to end. But what really matters to him is to learn to *logically distinguish* those elements which in Scripture are given to him in their unity and totality. He will make an analytical study of the nature, the being, the origin, the calling, the history, and the future of the Church. He will logically distinguish between the visible and the invisible Church (and between the very different meanings these terms can have); between God's counsels and Man's responsibility with regard to the Church; between the various descriptions of the Church as the body of Christ, as the house, temple, city, army, or vineyard of God, as the bride of the Lamb; between the worldwide Church and the local church.

The theologian is always *analyzing*. He wants to analyze the Church's meaning and purpose, its origin and development, its calling in this world, its composition, its practical functioning in its meetings and outside these meetings, etc. Please notice that "analyze" comes from Greek *analuô*, "loosening;" it means "taking apart" that which in common life belongs together and forms a unity.

It is typical of the theoretical thought attitude that it is logically qualified, and works in a methodic, systematic, logically correct way, in a continual confrontation with what earlier exegetes and systematic theologians have brought up on the same subject. The investigator "abstracts" from himself, so to speak, his own feelings (of joy, disgust, or discouragement), affections (both positive and negative), exaltations (whether they be religious, mystical or aesthetic), memories, prejudices, and preferences, which all belong to the *common experience* of the Church. For the time being, the theologian puts aside the sensitive, historical, social, economic, aesthetic, juridical, and ethical aspects of the Church. These modal aspects find hardly any place in a systematic theology, but they do come up in historical theology (church history), psychology and sociology of religion, canon law, and moral theology (or theological ethics).

It is of the greatest importance to realize that the results of such a theological analysis can never be presented as a "copy" of what

WHAT THEN *IS* THEOLOGY?

Scripture says (even though they were certainly *inspired* by Scripture). That is to say, the Bible must never be "theologicalized" by reading theological concepts and theories into it. Scripture does not contain a full-fledged ecclesiology that is simply waiting there to be lifted out by the theologian. The way in which he might present the ecclesial contents of the Bible in a systematic-theological way, in a certain theoretical-abstract-methodic-systematic order, is never the way this is done in Scripture itself. Every ecclesiology is the creative product of the mind of one or more theologians, although designed in such a way as to account for the Scriptural data. It is an error, if not outright *hybris*, to claim of any ecclesiology: "This is the teaching of the Bible about the Church." Instead, the theologian should say something like this: "This is the theoretical representation of what I think the Bible is saying about the Church."

The Bible not Abstract

To understand the last point a little better, let us take the Letters of the Apostle Paul. These are all concrete, practical writings, in which concrete, practical problems are addressed. A good example is First Corinthians, which deals with questions like these: Whom are we to follow, Peter, Apollos, or Paul? Can you drag a brother before an (unbelieving) judge? Should a male Gentile believer be circumcised? Is a widow allowed to remarry? Are we allowed to divorce our wives? Can we eat meat that has earlier been sacrificed to idols? How are we to use the Lord's Supper? How do the *charismata* of the Spirit work? How are we to interpret glossolalia? And so on. To be sure, Paul deals with all these questions against the background of doctrinal considerations, but he hardly ever seems to be concerned with doctrine as an aim in itself. He never gives a purely theoretical treatise on any subject, in order to consider it from the viewpoint of the cool, detached observer, as happens in science.

Some of the most "theological" Letters in the New Testament, such as Romans and Hebrews, still had a very practical reason for being written, and a very practical purpose. For example, the reason for writing Romans was, among other things, the libertarian attitude of some of the Christians in the church at Rome, and the strained relationship between Jewish and Gentile believers. The reason for writing Hebrews was in particular the inclination of some Jewish believers to fall back into Judaism because of the pressure of persecution. The authors deal with very *practical* issues, even though they do so against the background of many *doctrinal* considerations. Thus, it is quite striking how Paul was able to place very down-to-earth problems in a broad Christological (2 Cor. 8:9), or eschatological framework (Rom. 14:17-18; 1 Cor. 6:2-3).

Apparently, the New Testament authors never intended to transmit pure knowledge as such, not to mention theoretical knowledge. This is the enormous difference between the Bible and systematic theology, whose primary aim is not only to present knowledge *as such*, but to do it in a theoretical form, according to a self-determined systematics. It is the duty of every Christian to strive for practical Bible knowledge. But doing scientific systematic theology is definitely *not* the duty of all Christians. It is only the task of those who are called to it and who have a gift for theoretical work.

One may wonder: If the systematic theologian's way of speaking is so much different from Scripture's, how can the former be justified in the first place? I think the answer is that, from a historical, logical, and psychological point of view, systematic-theological work is simply *inescapable*. The question is not whether we may do this work—we simply must. Throughout the centuries and in all denominations, Christians have asked questions like these: What is the Bible precisely about? What is the doctrine of Scripture about God, about creation, about Man, about the fall into sin, about redemption, about the covenant, about the Kingdom, about the Church, about the end of the world, etc.? Time and again, such questions have arisen, not only to satisfy a lively curiosity, but also to offer resistance to emerging heresies. The product of the resulting reflection was, time and again, a systematic theology, no matter how elementary. This may have been academically simple or advanced, orthodox or heterodox, in the spirit of Scripture or of paganism, logically and methodically sound or weak—but at any rate it was some form of systematic theology.

As I have said before, theological knowledge is not a kind of "higher" knowledge, and thus never an aim in itself. It has to be "fed back" to practical faith knowledge. In other words, systematic theology has to be *subservient* to faith and to fellow-believers.

WHAT THEN *IS* THEOLOGY?

Practical faith-knowledge is tremendously deepened, clarified and enriched by the results of systematic theology. Just as linguistics deepens our practical knowledge of languages, as biology deepens our knowledge of the living nature, and as historical science deepens our knowledge of history, in the same way systematic theology deepens our practical knowledge of Scripture. This is the true aim, the most important purpose, of systematic theology. Along this road, the Church is enriched, and God is glorified. When treated as an aim in itself, science, including systematic theology, is nothing but a form of scientism, that is, a glorification of science. When systematic theology is inspired by the biblical ground-motive as a form of biblical service, it is useful for the whole community of believers and for the honor of God.

Abstraction and Theological Concepts

The abstract character of systematic theology comes to light in a striking way in the status of theological concepts. Take the biblical terms for "soul" (Hebrew *nèfesh*, Greek *psychè*) and "spirit" (Hebrew *ruach*, Greek *pneuma*), which have a tremendous variety of meanings. For instance, *nèfesh* is associated alternately with Man as a complete person, with his breath, with his blood, his feelings, his mind, his heart, and sometimes even with his dead body. From this variety, we see that biblical language is the language of practical, everyday life. And in our everyday speech, the word "soul" can mean many things; we use the word in such expressions as: the life and soul of a party, the soul of a company, soul music, soul brother, soul kiss, soul mate, etc. However, in psychology or anthropology, we could not make any use of such a diversity of meanings. Scientific terms are much "poorer" than everyday terms in that they have, and ought to have, only one well-defined meaning. All possible nuances in everyday concepts have been *abstracted* from it until one kernel meaning is left.

The same is true for systematic theology. In theological anthropology, the systematic theologian must account for such terms as "soul" and "spirit." In a theological theory these concepts necessarily will have to assume only one well-defined (modal-abstract, that is, physical, biotic, perceptive, sensitive, or logical, etc.) meaning, or else they will be replaced by other similar terms. The various aspects of human existence that are expressed in the many biblical meanings of "soul" and "spirit" will have to find a place somehow in this anthropology. This must take place in an unambiguous, well-defined, modal-abstract terminology, in which, for instance, the physical, biotic, perceptive, sensitive and logical aspects are clearly distinguished. There is nothing we can do about it; the better delineated theological terms become, the less they resemble the biblical terms—fluent as the latter are—and the more they resemble the language of science, that is, the more accurate they are and the better they fit into a system of strictly logical reasoning (Emil Brunner).

The Word of God has been communicated to us in thoroughly human language. However, because of the strong scientistic tendencies in Western society, theology tends to deal with biblical concepts as if they were theoretical. In this way, the Bible is "theologicalized," as if it were a theoretical treatise. However, strictly speaking the Bible never deals with theological subjects. It neither explains the concepts of soul and spirit, nor does it supply us with theories about them. Jesus did not give Nicodemus a theoretical-conceptual outline of new birth (John 3:1-5). The Apostle Paul did not write the Roman Christians a theoretical-conceptual outline of justification. The author of the Letter to the Hebrews did not give to the Jewish believers a theoretical-conceptual outline of propitiation. Likewise, the Bible does not supply us with (theoretical) treatises about concepts such as creation, sin, redemption, etc. All this work has been left to the theologians, who must develop *their own* theories about these matters. And when this is done, it will turn out in the end that God's revelation in Scripture with respect to such subjects is transcendent in character, so as even to *surpass* all human conceptualization.

As far as I can see, with regard to the nature of biblical language, we might make at least three mistakes, which unfortunately are quite common:

(a) We could *reduce* biblical language to nothing but a collection of logical concepts and logical propositions (a common fundamentalist claim, due to rationalism). What is so "propositional" about phrases like "Woe to me!", "Shame on you!", or "Do not fear!" which are as abundant in the Bible as in everyday parlance?

(b) Even worse, we could treat these biblical concepts as *theoretical*, that is, as if they were of the same nature as those of systematic theology. This overestimation of theology is a typically scientistic error. "Theologicalizers" see theology everywhere in the Bible, whereas in reality it is found *nowhere* in Scripture.

(c) We could misjudge the primarily revelational, transcendent meaning of biblical concepts as referring to God and his transcendent relationship with Man. Below, we will see that such alleged *concepts* are in fact *superconcepts* or *ideas*—a characteristic term of Christian philosophy, with which we will deal extensively.

Theological Concepts not Found but Formed

It would be a great mistake to view the Bible as a collection of *concepts* that lie waiting until they are *li ted* out by systematic theology. This amounts to saying that the Bible is a disorganized mass of concepts, which can only be ordered neatly and systematically by the systematic theologian. The ultimate consequence of this view is the idea that, in a sense, systematic theology is more orderly and more systematic than Scripture itself. Thus, Klaas Schilder (1890-1952), a well-known Reformed theologian from the Netherlands, suggested that after God has revealed himself, the systematic theologian may then come and *order* what he has read. Apparently Schilder did not realize that theology is not *more* orderly than Scripture but that it has an order of a *di erent nature* than the one found in Scripture. Theology imposes its own *order* upon the Scriptural data, which themselves are of a *higher* order, with the purpose of attaining, through this lower scientific order, a deeper understanding of the order of Scripture.

The order of systematic theology is a *designed* order. That is, theologians do not "lift" theological concepts "out" of the Bible but *form* them themselves. As far as their form is concerned, theological concepts and theories are human artefacts, just like *all* theoretical concepts and theories in *all* sciences. Ideally, theologians form them under the powerful guidance of the biblical ground-motive, in which case the resulting concepts can be supposed to be a reasonably reliable approximation of biblical truth. But even then, these results always remain fallible, flawed, preliminary human work. A systematic theologian can never claim a status of authority for his results because of the mistaken belief that his tenets have been "derived from Scripture," or would be a "simple copying" of what Scripture is saying. This is nothing but scientistic self-deception and self-overestimation, whether it comes out of naïveté or hubris, or both. God's Word is absolute, whereas our theories about it are relative, imperfect, and always preliminary (for further details, see chapter 10).

I repeat, theological concepts are not lifted from the Bible: they are creatively formed (designed) by theologians, although their purpose is to account for the biblical data. If a term is found in the Bible, a "concept" must then be made of it, that is, it has to be "defined"; its meaning has to be described. How is this done? In every concept, relevant universal properties of a certain entity are abstracted from non-relevant properties. To have a clearer idea of how this works, let us look at how the concept of an angel is formed:

(a) *Identification*: Through biblical investigation theologians *identify* which properties of an angel are relevant, and which are not. Important relevant properties turn out to be the following: an angel is a created, rational, celestial, sexless, immaterial being and a messenger (servant) of God. Irrelevant properties, i.e., those that do not necessarily belong to the definition of an angel, are the ideas that it is winged and fiery, and that it bears a sword, etc.

(b) *Distinction*: The relevant properties that are found are compared with those of other beings, and the similarities and differences are determined. For instance, an angel is similar to a human in that both are creatures and rational beings, and differs in that angels are immaterial, sexless, and celestial beings, whereas humans are material, sexual, and terrestrial beings. Angels resemble God in that God too is immaterial, sexless, and celestial, whereas they differ from him in that they are creatures, and he is the Creator; they are servants, and he is their Lord.

We can now come to the *concept* of an angel, which we can express in a *definition*. To such a definition belong the relevant characteristics that we have identified: "an angel is a created, rational, immaterial, sexless, celestial being." (Man, by contrast, is a created, rational, material, sexual, terrestrial being.) Again, please note that such a concept or definition is not *found* in the Bible and then lifted out, but is *formed* (designed) by theologians. Such concepts are creative designs produced by their brains, although of course in compliance with the biblical data.

Note that we cannot *define* God in this way, for instance, by saying that God is an uncreated, rational, immaterial, sexless, celestial being. When it comes to angels or humans, we can distinguish a higher category, namely, *beings*, of which angels and men are distinct examples. But although we cannot speak in a similar way of God, it *is* possible to form an *idea* of God. We now have to turn to the important subject of ideas.

Theological Ideas

One very special aspect of conceptualization is the distinction between (common) concepts and *superconcepts* or *ideas*. This distinction has either been neglected or misunderstood in theology. Strictly speaking, only things that belong to our immanent, modal-functional reality can be logical-analytically "conceived," i.e., contained in a "concept" (from Latin *concipere*, derived from *capere*, "seize, grasp," first in the literal, then in the metaphorical sense). However, when we think of the transcendent, supramodal, suprafunctional reality, it is different. We cannot conceptualize it, but we can form *ideas* of it. *Idea-wise knowledge*, i.e., knowledge in the form of ideas, is also knowledge, even rational knowledge, but it is a form of knowledge surpassing conceptual knowledge.

For every systematic theologian, it is of the utmost importance to realize that there are logical objects in theology of which no theological concepts can be formed. The most obvious example of such a logical object is God. We can give a *description* of him, but we cannot contain him in a (scientific) *definition*. The same is true for (a) the transcendent-religious meaning of Scripture, that is, the eternal Word of God; (b) Man's "heart" in its transcendent-religious meaning; (c) the religious relationship between this heart and God, or the idols; (d) the Church in its transcendent fullness and unity. About such *transcendent* matters we can speak only with words that normally refer to concepts belonging to our *immanent* reality, *since we simply do not know any other words.* In such cases, we use these same words to refer to *super*concepts in the sense of *pointing* to matters that surpass our immanent reality.

The clear exception is the word "God," which does *not* refer to some immanent-rational concept. But words like God's "mercy" or God's "descending" do refer to such concepts, as we will see below.

Also, some *immanent* notions like harmony, justice, love, goodness, which play a role in systematic theology as well, are not concepts but ideas. Such terms are directly related to the kernels of certain modal aspects (this is discussed in greater detail in my book, *Wisdom for Thinkers*). Think of distinction (logical aspect), power (formative aspect), communication (lingual aspect), fellowship (social aspect), value (economic aspect), harmony (aesthetic aspect), justice (juridical aspect), love (ethical aspect), confidence (pistical aspect). Of such modal kernels we can only form an idea, not a concept; that is, strictly speaking they cannot be *defined* (at best they can be *described*) because they cannot be related to a higher category. As a consequence, not only are we unable to conceptualize God's (transcendent) omnipotence, we cannot even conceptualize everyday (immanent) power, because it is the kernel of the formative aspect and, as such, it cannot be "defined."

It is now time to give you some examples to explain the difference between concepts and ideas, because good examples often tell us more than a thousand words. Think of a word that I used just a moment ago, as well as many other times earlier in this book: the word "transcendent." Literally, the Latin *transcendere* means to "rise above (or beyond)." When we speak of "rising above" in a strictly kinematic sense, we are dealing with a *kinematic concept*; that is, this concept is composed of literal kinematic features that determine the term "rising above" as a kinematic concept. Primarily, "rising above" is a literal movement such as the diver "rising above" the water level. The rule of thumb is that such literal "rising" can always be expressed in so many meters per second.

Now, the point is that this kinematic term can also be used to refer to something that surpasses its literal meaning, such as the transcendence of God or the human heart. In this case, we are no longer dealing with a concept but with an idea. The latter is definitely rational, for it is possible to imagine a mental representation of its content, and to consider this logically. But at the same time, it is only a *representation,* an *image.* We can only form a (rational) image of things that surpass rational concepts. We can only speak *idea-wise* (Dutch: *ideematig*) of the transcendence of God or the human heart. The *reality* of this transcendence *transcends* the limits of empirical reality! Yet we can only speak of it in modal terms, that is, in terms adopted from our immanent cosmic reality. As I said, we simply have no other terms. But these terms are used here idea-wise, not concept-wise. Only through the idea-wise use of such modal terms can we obtain knowledge about that which surpasses the limits of conceptualization. The image, like a photograph, *refers* to, *represents, approximates* reality, but is not identical with it. Thus, we form for ourselves an image of transcendence, but cannot rationally contain the latter in a concept.

God the Father

Let us take a very important term that the Bible uses for God, namely, "Father." The *concept* of *father* necessarily contains the following constitutive features: a father is a male, who has had intercourse with a female, and in this way has produced one or more children. A *good* father is one who not only begets children, but also cares about them, loves them, looks after them, feeds them, raises them, and trains them. Now, the *term* "father" can also be used as an *idea,* for instance when we speak of God as a Father. In that case, *some* vital features are applicable, *but others are not*: God is *not* a male, and has *no* intercourse with women, but he *does* have children, whom, as a good Father, he loves and looks after, whom he feeds, raises, and trains. This is characteristic of an idea: *some* essential features of a concept are applicable, while others are not.

Two points are of great importance here. First, God's Fatherhood is not *just* a metaphor. If that were true, we could simply drop it if we like, and try to find other metaphors, that could be used to express the same characteristics of God. However, as it turns out, not only is this virtually impossible, but also God's Fatherhood is even presented in the Bible as an essential aspect of his being. One of the purposes of Jesus, (God's Son!) was to reveal God as being "Father" (John 17:6, 26). "Father" is not just an arbitrary, interchangeable name for him, but Christians believe that God is Father (and Son, and Holy Spirit).

Second, we can now unmask a grave Scholastic error. Even today, there are theologians who claim that a logical inference from the Bible has the same divine authority as explicit biblical statements. This would only be true if we were dealing exclusively with *concepts*. If Moses is called a father, we can safely conclude from this that he *must* have been a male and *must* have had intercourse with a woman, because in his case we are dealing with the *concept* of a father. However, when it comes to God, we *cannot* draw such conclusions because in this case we are dealing with the *idea* of a father. If this is the case, we have to find out from the context which features of fatherhood are applicable, and which are not. We can never determine this from the idea as such.

Let us now take a different example. From the biblical given of the eternal election of the righteous, you cannot logically infer the eternal reprobation of the wicked. That would only be possible if "election" were just a concept; in that case, to elect some would imply rejecting the others. But with biblical ideas it does not work like that. Scripture itself will have to teach us explicitly whether there is such a thing as the eternal reprobation of the wicked; it does not follow from the notion of election as such. Also compare the words "it must necessarily follow" in the Heidelberg Catechism Q&A 48 (see chapter 5), where this phrase would only be true if we could speak of the deity of Christ in a conceptual way—which we cannot.

Anthropological Examples

Let me give some further examples, this time with regard to Man's transcendent-religious unity and fullness, which are of great importance for theological anthropology and theology proper (the doctrine of God):

(a) Man's *uniqueness* (from Latin *unus*, "one") and *individuality* (etymologically related to "indivisibility"), compared to God's uniqueness and individuality. Strictly speaking these are *arithmetical* terms, in this case not referring to concepts, for they surpass arithmetical laws (one cannot calculate with them). They refer to *ideas*, which try to express certain features of Man's and God's transcendent unity and fullness (the latter term refers to a spatial idea).

(b) Man's *eccentricity*. This is a favorite term used by the German anthropologist Helmuth Plessner (1892-1985) with regard to Man, to point out that Man's being is not enclosed within himself; his "center" lies outside himself (although Plessner understood this in a different way than Christian philosophy does). I take the term to indicate that Man's being is determined by his *eccentric*, i.e., transcendent-religious relationship with God. Eccentricity as such is clearly a *spatial* term, although here it does not refer to a spatial concept—there are no geometrical coordinates involved— but rather to a spatial idea. We are not dealing here with simple metaphors, for those are arbitrary; they could easily be replaced by other metaphors. Moreover, metaphors are lingual in nature, but ideas are logical in nature. Ideas represent true features of Man and of the ontic order that God has instituted for created reality. This follows from the fact that we cannot possibly express these same things in terms that do not somehow relate to the spatial.

(c) Man's *heart*; also his *soul* and *spirit* insofar as these biblical terms originally point to Man's breath. The Bible even speaks of the heart of *God* (Gen. 6:6; 8:21; 1 Sam. 2:35; 13:14, etc.). These are clearly biotic terms, although here they do not refer to biotic concepts—we cannot speak of the physiology of heart, soul, and spirit in the transcendent-religious meaning of these terms—but rather to biotic ideas.

(d) Man's *responsibility*. In its original meaning this is a strictly *lingual* concept; it refers to one person giving a "response" to another. Here, however, this term does not refer to a lingual concept—we cannot speak of grammatical errors in, or the sound volume of, this response—but rather to a lingual idea.

(e) Man's *dignity* (from the Latin *dignus*, "worthy"). Worth in its original sense is a strictly economic term, although here it does not refer to an economic concept—we cannot calculate the market price of Man's dignity—but rather to an economic idea.

(f) Man's *theonomous* character (Greek *nomos*, "law"). *Nomos* is a strictly juridical term, but here the term *theonomy* does not refer to a juridical concept—there is no legislation around this "law"— but rather to a juridical idea.

Idea-Wise Knowledge

It is very important to grasp correctly the difference between concepts and ideas. Rational knowledge is not limited to conceptual knowledge, as rationalism—also within theology—has always claimed, but it also includes idea-wise knowledge. Man's knowledge of God and his Word, and of the essential being of Man, is rational, but not conceptual. Where theologians have failed to grasp this, they have instead misunderstood this "higher" knowledge in either of two ways:

(a) *"Knowledge of the transcendent is irrational."* If knowledge of the transcendent were indeed non-rational, or irrational, this would imply that those claiming such knowledge end up in mysticism and bigotry. In order to avoid this, theology tries to manage without terms such as God's "transcendence" because of the allegedly mystical overtones.

(b) *"Knowledge of the transcendent is rational-conceptual."* If this were true–if such knowledge could indeed be conceptualized–it would mean that the transcendent belonged to the rational order that applies to the cosmos. This would imply, for instance, that the transcendent God is submitted to the logical laws that he himself as the Creator has established for the cosmos. In fact, this is an inner contradiction whereby the transcendent is drawn into our immanent world.

Many theologians do not see that there is a third possibility:

(c) *Knowledge of the transcendent is rational, but only idea-wise,* that is, it is knowledge that surpasses conceptualization. In this case, it is no longer a contradiction (whether real or apparent) to say that God has used *creaturely* terms in order to truly reveal his *being*, that is, *himself.* Knowledge of the transcendent is neither mystical, nor conceptual; there is a third way.

Let me add to this, though, that knowledge of God, his Word, Man's transcendent heart, etc., is never *limited* by this rational (idea-wise) knowledge. We do have idea-wise knowledge of God, but at the same time our knowledge of God ultimately surpasses all rational knowledge. This is the supra-rational knowledge of the heart. This is not irrational or mystical—our faith knowledge is constantly fed by practical and theological rational knowledge of God—but supra-rational, intimate, existential, and relational, in the full transcendent-religious sense. This leads to the interesting conclusion that the highest knowledge of the transcendent is itself transcendent.

I repeat here that it is very important to have a clear-cut idea of the differences between these four terms: *non-rational* (i.e., not referring to the rational), *rational* (i.e., logical, that which has to do with reason), *irrational* (i.e., that which goes against reason, the illogical), and *supra-rational* (i.e., that which surpasses the rational). I advise you to review these four terms until you are completely familiar with them.

Basic theological work is made up of concept-wise and idea-wise knowledge. It is limited to Scripture as the concrete book in our hands, or, to put it more neatly, to Scripture in the sense of the *immanent* expression—in human language—of the eternal, *transcendent* Word of God. At the same time, the theological investigator wishes to know more, to penetrate into this very *being*, the deepest nature, of Scripture as Word of God. However, this is more than theology as such can offer him. We are dealing here with knowledge of Scripture that is of a transcendent-religious character. It is a knowledge that does not exclude the brain, but primarily concerns the heart. The theologian's study is *directed* by such knowledge, that is, by an *idea* of the transcendent-religious fullness of Scripture as revealed in that same Scripture. This heart-knowledge of Scripture as divine revelation is the religious *faith presupposition* of all systematic theology. We gather theological knowledge of the immanent Scripture starting from the faith-knowledge that it is God's transcendent Word. The heart necessarily precedes the brain—as it always does.

Chapter Seven
THEOLOGICAL CRITERIA

What are the criteria needed to call a certain piece of theological work "scientific"? This is the central question of the present chapter, though several collateral questions will be dealt with too. I will try to do this with the help of so-called modal *analogies* (see the more detailed discussion in my *Wisdom for Thinkers*). For instance, the strength of a digging machine that displaces heaps of sand or uproots trees may be compared to the strength of faith that—spiritually speaking—displaces mountains and uproots trees (Mark 11:23; Luke 17:6). The term we use here, "strength," normally indicates a physical quality that can be expressed in newtons. However, when we speak of faith we are not using "strength" in its original physical sense but as a physical retrocipation within the boundaries of the pistical modality.

As we have seen, Christian philosophy does not consider this an accidental parallel but a piece of ontic coherence between the physical and the pistical aspect, laid down in cosmic reality by the Creator. Within each of the (approximately) sixteen modalities, we can find similar analogies with the other modalities, which we call *modal analogies*. When they refer to earlier modalities we speak of retrocipations, and when they refer to later modalities, we speak of anticipations. Thus, in the "strength" of faith we have to do with a physical retrocipation within the pistical aspect.

When we want to find out whether a piece of theological work is "scientific," we focus on the *logical* modality, that is, we apply logical *norms*. Whereas common Bible reading is pistically qualified, theological Bible investigation is logically qualified. On its law-side, the logical modality contains a number of modal analogies that can help us to get an idea of the criteria or *modal norms* of scientific work.

The Natural Retrocipations

Let us now look at the first seven analogies within the logical modality, which refer back to ("retrocipate upon") the natural modalities. I will use the adjective *epistemic*, which comes from Greek *epistèmè*, for logical "knowledge" (cf. epistemology):

1. *Epistemic multiplicity and identity* (arithmetical retrocipations). Each theological hypothesis contains a certain number of arguments, syllogisms, judgments, and theoretical concepts. These are not determined by arithmetical laws, but by logical laws; therefore, we speak of an arithmetical retrocipation within the logical modality. The greater the logical transparency with which a hypothesis has been formulated, the easier it becomes to map out this multiplicity. Good theological theories are those with increasingly complex and sophisticated multiplicity, that is, an ever finer specification of their internal structures.

Another arithmetical retrocipation is logical identity. In that which is analyzable, only A is A. This is an arithmetical retrocipation because it is the arithmetical modality that serves as a basis for the identification of every unit as distinct from all other units.

2. *Epistemic coherence.* The "hanging together" of arguments, their "belonging together," is clearly a spatial retrocipation within the logical modality. The same holds true for Karl Barth's "theological space" (chapter 4), or the "place" (Latin: *locus*; the favorite German term for this is *Ort*) of a certain theological subject. According to the coherence theory of truth, logical coherence is the primary criterion for a scientific theory (see chapter 10). The correct encyclopedic *localization* of theological elements is a clear criterion for theology (see below for our discussion of *systematization*).

3. *Epistemic progression and continuity.* Though often used in a historical-formative sense, progression (lit. "moving forward") is primarily a kinematic retrocipation in the logical modality, just like the "course" of a theological argument or of theological "development" (itself a biotic retrocipation); for instance, "In what direction is this theological school moving?" According to critical realism (see *Wisdom for Thinkers*), a theological movement is progressive if the newer theories are a better approximation of reality than the older ones.

Another kinematic retrocipation within the logical modality is analytical continuity. Even in the most drastic scientific revolutions, there must be some underlying continuity of theoretical entities and relationships so that the level of good science can be maintained.

4. *Epistemic interconnection, validity, force.* The interconnection of theological arguments, or their validity (the measure in which they are applicable to a given theological-empirical state of affairs), are physical retrocipations in the logical modality, just like the force of a theological argument, or the brainpower of a theologian.

Moreover, the relationship between logical ground and logical conclusion is a physical retrocipation in that it refers to the relationship between cause and effect within the physical aspect. Another example of a physical retrocipation is the logical principle of *sufficient reason* to determine the (non-)validity of theological theories.

5. *Epistemic vitality, fruitfulness, differentiation, integration.* This is obviously not vitality or fruitfulness in the original biotic sense but in the logical sense; we are dealing with biotic retrocipations here. Critical realism attaches great value to the "metaphors"—by which it actually means *ideas*—used in scientific theories, as well as to their fruitfulness; The most useful ideas are those which continually bear fruit and are capable of ever increasing extension (itself a spatial retrocipation) and refinement of a theory (for further discussion, see chapter 10). Fruitful theories are those that continually give rise to new investigation.

6. *Epistemic consciousness.* This is a perceptive retrocipation in the logical modality. Logical thinking has an intrinsic consciousness (awareness) of itself, though not based in this instance on sensory observations; consciousness here is a modal retrocipation. It is the awareness that thinking has of itself, of the "force" (itself a physical retrocipation) of its own arguments, and of weaknesses in its own reasoning, even if these cannot always be lingually formulated.

7. *Epistemic sensitivity.* This is a sensitive retrocipation within the logical modality. An example of this is that we sometimes say, "I feel," when what we really mean is that we have an opinion, a view, or a standpoint. Inevitably, the good theologian, like any good scientist, needs to have a certain *sensitivity* towards his field of investigation. He must have *feeling* for theology, otherwise he cannot be a good theologian. However, this is not "feeling" in the original sensitive (affective, emotional) sense but in the logical sense.

WHAT THEN *IS* THEOLOGY?

The Spiritive Anticipations

8. *Epistemic thought control and thought formation.* These are historical-formative anticipations within the logical modality. In the technical control over matter, and the formation of cultural products, we encounter the historical-formative in its original sense. In the formation of concepts, judgments, syllogisms, arguments, (working) hypotheses and theories, we are dealing with an anticipation in the logical modality. Such formations are a criterion of true theological work. As far as I can see, this activity cannot possibly be expressed in terms in which no analogy with the historical-formative modality comes to light.

9. *Epistemic symbolics and interpretation.* These are lingual anticipations within the logical modality, which can be seen most clearly in the ideas that play a central role in theological theories. These ideas "represent" certain states of affairs, they "point to" them in a symbolic way. The number of "strong" (physical retrocipation), "fruitful" (biotic retrocipation), "efficient" (economic anticipation), "creative" (aesthetic anticipation), "plausible" (juridical anticipation) and "credible" (pistical anticipation) ideas constitutes a criterion for a good theological theory.

10. *Epistemic thought interaction.* This is a social anticipation within the logical modality, referring to the exchange of thoughts and ideas, of arguments and counter-arguments, both within the theologian himself and within the theological community. No theology would be possible without this "lively" (a biotic retrocipation) traffic of viewpoints at conferences and in theological journals. This is a social criterion of theological activity: hypotheses are not *theological* hypotheses if they do not aim at solving problems which, on the basis of a common paradigm (see the following chapters), have been *acknowledged* by the theological community as theological problems. It is also true that theological hypotheses are not acknowledged as such if they do not produce new theological problems capable of affecting the scientific activity of other theologians.

11. *Epistemic economy* (economic anticipation). Theological "efficiency" is illustrated in "Occam's Razor" (attributed to the medieval British philosopher, William of Occam): *pluralitas non est ponenda sine necessitate* ("multiplicity is not to be posited without necessity"). To

put this another way, we should always prefer the simplest of alternative theories to more complex ones, and new phenomena should be in terms of ones we already know. Theological theories should be relatively "simple," that is, they should not contain superfluous suppositions and arguments. Theological hypotheses that are more complicated than is demanded by the facts we know so far do not give a clear picture of things or their mutual relationships, and therefore are not good scientific theories.

12. *Epistemic harmony and creativity* (aesthetic anticipations). A coherent theological thought system exhibits a certain intellectual beauty and harmony. Scientific theories (including theological ones) are not "deduced" from reality but are the free "inventions" of a creative mind, although they are, of course, designed so as to account optimally for the biblical data. This creativity comes to light especially in the theoretical ideas that form the heart of a good scientific theory. Scientific creativity is a criterion for good science. According to critical realism (see chapter 10), science offers true knowledge concerning cosmic reality, not only in its direct statements with regard to directly accessible empirical phenomena but also in these theoretical ideas. Although theories are creative inventions of the mind, critical realists maintain the view that one of the definite aims of science is to *discover* the structures of cosmic reality. Theology is an activity that does not try to *create* a certain pistical order but aims rather to *disclose* (unravel, reveal) the pistical order instituted by God.

13. *Epistemic evidence and plausibility* (juridical anticipations). These anticipations refer to another important criterion of good science in general and good theology in particular. This is the question of the extent to which the theories of science (including theology) are *justified* by the empirical data available. Do they do *justice* to them all, or are some sense data swept under the carpet? How far does the logical "evidence" of the theories in question satisfy our sense of plausibility? Or do we feel that another approach would have been more appropriate?

14. *Epistemic eros and integrity* (ethical anticipations). There is first of all the criterion of the theoretical *eros*, without which no good theology is possible. It is that peculiar affection, that love, that drive, that zeal for one's work, which the scientist has with

respect to his field of investigation. Someone who himself is not active in that field can hardly have a real understanding of this affection, this passion. I could not have written this book if the writing had not been enjoyable! If you do not *like* theology, it will be very difficult for you to produce any fruitful theological work. (This should not be confused with love for God; a person can love God without loving the theological work—and *vice versa* for that matter.)

Intellectual integrity is another ethical anticipation, and a norm for theological activity. A theologian is bound to a personal faith, and usually to a certain theological tradition. As a consequence, he may be tempted occasionally to sacrifice his intellectual honesty to the demands of his faith or tradition. However, good theology also needs a basis of intellectual integrity. The theologian must reveal the conclusions *he* has reached independently, not the ones he feels compelled by his tradition to find. This is in particular a temptation for doctoral students at theological faculties belonging to certain denominations. Fortunately there are positive exceptions. In his dissertation at the Theological University in Apeldoorn (Netherlands), Willem A. den Boer dared to call Dutch theologian Jacobus Arminius (1560-1609) a "Reformed" theologian in spite of heavy criticisms from the conservative side of his denomination (2008). Only after the board of the university had declared that "Reformed" is the name for a certain movement, and does not necessarily mean that Arminius was "orthodox," did the critics quiet down.

15. *Epistemic credibility.* This is a pistical anticipation within the logical modality, referring to the criterion of the ultimate credibility, veracity, reliability and certitude of science (including theology), and particularly of its logical axioms. We are dealing here with the logical confidence in the unprovable axioms from which all scientific activity starts, such as: (a) the trustworthiness of empirical observation ("do you read what you read, and how do you know you read what you read?"); (b) the reliability of logical thinking ("how do we ultimately *know* that, for instance, if A = B, and B = C, then A = C?"); (c) the fundamental knowledgeability of the cosmos ("how do we *know* that we can, and do, know [parts of] the cosmos?").

More generally, in epistemic credibility, it is ultimately the theoretical and pre-theoretical rational presuppositions of theology that matter. In the end, all our logical certitudes are founded in our pre-theoretical, and even pre-rational, or rather supra-rational convictions, which are of a transcendent-religious nature. We will come back to this later in this chapter.

Some Caveats

Please note again that modal analogies are never arbitrary metaphors that can easily be discarded or replaced. For instance, when we speak of the force of an argument, the plausibility of a hypothesis, or the elegance of a theory, it is virtually impossible to replace such terms with other terms that are *not* analogous to the physical, juridical or aesthetic modalities, respectively.

It should also be noted once again that all the norms and criteria we have listed must be found on the *law-side* of the respective modalities, not on the *subject-side* (for this distinction, see my *Wisdom for Thinkers*). This will help us to understand why we can never call the Bible a "norm" or "criterion" for theology, although this has been done by Karl Barth, Paul Tillich, Hans Küng, and so many others. The reason is that the Bible is on the subject-side of reality, not on the law-side. Facts can never be criteria. You can say that the Bible is the final judge over all our theological hypotheses and theories, but that is not what a criterion is. A criterion for theology is a kind of law that you have to follow in order to produce good theology. A thing can never be a law.

We *can* speak, though, of the universal and timeless significance of God's Word, and thus we may deduce the immanent-modal criterion of *logical continuity*, which we have identified as a kinematic retrocipation in the logical modality. As well, when we speak of God's Word in its transcendent-religious sense as the Law of Love that addresses the theologian's heart, this clearly involves a transcendent, supra-modal criterion for theological activity.

The Bible is not itself a norm. While it does *contain* a large number of norms (ethical laws); these are not norms for theological activity, but rather for the everyday practical life of the common believer, which is something the theologian should also be. However, for his scientific work as such they have no relevance.

WHAT THEN *IS* THEOLOGY?

Interestingly, you might say that the norms in the Bible are not on the law-side but on the subject-side of the theologian's field of study. That is, these norms are part of what he has to investigate. The Bible does not supply us either directly or indirectly with norms for theological activity, for it does not recognize this kind of activity. Instead, the Bible supplies us with immanent-modal norms for our practical life of faith, and these norms are in fact investigated by theologians.

Systematization

It is striking to see how often the *systematic* character of science has been considered to be *the* criterion of science. However, this cannot be correct because systematization also occurs in practical thought. Just think of the systematic character of a creed or a catechism, although these are not theological documents at all. As a boy, I began to classify and systematize all the prophecies that I could find in the Bible. This was a good training of my instinct for systematization, but it had very little to do with theology. Even the mechanic who has to detect a malfunction in the engine of my car goes about it in a systematic way, without this ever making him a scientist.

Yet, we can say that systematization *must* necessarily be a special characteristic in a discipline that calls itself *systematic theology*. One of the first questions to be raised is whether systematization always has to give rise to a *system*. Apparently, many older theologians thought so. The term *Summa* ("summary"), used by several medieval theologians (Albertus Magnus, Thomas Aquinas in the thirteenth century), and even before this the term *Sententiae* ("Statements," by Anselm of Laon and Peter Lombard in the eleventh and twelfth centuries), suggest the idea of a *system*. As far as I know, the first one to explicitly use the term "system" in theology was the German Reformed theologian Bartholomäus Keckermann, in his *Systema theologicum* ("Theological System," 1607).

Whatever meaning we attach to the term "system," it must be clear, firstly, that no system can ever be complete. And this is a very good thing too, for otherwise theologians would have nothing more to do as soon as the system was finished. Secondly, we must keep in mind that no system can ever fully cover God's revealed truth. Strictly speaking, the very idea of a system belies the fact that we only "know in part, . . . but when the perfect comes, the partial will pass away" (1 Cor. 13:9-10). Insofar as there can be any system, it has to account for the "in part" and the "not yet," always realizing that in the transcendent dimension there are things which "surpass knowledge" (Eph. 3:19). As Otto Weber noted, "dogmatics is eschatologically delimited; *that* is the actual counter-argument against any system." And as Hendrikus Berk-hof suggests, we can only observe God "from behind" (cf. Exod. 33:23). It is only *within* the framework of our immanent-theoretical thinking that systematization can lead to a certain system build-ing, in which the various subjects (Latin *loci*) of systematic theol-ogy are systematically correlated.

Snares

There are several dangers looming when any theological system tends to become too rigid. I see at least the following:

(a) *Closedness*. The first danger is that the dogmatic system becomes *strictly closed*. This may be a consequence of the fact that it is considered to be a totality of axioms, judgments, and conclusions, starting from a certain basic viewpoint, and as such complete and entirely self-contained. Euclid's geometry is a perfect example of this kind of closed scientific system.

The system may also be closed because it is dominated by a certain church denomination's peculiar views (see the following chapters), by the ideas of an (over)esteemed theological leader, or by those of an (over)esteemed theological school. For a time, such systems may seem very rigid and unshakable, but history teaches us that in the end they usually fall apart. True sustainability is not guaranteed by rigidity and confessional strictness, but by modesty, an open mind, creativity, and a clear awareness of the relative and provisional character of our theological constructs.

(b) *A limited starting point*. The second danger is that the longing for one mighty, all-encompassing system will entice its designer to build it on just one or a few theological ideas. I offer the following examples, which may serve to illustrate this tendency, without wishing to suggest that the theologians who developed the ideas in question were one-sided, or that the ideas to which they gave such prominence are not important: God's sovereignty (Augustine, John Calvin); nature–grace (Thomas Aquinas); law–gospel (Martin Luther); the covenant (Johannes Cocceius); religious feeling (Friedrich Schleiermacher); dispensations (John N. Darby); rebirth (Franz H. R. Frank); justification and reconciliation (Albrecht Ritschl); Christology (Karl Barth); the kerygma (Rudolf Bultmann); the "evangelical ground-principle," i.e., the doctrine of justification (Martin Kähler); etc.

The danger here is that the systematic unity and coherence that is gradually discovered becomes a principle from which the next step can be derived. At this point the system has become a slave to its own organizing principle (German: *Systemzwang*; Dutch: *systeemdwang*). The most prominent ideas are overloaded, while other essential ideas are neglected. The systematic theologian must allow room for all different aspects of his field of investigation.

(c) *A system as such*. If we, as a matter of principle, give up the ideal of an all-encompassing system, this does not mean that systematic theology can no longer be systematic. One traditional way to prevent any theological idea from dominating the system is to deal with the various articles of faith in the form of distinct loci (Latin sing. *locus*, "place"; here: "chapter," "subject"; see above). In Protestantism, Philip Melanchthon (*Loci communes*), and John Calvin (*Institutes of the Christian Religion*) were the first to employ this method. Since then, many systematic theologians have followed their lead by writing separate monographs on various dogmatic subjects without trying to place them in their own coherent systems. Notable examples are Reformed theologians Karl Barth (1886-1986) in Switzerland and Gerrit C. Berkouwer (1903-1996) in the Netherlands.

Foundationalism versus Fideism

There are several influential views with respect to faith and reason. I think of such confusing terms as foundationalism, evidentialism, presuppositionalism and fideism. Let us try to bring some order into this chaos. The errors committed by these various "-isms" can help us to get a clearer picture of what I view as the proper relationship between faith and reason. As far as I can see, we can make the following distinctions between the confusing "-isms" just mentioned:

1. *Foundationalism*: Truth—whether we mean the truth of God or truth in general—rests on a fixed, unassailable, axiomatic foundation. Although it is seldom mentioned, this foundation is of an emphatically immanent nature. Here we find several concepts placed in juxtaposition to each other:

(a) *Presuppositionalism*: Faith is founded on clear and obvious presuppositions of a rational nature. This view goes back to Aristotle and Thomas Aquinas, and in more modern times to the French philosopher René Descartes (1596-1650), who built his whole philosophy on an axiom which, to him at least, was obvious: *Cogito, ergo sum*, "I think, therefore I am." Truth is considered to be a pyramid, in which one truth is deduced from the other, and built on one or more axiomatic truths. These axioms are for all thinking people immediately obvious truths (think again of Euclid's geometrical system). Recent representatives of presuppositionalism are the American theologians Cornelius Van Til (1895-1987), Francis A. Schaeffer (1912-1984), Rousas J. Rushdoony (1916-2001), and Greg L. Bahnsen (1948-1995). In their thinking, the most important axiomatic *presupposition* is Scripture as the Word of God; presumably, he who starts from the authority of Scripture will come automatically to knowledge of the truth.

(b) *Evidentialism*: Faith is founded not on rational proofs but on empirical evidence; we accept as true only that which relies on facts that are observable for everyone. This view does not automatically lead to empiric*ism* or natural*ism*. On the contrary, this kind of empirical evidence—think of the resurrection of Christ (established on the basis of the empty tomb and the testimonies of witnesses), of prophecies fulfilled so far, or of striking radical conversions—is also used as evidence in apologetics. According to this view, truth is not reached deductively, as in (a), but inductively, by proceeding from individual facts to general principles. In philosophy, this view goes back to British empiricism. Recent representatives of evidentialism are the American theologians John H. Gerstner (1914-1996), John W. Montgomery (b. 1931), Norman L. Geisler (b. 1932), Richard Swinburne (b. 1934), Josh McDowell (b. 1939), Robert C. Sproul (b. 1939), and William L. Craig (b. 1949).

2. *Non-Foundationalism*: Truth and apologetics are based neither on (immanent) reason, nor on (immanent) observation, but on faith, whether in the irrational or the supra-rational sense. Now that it has become clear that, strictly speaking, presuppositionalism and evidentialism can no longer be maintained, some people go so far as to speak of the *post-foundationalist* task of theology. We distinguish between the following:

(a) *Fideism*: In line with (pre-)existentialism, especially as expressed in the thought of Danish philosopher Søren Kierkegaard (1813-1855), faith is taken here to be an *irrational* condition of all knowledge of the truth—Kierkegaard's well-known "leap in the dark"—which stands over against reason. We are dealing here with a genuine *sacrificium intellectus* ("sacrifice of the intellect"), which goes all the way back to the early church father Tertullian (c. 160-c. 225) and the medieval thinker William of Occam (c. 1287-1347) and links faith with the absurd.

(b) The *Reformational epistemology* of the American philosophers Alvin Plantinga (b. 1932), Nicholas Wolterstorff (b. 1932), and others: Truth starts with faith, but it is neither an immanent faith that can be primarily based on reason or observation, nor an irrational faith. This view is closely related to the Christian philosophical view that I have summarized in my *Wisdom for Thinkers*. Faith in the sense of the *fides qua* is neither rational, nor irrational, but supra-rational. Therefore, faith does not stand in opposition to reason and observation, but only in opposition to the absolutization of them in presuppositionalism and evidentialism, respectively. Plantinga and Wolterstorff try to make this faith acceptable by appealing to the natural awareness of God that all humans allegedly possess.

Faith and Reason

Of course, the distinctions I have just made are only relative. In an extremely simplified form, the choice is simply between four starting-points: the empirical, the rational, the irrational and the supra-rational. The names of the various "-isms" are very confusing because *all four* viewpoints could be described as *fundamentum*, as *presuppositio*, as *evidentia*, or as *fides*, if we so wished. In my view, it all amounts to this: rational thought (including irrational thinking) and empirical perception are nothing but immanent functions of the transcendent heart, and as such, they always presuppose the transcendent-religious attitude of the heart, that is, a *fides qua*. In my view, this insight is of the greatest importance for all theology, all apologetics and all philosophy of religion.

The problem of the relationship between faith and reason, between *pistis* ("faith") and *gnosis* ("[rational] knowledge"), or, as the church father Augustine put it, between *credere* ("believing") and *intelligere* ("understanding"), has been around for centuries. In 1998, Pope John Paul II (1920-2005) even devoted an encyclical (*Fides et ratio*) to the problem of faith and reason. I touched upon the matter in my *Wisdom for Thinkers*, but now we must consider it in a little more detail. I am convinced that this problem can only be dealt with in the context of a radically Christian philosophy.

The relationship between reason and faith is to be considered from two different angles, which we could call the vertical and the horizontal viewpoint:

1. *Vertical*: This is the relationship between reason in the sense of the modal-logical function and faith in the transcendent-religious sense (*fides qua*). The logical function is just one of many modal functions that arise from the human heart, that is, from the transcendent-religious Ego. Logical thinking is directed by the religious ground-motive that governs the human heart. In other words, there is no such thing as a neutral, objective theological argument because this is *a priori* dominated by the transcendent-religious attitude of the theologian's heart. We have dealt with this before.

2. *Horizontal*: This is the relationship between reason in the sense of the modal-logical function and faith in the sense of the modal-pistical function. Let us investigate this relationship a little more closely by studying the various modal analogies (which are all retrocipations) within the pistical modality. We will first look at the analogies with, or retrocipations upon, the natural modalities, then at the analogies with, or retrocipations upon, the spiritive modalities.

WHAT THEN *IS* THEOLOGY?

Natural Pistical Retrocipations

1. *Faith unity and multiplicity* (arithmetical retrocipations within the pistical modality): There is a multiplicity of beliefs, dogmas, creeds, and confessions, and at the same time "the unity of the faith" (Eph. 4:13) and "the [one and only] faith that was once for all delivered to the saints" (Jude 3). There is a multiplicity of faith truths, and yet only one Truth (John 1:14, 17; 14:6; 17:17). The whole is more than the sum of its parts, just as the Church is more than the sum of all its members.

The idea of the Trinity is internally contradictory if it is taken in the original arithmetical sense (something cannot be one and three at the same time) but not if it is viewed as an arithmetical retrocipation within the pistical aspect. In that case, the subject is primarily a pistical one and not an arithmetical one, though there is an analogy with the arithmetical modality. The Trinity is not a matter of counting but of believing.

2. *Faith sphere* (spatial retrocipation): We speak of the typical *space* in which faith can function, the sphere in which the life of faith unfolds and communion with God takes place (Eccl. 5:1; Ps. 139:5-10). Other examples are the "wide open" heart of the apostle Paul, and the Corinthians who, being too "restricted" (narrowed) in their affections, must "widen" their hearts as well (2 Cor. 6:11-13). Jesus speaks of a "little faith" (Matt. 6:30ff.) and a "great faith" (Matt. 15:28). We can also think of the sitting "at God's right hand" (e.g., Matt. 26:64), the "outer darkness" (e.g., Matt. 8:12), heaven "above" the earth (Ps. 103:11), etc. None of these matters is to be understood in a strictly geometrical way but as retrocipations within the pistical aspect.

In theology, we are familiar with terms like *locus* (a chapter in dogmatics), or *center* (Christ as the "center" of biblical thought), in contrast to more "peripheral" faith truths. Comparable terms are *focus* (itself a physical retrocipation), and *scopus* (itself a perceptive retrocipation).

3. *Faith constancy, mobility, progress* (kinematic retrocipations): On the subject-side of cosmic reality, there is on the one hand the constancy of beliefs, and on the other hand for instance the mobil-

ity, progress (and sometimes regress) in confessional and theological developments, and the course of Christian faith throughout the world (cf. Rom. 10:18) and through the ages. Another example is the fact that faith sets humans and things in motion.

On the law-side of reality, faith offers the norm for the proper constancy (as opposed to false obduracy), and for the right pace of faith in human lives (as opposed to rushing or excessive slowness): "Whoever believes will not be in haste" (Isa. 28:16).

4. *Faith power, energy, dynamics* (physical retrocipations): Jesus speaks of a faith so strong that it can displace mountains and uproot trees (see above), and the Letter to the Hebrews speaks of a faith that can conquer kingdoms, stop the mouths of lions, quench the power of fire, make people "strong out of weakness," etc. (Heb. 11:33-38). James tells us: "The prayer of a righteous person has great power as it is working," (James 5:16). "I can do all things through him who strengthens me," says Paul (Phil. 4:13). These are just a few examples.

5. *The life of faith* (biotic retrocipation): We can think of the *vitality* (from Latin *vita*, "life") of faith, the *development* of our beliefs, the *nourishing* of faith (the Bible has various references to "milk" and "solid food," (1 Cor. 5:2; Heb. 5:12-14; 1 Pet. 2:2), the *organic* coherence of our beliefs, our spiritual growth (Eph. 4:13; 2 Pet. 3:18).

6. *Faith perception, susceptibility, awareness* (perceptive retrocipations): Faith is conscious of itself and of its sources. Faith comes by "hearing" with the ears of our heart (Rom. 10:17), by "seeing" with the enlightened eyes of the heart (Eph. 1:18), and even by "tasting" the goodness of the Lord, or of his Word (Heb. 6:5; 1 Pet. 2:3).

7. *Faith sensitivity* (sensitive retrocipation): By this we mean the "warm" (itself a physical retrocipation), affective confidence of faith. This is not to be confused with the joy or the anger of faith, for these are true emotions, and are therefore to be viewed as pistical anticipations within the sensitive modality (the opposite of sensitive retrocipations within the pistical modality). The confidence of faith is a *pistical* matter, though retrocipating upon the sensitive aspect, whereas the ecstasy of faith is a *sensitive* matter, though anticipating the pistical aspect.

Spiritive Pistical Retrocipations

8. *Faith thinking* (logical retrocipation): "Distinction" is the distinctive mark of the logical aspect. Yet, on the law-side of the pistical modality, there are pistical distinctions that are often not logical at all. It is as Paul says: "The natural person does not accept the things of the Spirit of God, for they are folly to him, and he is not able to understand them because they are spiritually discerned" (1 Cor. 2: 14). Some examples are the distinctions between the three persons within the Trinity, between the divine and the human natures of Christ, and between God's sovereignty and Man's responsibility.

On the subject-side we notice that faith is never a "leap in the dark," as though we must leave our reason at home or turn it off the moment we begin to believe. Faith is never limited to logical distinctions (on the contrary, cf. Isa. 55:8; Rom. 9:19-20; 11:33); but it definitely contains such distinctions. In fact, it could hardly manage without them. For instance, the contrast between faith and unbelief is only possible through the analogy with the logical principle of contradiction (cf. Rom. 11:20: "They were broken off because of their unbelief, but you stand fast through faith").

9. *Formation of faith* (historical-formative retrocipation): This comes into play when you give shape—consciously or unconsciously—to your life of faith, your beliefs, your spiritual growth, the relationship to your church, etc. We may also think of the formative or reforming power of faith, often embodied in certain *authorities* (i.e., persons who exert formative power), whom God has placed within a faith community. Some examples are the reformers such as the German Martin Luther and the Frenchman John Calvin, but also, for instance, the German Nikolaus L. von Zinzendorf (1700-1760), the Englishman John Wesley (1703-1791), and the Anglo-Irishman John N. Darby (1800-1882). This formative work depends on many factors: character and disposition, upbringing and education, regional and church culture.

10. *Faith language and interpretation* (lingual retrocipations): We are not referring here to language in the literal sense, which is qualified by the lingual modality, but to the process by which we signify the meaning of Christian beliefs, which are supposed

to represent God's thoughts (cf. 1 Cor. 2:9-13). It is because of this lingual retrocipation within the pistical modality that theology is more than just a literary science. In theological exegesis, we are primarily interested in the pistical significance of the text, not just the literary (grammatical-historical) aspects, though there is an interconnection with the literary and historical sciences.

11. *Faith communion and interaction* (social retrocipations): We can think here of the believer's communion with God and with fellow-believers, so that a faith community arises. Faith creates horizontal bonds and fellowship with all those who experience the same vertical relationship with God. Believing in isolation, outside any form of faith community, means a serious impoverishment for the person himself. We could even say that this is in fact impossible, since even the most individual faith is marked by the faith community in which the person is rooted.

12. *The sacrifice of faith, faith evaluation* (economic retrocipations): The Bible gives many examples of the willingness of faith to bring sacrifices (cf. Luke 18:22; Rom. 12:1; Heb. 3:15-16; 1 Pet. 2:5), of weighing the value of temporal as against eternal goods (2 Cor. 4:16-18), of "making the best use of time" (Eph. 5:16; ASV: "redeeming the time"), and of "counting the cost" of faith (Luke 14:28).

In another sense we may think of the *efficiency* of certain faith aphorisms, which express all-encompassing truths in a few words, such as: "The saying is trustworthy and deserving of full acceptance, that Christ Jesus came into the world to save sinners" (1 Tim. 1:15).

Another economic retrocipation is also avoiding "excesses." For instance, we should not believe more than God's Word demands (an idea which is humorously expressed in the saying, "Don't try to be more Catholic than the Pope"). Or, to use another example, one may think of the debt of faith: "Owe no one anything, except to love each other" (Rom. 13:8).

13. *Faith harmony* (aesthetic retrocipation): We may consider the inner harmony (or lack thereof) in our life of faith, or between our various beliefs. It is important not to over-emphasize one or two faith elements.

Harmony is also an important element in the peace of God (Phil. 4:7), in the peace of Christ (John 14:27; Col. 3:15), and in the rest promised for the souls of those who follow Jesus (Matt. 11:29-30).

Last but not least, harmony exists within the Bible itself. We can speak of the harmony between the Old and New Testaments, between the four Gospels, between the Apostles Paul and James, etc.

14. *The right of faith, faith authority* (juridical retrocipations): Let us think here of whether or not certain beliefs are *justified*. This is something very different from justification by faith, in which by the way, we also encounter a juridical retrocipation in the pistical modality. There is also the *right* of faith, being *entitled* by God to his promises, and conversely, God's right to our service and worship.

Please note that in the righteousness of God, whether the condemnation of the wicked or the justification of the righteous, we are not dealing with juridical ideas as such, but with juridical retrocipations within the pistical modality. This is different from canon law, where we find justice in its original juridical sense, though clearly anticipating the pistical modality.

Another important term is authority (Greek *exousia*, also "power, authorization"): In the authority of Scripture, to which every human must submit himself, and in the authority of the office-bearers in the church, to which church members must submit themselves, we meet a juridical retrocipation within the pistical modality. Because this authority is formally established in the sense of canon law, there is also a truly juridical aspect to it.

15. *Faith affection* (ethical retrocipation): Think of the affection and love inspired by the confidence of faith, for God and his Word (Ps. 119:47-48, 97, 113, etc.). True faith cannot be anything other than "faith working through love" (Gal. 5:6). Here again, we can say that in Christianity we never deal with faithfulness or morality in themselves, apart from their connection to faith. It is this faith that marks every form of faithfulness and love. There is no true faith without true love, for "whoever loves has been born of God and knows God. Anyone who does not love does not know God, because God is love" (1 John 4:7-8).

No Confusion!

It is essential for the theologian to be conscious of the proper pistical sense of the analogous retrocipatory or anticipatory terms of which he makes use, and of which I have just given some examples. This pistical sense is never to be confused with the meanings that other sciences attribute to these same terms. I have already used the example of the Trinity. If we take "Three-In-One" in a strictly arithmetical sense—as the Jehovah's Witnesses do, who therefore reject it—this will lead to an absurdity. But this is *not* an arithmetical matter; it is merely an arithmetical retrocipation within the pistical modality. That is, it is primarily a pistical matter, though retrocipating upon the arithmetical modality.

Let us look at another example. As I mentioned earlier, in the joy of faith we are dealing with a sensitive matter, in which the sensitive modality anticipates the pistical modality. If this pistical anticipation is not recognized, this joy—as a pure emotion in itself—will be considered identical to any other joy. One consequence will be that people will try to reduce religious feelings entirely to the sensitive aspect, as has been done, for instance, by the Austrian psychologist Sigmund Freud (1856-1939). In this case, we speak of sensitivism (or psychologism), which is a way of absolutizing the sensitive modality.

If, conversely, the warm confidence of faith—a sensitive retrocipation within the pistical aspect—is confused with emotions in their original sensitive sense, people begin to search for such emotions as the true test of faith. This is a mistake. To put it bluntly, we can experience the joy of faith without any activation of the sympathetic nervous system. In order to rejoice in the Lord *always* (Phil. 4:4), no continuous gland secretions are needed (for after all, they really would be a little unhealthy). Study of the modal analogies is a means to help us distinguish between different kinds of joy, and a thousand other things.

A further example has to do with the matter of justification by faith. In the so-called "forensic" doctrine of justification (based on ideas found in the writings of Anselm of Canterbury, (c. 1033-1109), the emphasis is laid too strongly and too one-sidedly on the juridical element in justification, i.e., the acquittal and rehabilitation of the one justified. But an ethical doctrine of justification underscores too strongly and too one-sidedly the moral element, i.e., the idea that one becomes a *tzaddiq* (a righteous person), whose righteousness comes to light in his words and deeds of love (cf. "faith working through love" mentioned by Paul in Gal. 5:6). However, justification by faith is qualified neither by the juridical nor by the ethical modalities, but by the pistical modality. Righteousness and love in their original modal (i.e., juridical and ethical) sense are confused here with juridical and ethical retrocipations within the strict boundaries of the pistical modality. In other words: justification by faith can never be explained in purely juridical or ethical terms (although this has often been tried), because it is of a specifically pistical nature. Again, study of the modal analogies can make these states of affairs transparent.

The Logical Within the Pistical

The relationship that interests us most, when we think of faith and reason, is the one between the logical and the pistical modalities, particularly the logical retrocipation within the pistical modality. As I said before, logical distinction in faith matters is to be understood, not according to strictly logical norms but as a logical retrocipation within the pistical modality, and thus according to pistical norms.

Unfortunately, this relationship is often viewed in a very different way. Faith and reason are usually viewed as two activities that allegedly first have to be *theoretically* severed. Subsequently, having been forced to stand in a *theoretical* antithesis to one another, they are compared and contrasted. Then the results of this comparison are imposed upon our *practical* thinking, to which such a theoretical antithesis is totally foreign. In this way, especially after the Enlightenment, people became accustomed to the stark distinction, or even separation, between faith and reason. This explains why many people have been brainwashed to think that if you believe, you cannot be rational, at least not *within* your belief-system, and conversely, if you want to think logically you have to keep your beliefs as far away as you can.

As I explained before, the underlying error here is not distinguishing between practical and theoretical thinking. Practical thinking is theoreticalized, and theoretical thinking is in turn absolutized at the expense of the practical. In fact, faith and reason are intrinsically interwoven within immanent reality, and integrated in the transcendent-religious human heart. It is in the heart that faith and reason converge and are grasped in their unity, identity, and fullness. And it is *from* the heart that faith and reason emerge as distinct, though not conflicting, modalities, and diverge within the diversity of immanent life.

I spoke about the logical modality on the one hand and the logical retrocipation within the pistical modality on the other. If *distinction* is a main feature of the logical, we may distinguish two kinds of distinction, which are both present in matters of faith:

(a) Faith in its immanent sense is not possible without logical distinction as such, that is, distinction in its original modal-logical meaning. The believer is never to switch off his logical thinking. How would he be able to understand the Bible if he could not make necessary distinctions, such as between an apostle and an evangelist, between a Jew and a Gentile, between faith and sight, between authority and submission, between the ox and the donkey, between the cedar and the hyssop, etc.? This does not apply only to theoretical thinking, but also to practical Bible reading. Even though this is a pistical matter, it cannot manage without continuous logical distinctions. There is no faith without logic and reason.

(b) We also speak of "distinction" in a typically pistical sense, that is, as a logical retrocipation within the pistical modality. I have already mentioned the examples of the distinctions between the three persons of the Trinity, between the two natures of Christ, or between God's sovereignty and Man's responsibility. From a purely logical viewpoint, such distinctions are full of contradictions. In a purely logical way, we cannot reconcile the truth that Christ is really God with the truth that, when he was here on earth, he was a humble man, dependent on and subservient to God, all the while existing not as two persons but as one person.

In a purely logical way, we cannot reconcile the truths of election and rebirth, which are dependent on God's sovereignty, with the truths of repentance and conversion, which, though not severed from God's sovereignty, are primarily dependent on Man's responsibility. The solution cannot be fifty-fifty. Man's redemption is one hundred percent a matter of God's sovereign grace, and one hundred percent a matter of Man's own responsibility. This is a paradox that cannot be solved by the strict use of logic.

WHAT THEN *IS* THEOLOGY?

In a purely logical way, we cannot reconcile the truth that God did not desire sin, forbade it and was not responsible for it, with the truth that his eternal plan of salvation definitely presupposed Man's fall into sin. In my book *Power in Service*, I quoted the church father Augustine (354-430) who spoke of *felix culpa*, the "fortunate fall": "God judged it better to bring good out of evil than not to permit any evil to exist." His teacher, Ambrose (c. 340-397), also spoke of the "fortunate ruin" of Adam in the Garden of Eden, in that his sin brought more good to humanity than if he had stayed perfectly innocent. But, as far as I am aware, neither of them concluded that for this reason God was responsible for the fall of Man. They let the paradox stand as it was.

Two Ways Out

Traditionally, the paradoxes just mentioned have led to two different ways out, which are comparable with the two ways in which people speak of the transcendent in general. In brief, we find again that the supra-rational is reduced either to the rational or to the irrational:

1. *The supra-rational rendered rational:* The first way out is that of rationalism, as we find it in the strains of Scholastic theology persisting in both Catholicism and Protestantism. This approach cannot resign itself to the idea that there are mysteries of faith that surpass human logic, because this is considered mysticism. In the end, all alleged mysteries must be reduced to their logical components, so that they can then be incorporated into purely rational, closed theological systems. Logical contradictions are simply eliminated, for instance, by denying either Christ's divine nature or his human nature. Either God's sovereignty in predestination is denied (being reduced by Arminians to foreknowledge—however, see the distinction in Rom. 8:29), or Man's responsibility is repudiated (as in hyper-Calvinism). Either God is made the factual "author" of sin, or the plan of salvation is severed from the problem of sin (supra-lapsarianism). And so on.

All of these are merely attempts to reduce the supra-rational to the rational. Nowadays, we can hardly imagine how thoroughly rationalistic Reformed and Lutheran theology were in the seventeenth century. Many people have suggested that early Protestantism made such a smooth transition to Enlightenment theology because it did not have to change its rationalistic methodology.

2. *The supra-rational rendered irrational:*. The second way out is to emphasize the "mysterious" or "mystical" character of the great truths of faith. Thinkers advocating this view underscore the idea that theology deals with matters that are ultimately absurd (Tertullian, William of Occam). They even boast that this is what faith demands of them: believing things that are strictly irrational. In his book, *The Reasonableness of Christianity, as Delivered in the Scriptures* (1695), the British philosopher John Locke (1632-1704) argued that, while Scripture does ask us to believe in things that surpass reason, it never asks us to believe things that go against reason. This corresponds entirely with the distinction we are making between the supra-rational and the irrational.

The "mysterious" here is not that which is simply hidden, but rather that which is illogical, irrational, and thus mystical, fantastic, speculative, esoteric, bizarre, or absurd. The longing for this kind of mystery dishonors faith and God just as much as does the rationalism that I mentioned in point 1. Neither rationalism nor irrationalism is the answer to the fact that there are indeed mysteries of faith that surpass human reason. Please note, this surpassing or transcending means that it surpasses *both* the rational *and* the irrational. The supra-rational is transcendent, whereas both the rational and the irrational are immanent, because they both presuppose the immanent logical laws. The irrational implies disobedience with respect to logical norms, whereas the supra-rational implies that which is elevated above the logical norms.

The whole matter of distinction looks very different if we do not see it as a matter qualified by the logical modality, but as a logical retrocipation *within* the pistical modality. In other words, it is something that is not subject to the laws of logic but to pistical norms. Precisely because it is a logical retrocipation *within* the pistical modality it refers continually to the *supra*-logical (supra-rational). The supra-logical differs from the illogical (irrational) as much as the transcendent differs from the immanent, the infinite differs from the finite or unity, fullness, totality, and integrity differs from modal-functional diversity and variability.

Chapter Eight

Paradigms & Ground-Motives

When we speak of "theology" this term can have two different meanings. We may be referring to an academic discipline called "theology," but we may also be referring to one of a multitude of "theologies" consisting of the views of theologians (many of them major figures), from the Apologists in the second and third centuries (or, as some say, from the post-apostolic period) up to the present.

There is such a thing as the *history* of theology: the succession of the various theological currents throughout church history, and the sometimes drastic way in which one school made way for a subsequent one. Therefore, we can speak of the "theology" of Augustine, of John Calvin, of Friedrich Schleiermacher, of Karl Barth, or of Wolfhart Pannenberg. And, as we have seen, some would even like to speak—erroneously, I believe—of the "theology" of New Testament writers such as Luke, Paul, John, or Peter.

The Paradigm Concept

The well-known philosopher of science Thomas S. Kuhn (1922-1996) has left a seemingly permanent mark on the discussion about this phenomenon of various theologies (and philosophies, for that matter) by introducing the term *paradigm*. In his view, the choice of scientific theories is ultimately determined not only by rational, but also by psychical, social, economic, cultural, political, and religious factors. In a revolutionary publication in the 1960s, *The Structure of Scientific Revolutions*, Kuhn explained why he rejected the standard view of some continued gradual progress in science. He pointed to long periods of "normal science" in the history of the various special sciences, which alternated with short periods of scientific revolutions.

During periods of "normal science," scientific investigation takes place entirely within the framework of a so-called paradigm. This is a model of problem solving with which a scientist approaches a certain field of study. It involves a *disciplinary matrix* in the sense of a systematic theoretical framework with which a scientist approaches his science. American philosopher John D. Caputo (b. 1940) remarked that during this time it was not a philosopher who accused religion of mythologizing, but rather the "apostles of scientific objectivity." In his view, a paradigm is a kind of myth which all practitioners of a given special science believe during a certain period, until this myth evaporates, and is replaced by a new one. Science is not objective or unprejudiced, but always paradigmatically determined.

Kuhn was not alone in claiming that, among the many things which influence the practice of science, there are, aside from the rational factors, also faith factors. As long ago as 1913, the great physicist and Nobel Prize laureate Max Planck (1858-1947) said that even in the most exact of all sciences the investigators cannot do without a preceding worldview. That is the same as saying that they cannot do without unprovable presuppositions. Planck said that even in physics one cannot be "saved without faith" (cf. Eph. 2:5, 8), at the very least the faith in a certain reality around us. The Flemish-South African philosopher Herman Jan de Vleeschauwer (1899-1986) wrote that even from a purely rational viewpoint, an unprejudiced science is impossible; it always starts with an act of faith in our thinking.

The German philosopher Hans-Georg Gadamer (1900-2002) described how all "prejudices" had been "discredited" by the Enlighten-ment, but that this condition was now changing in contemporary thought. Gadamer called for the renewed recognition that there are "legitimate prejudices," including faith prejudices. Let all rationalists, positivists, and naturalists pay attention, for I believe Planck, de Vleeschauwer, Gadamer, and so many others were right: *there is no science without some preceding faith.* Theology especially *studies* faith; but there is no theology that is not itself based on faith. Below, we will analyze more accurately what this entails.

In the broadest sense, a paradigm is a framework of reference, a tradition of investigation, which consists of a common world-view, general-philosophical and special-philosophical prejudices, a methodological consensus, scientific values, and special-scientific theories. More precisely, Kuhn uses the paradigm concept in two senses, which I express here in the modal terminology that we are by now familiar with: (a) a *socially* qualified meaning, which includes a number of convictions, theories, values, and methods that are shared by the members of a certain scientific community, and (b) a *logically* qualified meaning (*disciplinary matrix*), referring to the concrete *solutions* which as theoretical-methodological models create a basis for the solution of the puzzles that remain in normal science.

This second meaning is more in correspondence with the original meaning of Greek *paradeigma* ("example, pattern, specimen, sample"), but the first meaning has become by far the best known. Nowadays, most thinking Western humans have incorporated the word "paradigm" into their vocabulary in the often rather vague sense of a philosophy, an intellectual framework, a mental outlook, etc.

Once Again, Rational, Supra-rational, and Irrational

One fundamental starting point for an analysis of the philosophical paradigm concept is the insight that beliefs are never exclusively the subjective choice of an individual. For the most part, they are what we call the inter-subjective choice of a *community*. The thinking and experiencing human Ego not only stands in an I–thou relationship to God, but also in a we–thou relationship. This is because of the I–we relationship inherent in all societal relationships, including a Christian church denomination or a scientific community. Not only the Christian faith but also the apostate faith of secular thinking is almost always the faith of a certain community. This is also true for a scientific community which in a period of "normal science" works within a certain paradigm. It is a confession (written or unwritten) that keeps a church denomination together; Similarly, it is an (unwritten) paradigm that keeps a scientific community together.

In the broadest sense, such a paradigm necessarily includes not only philosophical and special-scientific theories, but also pre-theoretical beliefs of various kinds. According to our Christian philosophy, such theories and beliefs are ultimately of a transcendent-religious character—that which Paul Tillich called the "mystical *a priori.*" The term "mystical" is unfortunate here, for the mystical is only one form of manifestation of the transcendent-religious. But Tillich's basic idea of a (transcendent-)religious *a priori* seems to me to be correct.

Before I describe Kuhn's view in more detail, I have to emphasize that the idea that all scientific thinking is based upon pre-scientific, non-rational prejudices did not originate with him. Long before Kuhn, the Hungarian thinker Michael Polanyi (1891-1976) pointed out that all our scientific work exhibits almost systematically the traits of a hidden personal commitment (1958). To this belong the originality, intuition, and scientific passions of the investigator, but especially his partly non-rational or semi-rational presuppositions, convictions, commitments, and beliefs. However, even Polanyi brought this up only twenty years after the Dutch Christian philosopher Herman Dooyeweerd (1894-1977) had pointed out the supra-rational and supra-theoretical, transcendent-religious root of thinking.

But there is more to be said here. Dooyeweerd broke more radically with the dogma of rational autonomy than Polanyi did. Even Polanyi could not fully extricate himself from the rationalism pervading Western culture at the time, as we see from the fact that he described knowledge as primarily rational. For Dooyeweerd, however, rational knowledge is only one of several forms and kinds of knowledge, such as aesthetic knowledge, moral knowledge, and pistical (or faith) knowledge. The latter must not be confused with ethical and theological knowledge, for ethics and theology are special sciences. Therefore, knowledge belonging to these sciences is rational in nature. But moral consciousness for instance, although it *is* a form of knowledge, is non-rational (please note that it is not irrational!) There are Christians "who have their powers of discernment trained by constant practice to distinguish good from evil" (Heb. 5:14), often without being able to analyze logically why this is good and that is evil.

After Dooyeweerd, Thomas Kuhn was—as far as I am aware—the *first* who really broke with the idea of the strict rationality of science. However, although Dooyeweerd and Kuhn may seem to be allies, they are not. For Kuhn, knowledge is ultimately an *ir*rational matter, while for Dooyeweerd it is a *supra*-rational one. The two kinds of knowledge could not be more different (see chapter 7): the *supra-rational*, which surpasses reason and is *transcendent*, is essentially different from the *irrational*, which goes against reason and is *immanent*. What is lacking in Kuhn's thinking is the view of the transcendent dimension in all knowledge, and thus the notion of the transcendent and the supra-rational, which surpasses both the rational and the irrational. But despite this basic lack of understanding, there is still much we can learn from Kuhn.

Scientific Revolutions

Let us now examine a little more closely Kuhn's view with regard to the development of science. As long as a certain paradigm governs a group of scientists and binds them together, that science enjoys great harmony and stability. However, through further research such a paradigm can enter into a crisis. This occurs when more and more puzzles turn out to be unsolvable in terms of the governing paradigm. In that case, the paradigm will still be obstinately defended for some time, if need be with all kinds of auxiliary hypotheses and other mental gymnastics, especially as long as no new paradigm is in view. "Don't throw away old shoes until you have got new ones," as the old saying goes.

In the end, however, the paradigm will come under so much pressure that inevitably a *scientific revolution* will take place. Within a few decades, the paradigm will be creatively replaced, in whole or in part, by a new, alternative paradigm, which inaugurates a new period of "normal science." In such a revolution, scientific factors do play some role but, according to Kuhn, the most decisive role is the one played by the non-rational factors we have mentioned. This view flatly contradicts the previous view of science as a fully rational process: at decisive moments, this process is not rational at all, since other factors play the main role.

Interestingly, Kuhn compared "normal science" to religious dogmatism. You have to subscribe to the governing paradigm, otherwise you are not accepted by the scientific community. No one would even dream of contradicting it. Figuratively speaking, you would be burned at the stake if you did, just as they did with heretics in the Middle Ages. Such religious dogmatism can only be broken by a *reformation*, that is, a radical *conversion* or *Gestalt switch*. Hence the popular terms *paradigm switch* and *paradigm shift*, which are used nowadays for many different sorts of changes of opinion.

A new paradigm is not accepted primarily because of its success, but rather because of its *potential* for success. Scientists cling to the conviction that the new paradigm *must* be better than the one now outdated because it no longer works. This attractive feature of the new paradigm is based not so much on rational arguments, but rather on an almost religious faith or conviction, which is shared by its adherents—one might almost say its "converts" who now form the new "denomination," i.e., the new scientific community. It is often the case that the older scientists do not have the mental capacity (no matter how bright they are) to give up the old paradigm and accept the new one. The new paradigm is a matter that appeals in particular to the younger scientists—especially those under, say, thirty-five—within the special science concerned. When the French chemist Antoine Lavoisier (1743-1794) introduced a new paradigm in chemistry, *none* of the older chemists—some of them very famous—accepted it, whereas afterwards *all* of the younger ones did. Here you see what prejudice can do in even the greatest thinkers.

As a consequence of such a scientific revolution, entirely new problems are discovered, acknowledged and tackled. New criteria for testing scientific theories are developed. The earlier as well as the more recent data are interpreted in a fresh way, in the light of the new paradigm. The older concepts, ideas and theories are reformulated. The way is opened for entirely new observations, experiments and theories. In short, the whole scientific perspective of the scientific community in question is drastically reformed. If periods of "normal science" are characterized by a kind of religious dogmatism, as Kuhn says, periods of scientific revolutions may be compared with "great awakenings" or true "revivals," of the kind we see in the course of Protestant history.

In the twentieth century, the idea of a neutral, objective, fully rational science has been combated as well by other philosophers of science, each in their own way, on the basis of their own philosophical and pre-theoretical presuppositions. I only mention the critical rationalists Karl R. Popper and Imre Lakatos, the scientific "anarchist" Paul K. Feyerabend, the Neo-Marxist and pragmatist Jürgen Habermas, the representatives of philosophical hermeneutics (Paul Ricœur, Hans-Georg Gadamer), and the post-modern philosophers (Jean-François Lyotard, Jacques Derrida, Richard Rorty). It is mainly staunch physicists who still believe in the old idea of a neutral, objective, fully rational physics—either because they are simply not interested in philosophy, or else because they actually despise it.

Kuhn and Dooyeweerd

For a Christian philosophical view of science, Herman Dooyeweerd is undoubtedly one of the most important and most influential thinkers. This is because he was the first and the most thorough philosopher to point out that all pre-theoretical presuppositions are ultimately of a supra-rational, transcendent-religious character. The word "religious" here does not have the meaning that Thomas Kuhn attaches to it. To him, "religious" is nothing more than—as Dooyeweerd would put it—another one of the immanent-modal-functional aspects of our empirical reality, i.e., the pistical modality. In other words, "religious" for Kuhn refers only to facets of our immanent living and thinking.

For Dooyeweerd, however, the *entire* immanent-modal-functional life is religious in the sense that people have been called to serve God in every facet of their everyday lives, including their scientific activity. The reason is that our entire immanent-modal-functional life converges in the *transcendent*-religious life of Man's supra-modal and supra-functional Ego. As we have seen, this is what the Bible calls the "heart," in which Man stands in a relationship either with the God of the Bible, or with the false gods of society, whether that society be primitive or modern and sophisticated. For Kuhn, the "religious"—that is, pistical— factors have a place alongside the psychical, rational, social, economic, and other factors. Dooyeweerd sees this the same way. But beyond all these immanent factors, of which the pistical are just a few, he is aware of that transcendent-*religious* heart, in which all these immanent functions are concentrated.

Yet, there is a clear connection between Kuhn and Dooyeweerd, namely, between Kuhn's idea of the *paradigm* (especially in its philosophical sense), and what Dooyeweerd calls the *transcendental ground-idea* or the *cosmonomic* idea (Dutch: *wetsidee*). According to Dooyeweerd, a transcendent-religious ground-motive—the driving force of the human heart—expresses itself theoretically in just such a transcendental ground-idea (see my *Wisdom for Thinkers* for the difference between "transcendent" and "transcendental"). In this ground-idea, Dooyeweerd distinguishes three *transcendental theoretical ideas*, which underlie and pervade all scientific thinking (and even, one might add, all scientific paradigms). They concern, respectively, the three *transcendental ground-problems* of theoretical thought:

(a) The problem of *coherence*, that is, the mutual relationship and coherence of the various modalities of immanent reality.

(b) The problem of *unity*, that is, the deeper root-unity of these modalities, and thus of the entire cosmic reality.

(c) The problem of *origin*, that is, the ultimate origin of the diversity and coherence of immanent reality.

Applied to Kuhn's paradigm idea, taken in the broadest sense of the word, this means that every paradigm must somehow provide solutions to the problems of the coherence, the unity, and the origin of things. As an example of how this is sometimes done, let us take materialism. This philosophy solves the first problem by reducing all modalities to the physical aspect; i.e., according to reductionism, all cosmic phenomena are in the end nothing but material and physical. It solves the second problem by absolutizing this physical aspect and elevating it above all the other modalities. In this way, matter (the physical) becomes a kind of idol. Materialism solves the third problem in an evolutionistic way. Evolution is a physical matter in that biotic life too is reduced to the properties of atoms and molecules. All inanimate and animate things in the universe are the product of an evolutionary development.

Compare this with the radical Christian philosophical approach. Christian philosophy solves the first problem by accepting all the various modalities of immanent reality on the same footing, in all their divergence and variability, without ever attempting to reduce them to one another. It solves the second problem by maintaining that all immanent-modal aspects, all modal functions, find their unity, fullness and integrity in the supra-modal, supra-functional, transcendent human heart, Man's Ego. Please note that in the entire universe, Man's heart is the *only* location where such a convergence of all modal aspects takes place. This view assigns to Man a special and unique position in the whole of cosmic reality, in accordance with biblical revelation. Christian philosophy solves the third problem by its faith in God, the Creator, Lawgiver, and Sustainer of the universe. The diversity and coherence of immanent reality belongs to the law-order that God has instituted for it.

A Christian Super-Paradigm

The three transcendental ground-problems and other ideas I have mentioned could be brought together in a kind of a Christian super-paradigm. This is a general Christian theoretical frame of reference for philosophical and special-scientific, including theological, thinking (I touched upon this in my *Wisdom for Thinkers*, but here I deal with it more extensively). In my view, besides the three transcendental ground-problems of theoretical thought, some of the most important pre-theoretical and theoretical elements of such a paradigm are the following:

(a) Every (thinking) person, not least the scientist, is in his deepest existential being focused on the vital question concerning the absolute Origin and Ground of the whole of empirical reality. In his heart, every (thinking) person has a deep existential longing for this kind of solid support for his thinking. No wonder this orientation is a real "drive." Therefore, Dooyeweerd speaks of a *ground-motive* (from Latin *movere*, "to move"), a basic driving force that "moves" (steers, governs) Man in the depths of his heart. From his heart, Man orients his entire existence toward this Origin and Ground, which can be either true or false, God or idols—and by idols we mean either gods or ideologies.

This discussion of Man's being driven to his Origin and Ground is a philosophical way of describing *religion* (see my *Wisdom for Thinkers*). Therefore, we speak of a *religious* ground-motive. This is what others have called the *ultimate commitment* of every human being. Religion is "the relationship to the Absolute" (Hendrikus Berkhof). The genuinely ultimate commitment is therefore necessarily religious, and every human is therefore necessarily religious in the transcendent sense (which I have called "transcendent-religious," in contrast with the "immanent-religious," which is the same as pistical). This transcendent religiosity of Man is simply the way God has made him; God has designed Man for communion with him. Man cannot help being religious in this transcendent sense; he cannot live without this religious driving force. There is a "hole" in him that can only be filled by God (Francis A. Schaeffer)—or, since the fall, by the gods.

(b) In point (a) above, I indicated that this religious ground-motive is not the same in all humans. It may be _anastatic_, i.e., in the grip of God's Word-revelation concerning God, Christ, creation, fall, redemption, Kingdom, the end of the world, etc. It also may be _apostatic_, this is, in the grip of a pagan idea, or in the grip of mixed ideas, in which God's Word-revelation is not fully honored, or even rejected outright. (Of course, because of sin, no person on earth can be _fully_ in the grip of God's Word; I refer only to the fundamental intention and tendency of the heart.) Ultimately, there are only these two ground-motives: one is in the spirit of Scripture (anastatic), while the other goes against it (apostatic). That is, either Man has committed himself to the Bible's self-testimony as the inspired, authoritative, reliable, and trustworthy Word of God, or else he has not.

Here we touch upon the deep _antithesis_, which was already emphasized by the Dutch polymath Abraham Kuyper (1837-1920), but which was not always properly understood. This is not an antithesis between the church and the world, or between the church and the state, or between Christians and society, etc., which would be _structural_ antitheses. No, it is a _directional_ antithesis between regenerated and non-regenerated hearts. Or rather, because of the sinful nature that Christians on earth still possess, it is the antithesis between flesh and Spirit, which runs right through the heart and the life of believers (John 3:6; 6:63; Rom. 8:4-14; 2 Cor. 7:1; Gal. 5:16-26; Phil. 3:3; 1 Pet. 4:1-6).

(c) This _pre-rational_ and _pre-theoretical_ ground-motive colors, pervades, or even determines our _background assumptions_, our rational, but pre-theoretical worldview (John Wisdom), our "global assumptions" (Gerard Radnitzky), our _sensus communis_ or "common consciousness" (Hans-Georg Gadamer), our ideology

(Jürgen Habermas), our "first order principles" (John F. Miller), our "control beliefs" (Nicholas Wolterstorff), our life perspective or confessional view (Al Wolters), our "ultimate commitment" (Wentzel van Huyssteen), or whatever you wish to call it.

For the Christian it is self-evident that this worldview is indeed governed by his religious ground-motive. It is difficult to see how his deepest convictions concerning God, Christ, creation, fall, redemption, Kingdom, the end of the world, etc., could *not* strongly determine his views concerning the cosmos, nature, culture, history, Man, etc. Every rational view with regard to all these various facets of our world is necessarily governed by Man's pre-rational, or rather supra-rational ground-motive. Man's reason is not autonomous; on the contrary, it is dominated by his supra-rational faith. On the basis of his presuppositions, Man could not on the one hand confess his finiteness, including the finiteness of reason, and on the other hand view reason as autonomous. Reason is *a priori* existentially governed and determined by that which transcends its own finiteness: the *fides qua*, in which Man may account in a supra-rational manner for his own rationality. In this faith he is able to find in every possible respect his ultimate ground and certainty.

(d) In point (c) many expressions have been quoted that all more or less express the same idea of a pre-theoretical view of knowledge and of the world. However, it is not always clear to what extent the respective authors themselves make a distinction between pre-theoretical and theoretical, or between immanent and transcendent elements. At any rate, Kuhn's idea of a scientific paradigm seems to suggest rather a theoretical matrix, but, here too, pre-theoretical elements are certainly included, not to mention transcendent elements. Be that as it may, I would like to make two clear distinctions. The first is a distinction between, on the one hand, a general Christian *pre-theoretical* worldview, and, on the other hand, a *theoretical* paradigm, which is inspired and pervaded by this underlying worldview and which forms the foundation for a certain scientific community in a given period of "normal science." The second is a distinction between a pre-theoretical worldview, which is immanent, and the supra-theoretical ground-motive of the heart, which is transcendent.

(e) All special-scientific work takes place within the framework of paradigms as I have explained earlier. In contemporary philosophy of science, this seems to be rather generally accepted. The greatest difference between the consensus in the philosophy of science and the view that I represent is the central and fundamental place I assign to Man's "ultimate commitment," which is emphatically of a supra-rational, transcendent character. I certainly believe that all scientific activity takes place within the framework of a paradigm, but I believe even more strongly that all paradigms, through certain pre-theoretical worldviews, are ultimately founded in the individual's religious commitment.

"Christian" Theology

You will understand by now my central thesis that all scientific activity is ultimately determined by someone's ultimate commitment. In this simple but fundamental statement, the entire justification for a "Christian" science is given. Only in this way can we also theoretically account for the notion of a "Christian" theology. Interestingly, when we speak of a Christian mathematics, or even a Christian linguistics, many people shake their heads. They think Christian sociology is nonsense. And they would greet with similar skepticism the subjects which will be discussed in the upcoming volumes of this series, such as Christian psychology and Christian biology. But the notion of a Christian theology is usually taken for granted.

This distinction is still a by-product of the age-old Scholastic Nature–Grace dualism: Christian theology obviously seems to belong to the "upper storey" of grace, while Christian economics, relegated to the "lower storey" of nature, is considered to be absurd. However, if this scheme is faulty, and a Christian aesthetics is absurd, then why would a Christian theology not be absurd as well? As a matter of fact, some philosophers of science would maintain that there can indeed be a theology of Christianity, but not a "Christian" theology. Or they would say that if something like "Christian" theology existed, it could never be called a "science."

I believe they are wrong. If all science is rooted in some ultimate commitment—and I definitely believe it is—this could very well be a Christian commitment. We even believe that this is the most desirable commitment possible. But that then makes possible not only a Christian theology, but also a Christian physics, a Christian biology, a Christian psychology, a Christian linguistics, etc.–in other words, a theology, ethics, juridical science, aesthetics, economics, sociology, linguistics, psychology, etc., rooted in the Christian ground-motive. Of course, I will explain this further in the succeeding volumes.

As I emphasized in my *Wisdom for Thinkers*, the interesting implication of my standpoint is that both the arguments *for* the claim that science has a transcendent-religious foundation, *and* the arguments *against* it always function within an individual's religious commitment. The Christian thinker who believes that all science is ultimately governed by Man's ultimate commitment does so because of his own ultimate commitment. And a non-Christian thinker who believes that all science is *not* ultimately governed by Man's ultimate commitment does so because of his own ultimate commitment. There is no way to escape from this conclusion: you are either for or against the idea of a religious commitment on the basis of your own particular religious commitment. From the outset, the question whether a Christian theology is at all possible is determined by an individual's pre-theoretical ultimate commitment.

If it is a Christian thinker who denies that anyone's scientific work is necessarily governed by the latter's (anastatic or apostatic) ultimate commitment, he separates a part of his life, namely, his scientific work, from his ultimate commitment. In fact, this is a denial of one of the fundamental theses of the Reformation: the thesis that Man's entire life is under the dominion (objectively speaking) of God and his Word, or under the dominion (subjectively speaking) of his faith or his unbelief (or of the Spirit or the flesh). Such thinkers thus place themselves outside the Reformational tradition by assuming that there must be some neutral ground— science perhaps, or some other domain, such as the arts, or the national economy—where God and his Word have nothing to say.

Ground-Motive and Dogmatism

In our approach to systematic theology, the notion of a pre-theoretical, biblical, transcendent-religious ground-motive plays an essential role, as you will have realized by now. The same is true for the Christian view of reality and knowledge, rooted in this ground-motive. Along these lines, radical Christian philosophy makes a sharp distinction between the following two matters:

(a) The *a priori* (i.e., preceding not only all theoretical thought, but even all faith), supra-rational truth of God, embodied in the divine Word-revelation. This truth is granted to the believer's heart by the power of the Holy Spirit, and works there as a transcendent-religious ground-motive. Although every (rational) formulation or summary of the import of this truth is humanly flawed, ideas such as creation and preservation, the fall into sin, the redemption through Christ's work of atonement, Christ's resurrection and glorification, the Kingdom of God, and the end of the world in Christ, certainly form an essential part of it.

(b) The *a posteriori* (i.e., following upon faith) logical-rational-analytic theories, produced by theological reflection upon the ideas I have just mentioned, and many others. Each of these ideas can and must become the object of theoretical-theological reflection, and as such they will, we hope, yield useful, but at any rate humanly flawed theological theories. However, the supra-rational, supra-theoretical truth of God is not in the least affected by such flawed theoretical reasoning.

The above distinction poses an enormous challenge that should not be overlooked. The problem is that, on the one hand, we do not wish to risk ending up in mysticism and irrationalism. That is, we do not want to shy away from all the risks and traps in theology by falling back, time and again, upon our ultimate commitment. We should not appeal prematurely to "impenetrable mysteries" just to cover up the fact that we are simply too lazy to do hard theological work. On the other hand, we do not wish to fall into the danger of rationalism, scientism, or positivism, which believes it to be possible to enclose the whole truth of God in theological dogmas and theories, thus ignoring or denying the supra-rational, transcendent dimension in this truth.

This is a tricky dilemma! On the one hand, if we put too much emphasis on our pre-theological, supra-rational ultimate commitment (and especially if we do so without even bothering to account for it rationally), people may accuse us of things like biblicism, mysticism, irrationalism, dogmatism, fideism, or obscurantism. In short, our opponents will accuse us of hiding behind our ultimate commitment which in their opinion renders our own work unscientific. On the other hand, if we conceal the importance of our supra-rational ultimate commitment and emphasize the rationality of our theological work, other people may accuse us of things like rationalism, positivism, immanentism, scientism, or liberalism.

First, we should point out that rationalists have the habit of calling every standpoint that tries to transcend the limitations of our rationality "irrational," or "irrationalist," or "existentialist," or something like that. The reason for this is that many thinkers distinguish only between rational (logical) and irrational (illogical). They are unaware of, or do not accept, ideas such as the supra-rational, i.e., that which is neither non-rational nor irrational but surpasses the immanent world to which the rational and the irrational belong. The logical function is just one of the many immanent modal functions that arise from the heart, whereas the supra-logical belongs to the existential, transcendent domain of the heart itself. As I have said before, the irrational implies disobedience to the law-side of the logical modality, whereas the supra-rational transcends everything that is non-rational, rational or irrational.

Retreat into Commitment

In 1962, the American philosopher William W. Bartley III (1934-1990) wrote a book called *The Retreat into Commitment*. In this work, he rightly warns us about the danger of fleeing into the safe fortress of our supra-rational faith, just to render ourselves immune to criticism. Bartley refers to what people accept as a body of "unassailable truths" considered to be essential. These truths are often summarized in a "confession," a collection that, for its adherents, is non-negotiable. Similarly, the German theologian Wolfhart Pannenberg (b. 1928) refers to the danger of a "ghetto theology," which has only esoteric meaning—a meaning for the initiated only—but which does not deserve the name of science. The German theologian Gerhard Sauter (b. 1935) speaks of the danger of an authoritarian "standpoint theology," which refrains from arguing, either because it has no good arguments, or because it feels it is too superior to stoop to this.

WHAT THEN *IS* THEOLOGY?

The South African-American theologian Wentzel van Huys-steen (b. 1942) claims that every form of dogmatic exclusivism is not only unrealistic and irresponsible, but based on an intentional blindness with respect to God's presence and activity in ways for which traditional theology often has not prepared us. To use a biblical picture, dogmatic Christians camp at a certain theological location because at some time in the past the pillar of cloud settled there. They cannot possibly imagine that one day the cloud might lift and settle down at some other place (cf. Num. 9:15-23). And so they remain camped at their oasis while the rest of God's people move on.

One main argument of dogmatism is always, "Who are we to think we know better than the great men of God in the past?" They forget that these great men themselves never argued this way, and that was one reason why they were great. Imagine what might or might not have happened if Thomas Aquinas had thought, "Who am I to know better than Augustine?" Or if Martin Luther had thought, "Who am I to know better than Thomas Aquinas?" Or if Friedrich Schleiermacher had thought, "Who am I to know better than Martin Luther?" Or if Karl Barth had thought, "Who am I to know better than Friedrich Schleiermacher?" Or if Wolfhart Pannenberg had thought, "Who am I to know better than Karl Barth?" If these men had argued this way, theology would not have made much progress. Moreover, the point is not so much that these men "knew better" than their predecessors. It was rather that they lived in different times and cultures, with different challenges, which demanded different answers, or the same answers reformulated in different ways.

I once bought a second-hand theological book from a fairly conservative group of people. At the beginning of the book, I read this verse: "[N]o one after drinking old wine desires new, for he says, 'The old is good'" (Luke 5:39). I am sure that the author or the publisher wanted to express the idea that older theological ideas are better than newer ("modern") ones. Apparently, they did not realize that Jesus meant this saying in a negative sense; he was in fact condemning the attitude of the scribes and Pharisees, who, stubbornly sticking to their ancient views, refused to open themselves to any new light of the Spirit.

In reacting to this, or any, dogmatic attitude, we have to make two quite important distinctions. One is the distinction between, on the one hand, our supra-rational and therefore "unassailable," ground-motive, and, on the other hand, our rational beliefs, even our most precious ones, which must always remain open to scrutiny. The other distinction is the one between our beliefs and the way in which we formulate them. None of the formulations of our beliefs, no matter how firmly they may be anchored in our confessional tradition, are beyond criticism. This holds even more strongly for our theological theories. They can never be the last word on any subject, no matter how highly exalted a theologian may be in a certain church denomination.

I realize that many laypeople are scared when anyone tries to shake some of their firm beliefs, particularly when this person wields strong arguments. But professional theologians at least should not be afraid of this. On the contrary, they should love it because it is part of the theological "game." "Iron sharpens iron, and one man sharpens another," says Proverbs 27:17. There is nothing wrong with that. Dogmatism is one of the things that are forbidden to an academic theologian. He should never be afraid of strong arguments (unless, of course, he feels that his academic reputation is at stake). And he will not feel nearly as threatened if he realizes that, while rational arguments may shake his theological paradigm, they cannot so easily shake the deepest (supra-rational, existential, transcendent) convictions of his heart.

Various Viewpoints

I repeat that our supra-rational ground-motive is indeed beyond criticism, not because we dogmatically wish it to be so but because it simply could not be otherwise. On the basis of what "deeper" ground-motive can we criticize our own ground-motive? It is our ground-motive that judges all our beliefs and theories, not the other way around. It cannot be criticized for the very reason that it *precedes* all criticism. But please keep in mind that this does not release us from the obligation to *account rationally* for this ground-motive as best we can. Try to formulate it, and do your best to tell us what it entails. We know that your formulations will be always humanly flawed, but this is always better than not formulating at all. In the latter case, you might end up in some kind of esoteric mysticism, where you will perhaps be understood by a group of the initiated, but not by anyone else.

However, the opposite is also true. In all the discussions about your Christian beliefs, it is always possible that you reach a point where you have no further arguments, and you have to say (as Martin Luther is supposed to have done in 1521): "Here I stand, I can do no other." This is a "retreat into commitment," but this time you cannot help it. The foundations of the gospel are at stake, and even if you have no further arguments, you must stand your ground. In such a case, you speak in *statu confessionis*, that is, as a firm confessor of your faith. And even then, as a witness of the truth you do not have to accept the reproach of irrationalism. You say with the Apostle Paul, "I am not out of my mind . . . but I am speaking true and rational words" (Acts 26:25), although in this particular case, Paul's intention was not so much to *prove* anything as to give his personal testimony.

In principle, it *is* possible to criticize someone's ground-motive, of course. How else could we mark certain ground-motives as apostatic? But if you begin to question *your own* ground-motive, in the end you may throw it overboard and adopt another one. Do you realize, though, how drastic it would be to do this? A replacement of this kind has the character of a true existential conversion (or, if you like, a *paradigm shift*) from some other religion or ideology to Christianity, but possibly also from Christianity to some other religion or ideology, or from Catholicism to Protestantism and *vice versa*. Such conversions have happened many times.

We can understand why the idea of the supra-rational—however it is called—has so often met with severe criticism. William W. Bartley was among the many who pleaded for a thorough, consistent rationality. He argued that the commitment to such rationality is more rational than other, more "ideological" starting points. However, this is a circular argument. It has been pointed out by several philosophers, Karl R. Popper for one, that such rationalism cannot *itself* be rationally defended because that would be begging the question. Ultimately, the choice for rationality cannot be rationally accounted for. This is what Michael Polanyi called the faith-rootedness of all rationality. After all,

Bartley's view—his choice for rationality and his denial of the supra-rational—is also rooted in an ultimate commitment. As Wentzel van Huyssteen put it, Bartley was committed to non-commitment. In this way, Bartley became guilty of the same kind of "retreat into commitment" for which he blamed others. Bartley's own arguments simply demonstrate that an ultimate commitment is inescapable, even if it is "only" a commitment to non-commitment.

Van Huyssteen himself is not accurate enough in his rebuttal, though, because he does not distinguish (a) between faith (our supra-rational *fides qua*) a nd (rational) b eliefs, (b) b etween p re-theoretical beliefs and theological theories, or (c) between first, our pre-rational, pre-theoretical commitment; second, our rational, pre-theoretical worldview; and third, our rational, theoretical paradigm. What he lacks, as is the case with so many philosophers and theologians, is an underlying radical Christian philosophical view of reality and knowledge. As a consequence, our common everyday knowledge is theoreticalized, and the supra-rational is not acknowledged, or else it is confused with the irrational.

Ground-Motives and Mixtures

As I have argued before, basically there are only two kinds of ground-motives in the truly transcendent-religious sense of the word: the *anastatic* and the *apostatic*. Such ground-motives are existential attitudes of Man's transcendent-religious heart. They express themselves in certain immanent thought-contents, which the Dutch theologian and philosopher Andree Troost (1916-2008) attributed to what he called the *ethos*. All scientific work, carried out within a certain paradigm, requires such a ground-motive, as I have argued earlier in great detail.

When it comes to these "immanent thought-contents" of which Troost spoke, we may distinguish between the following "pagan" schemes:

(a) In *Greek antiquity*: the dualism of matter and form (which comes to light, for instance, in the alleged duality of the body substance and the soul substance).

(b) In *Renaissance and Enlightenment humanism*: the ground-motive of nature and freedom, i.e., on the one hand, the ideal of science with its fixed natural laws, and, on the other hand, the ideal of the "free" (autonomous) human personality, which is not subject to natural laws.

Only seldom could the anastatic ground-motive work in an almost pure form; perhaps it did in the early Church, and in the time of the Reformers, or during other great awakenings and revivals—which were "flashes of light." In practice, unfortunately, the anastatic ground-motive was, and is, easily contaminated by the pagan schemes of various earlier epochs:

(c) The *Scholastic* dualism of nature and grace was based on just such an intermingling of the anastatic ground-motive and Greek matter–form dualism. The great church father Augustine (354-430 A.D.), as well as the great Greek philosopher Aristotle (384-322 B.C.), inspired this type of thinking, not only in the medieval Roman Catholic Church, but also in the early Protestant churches. Aristotle was *the* authority for the domain of nature, Augustine for the domain of grace.

(d) Since the time of the Enlightenment in the seventeenth and eighteenth centuries, many Christians thinkers mixed humanistic elements into their Christian thought: both rationalism and irrationalism, German idealism, scientism, historicism, both positivism and neo-positivism, process philosophy, existentialism, neo-Marxism, linguistic philosophy, phenomenology, postmodernism, deconstructionism, and many others.

To give some examples: dialectical theology (adopted by Karl Barth, Friedrich Gogarten and Emil Brunner) was influenced by the (pre-)existentialists, especially Søren Kierkegaard and Karl Jaspers. The atheist theology of Thomas J. J. Altizer and Harvey Cox was influenced by Auguste Comte's positivism and the neo-positivism of the Vienna Circle (German: *Wiener Kreis*). Jürgen Moltmann's theology of hope was influenced by the neo-Marxist Ernst Bloch. Wolfhart Pannenberg's theology was influenced by the historicism of Ernst Troeltsch and Wilhelm Dilthey. What is now known as process theology was influenced by Alfred N. Whitehead's process philosophy. Rudolf Bultmann's demythologization theology was influenced by Martin Heidegger's *Being and Time*. And what would Friedrich Schleiermacher, Albrecht Ritschl and Ernst Troeltsch have been without the German philosopher Immanuel Kant?

The more recent forms of existential theology were influenced by the twentieth-century philosopher Heidegger. Liberation theology was influenced by the Frankfurt School of neo-Marxism. The newer type of irrationalist theology was influenced not only by historicism and the relativism of Thomas Kuhn, but more particularly by the postmodernism of Jean-François Lyotard and the deconstructionism of Jacques Derrida. The newer emphasis on philosophical hermeneutics and the alleged metaphorical character of all language (including the language of theology) is closely related to the anti-logical linguistic philosophy of the later Wittgenstein. Hendrikus Berkhof's dogmatics is rooted in a phenomenological analysis of the idea of religion by Edmund Husserl, etc. And what would present-day (German) Lutheran theology have been without Wilhelm Dilthey, Edmund Husserl, Oswald Spengler, Ernst Bloch, Franz Rosenzweig, Martin Heidegger, Karl Jaspers, and Martin Buber?

Let no one think that modern fundamentalist theology can escape from this list because of its allegedly "biblical" character. In my opinion, many of its claims are inconceivable without positivism and the age-old rationalism which characterized orthodox Protestant theology almost from its beginning. One need only listen to the vehemence with which some fundamentalists accuse their opponents of all kinds of "-isms," whereas they themselves in truly positivist fashion ostensibly stick to the "solid facts" of the Bible. As if such "objective facts" could ever exist! Facts are always facts-for-people. What we consider to be facts depends on our frame of thought.

Strictly speaking, of course, there is no such thing as a purely biblical systematic theology in the absolute sense of the word, existing as a timeless cloud floating in the air. Even the most "orthodox" or "biblical" theologian (normally self-appointed to his task) is always a child of his time, embedded in his own culture, and thus—often unconsciously—exposed to all kinds of influences on his thinking. The only way one could possibly rid systematic theology of these flaws is to rigorously hunt down such cultural and other influences, unmask them, and remove them. But even then, no matter how successful one is, systematic theology will always remain a tentative, provisional, humanly flawed piece of work.

WHAT THEN *IS* THEOLOGY?

No Mini-Confession, No Mini-Theology

It is important always to keep in mind the distinction between a ground-motive and people's beliefs. A ground-motive is *never* a kind of mini-confession in which the content of Scripture is "summarized." Remember that a ground-motive is a supra-rational transcendent driving force of the heart, put into operation by the Holy Spirit or the spirit of darkness, whereas a confession is a rational-immanent, necessarily humanly flawed formulation of beliefs. Moreover, a confession as such does not tell us anything about the attitude of the confessor's heart, and this is the very thing that matters in a ground-motive. A truly ecumenical community of Christians is built on such a common ground-motive, but *not* necessarily on a common confession, such as, for instance, the Apostles' Creed, no matter how useful and powerful it might be. You may *confess* that Jesus is Lord, and you may rationally mean it, you may "demonstrate" it from Scripture, and yet, "no one can say 'Jesus is Lord' except in the Holy Spirit" (1 Cor. 12:3). What you say as a confessor is truthful, but do you also speak the Truth? Without the guidance of the Holy Spirit, even the best confession will not help such a community (cf. chapter 5).

A ground-motive (whether it be anastatic or apostatic) can, with even less justification than a mini-confession, be considered a mini-theology, from which a full theology could be "developed" or "deduced." First, I cannot repeat often enough that theological theories are in no way "deduced" from any Christian beliefs, but are *designed to account for these beliefs.* Second, a ground-motive is not theology at all, nor is it theoretical knowledge, pre-theoretical knowledge, a rational belief, or a pre-rational belief. It is our ultimate, transcendent, existential, supra-rational *unassailable certitude*, which cannot be verified against anything else, otherwise it would not be our ultimate commitment. It is this certitude of the heart that underlies, steers, governs, and dominates all our beliefs, all our knowledge and all our theology.

We cannot get this ground-motive under our control because this ground-motive *itself* has all *our* beliefs and theological theories in its control; at the same time, it surpasses all our formulations, beliefs and theories. For instance, it is nonsense to speak of an "orthodox" ground-motive. The word "orthodox" refers to our rational beliefs, measured according to what Christians have always believed. One may be orthodox (literally, straight in doctrinal matters) and yet be in the grip of a mixed ground-motive. Conversely, one may be under the control of the biblical ground-motive (a state instinctively recognized in such phrases as "His heart is in the right place") but through ignorance and faulty education one could at the same time be less than orthodox.

Herman Dooyeweerd saw a parallel between the biblical ground-motive and what Jesus called the "key of knowledge" (Luke 11:52). This is the key that the scribes and Pharisees did not possess, even though they were the smartest Bible scholars of their time. They believed all that the Scriptures said, but they did not possess the "key" needed to really understand it. Therefore Jesus reprimanded them with the words, "You are wrong, because you know neither the Scriptures nor the power of God" (Matt. 22:29). This is the power of the Holy Spirit, who alone guides us into all truth (John 16:13). Nicodemus was "the teacher of Israel," yet he did not even understand such a basic truth as that of rebirth as a condition for entering the Kingdom of God (John 3:1-10; cf. Ezek. 36:25-27).

I must emphasize again that a ground-motive is not open for discussion because any discussion is possible only *through* this ground-motive. It is that which pre-rationally precedes and underlies any rational discussion. No discussion can be used to judge our ground-motive because it is this ground-motive that judges all our discussions. We cannot theologically check it because it checks our beliefs and theories. It cannot be interpreted because it interprets us. It is the only true ecumenical foundation of the Church, which in its immanent institutional manifestation is hopelessly divided, whereas in Christ its unity is always preserved on the transcendent level. And in this sense at least, we may say that Jesus' prayer—"that they may all be one" (John 17:21, 23)—was definitely granted by the Father.

Last but not least, I must underscore again that ground-motives have to be *made* the objects of theological and philosophical reflection. Otherwise we could never arrive at a philosophical theory of religious ground-motives. At the same time, we realize that this theological and philosophical reflection, and any philosophical theory of religious ground-motives, is always *a priori* steered and governed by our own (anastatic or apostatic) ground-motive. As I have said before, we can never escape from this hermeneutical circle.

Chapter Nine
PARADIGMS IN THEOLOGY

In the light of our discussion of the religious ground-motives (see chapter 8), we can now attempt to distinguish various paradigms of systematic theology in the Christian tradition. I use this word "tradition" on purpose. The views of Thomas Kuhn and others imply that tradition is in fact the main source for the origin of paradigms, not only in theology but in all sciences. All thought models in the sciences (including theology) find their origin in some thought tradition. We are less innovative than we may think!

Two Examples in the Literature

Long before Kuhn, the well-known German-French theologian and philosopher Albert Schweitzer (1875-1965) already distinguished in his *Geschichte der Leben-Jesu-Forschung* (translated into English as *The Quest of the Historical Jesus*) certain phases, each with their inherent alternatives:

(a) David Friedrich Strauss (1808-1874): He advocated a purely historical and "scientific" approach to the life of Jesus as opposed to a purely supernatural and believing approach.

(b) The Tübingen school, as well as the German theologian Oskar Holtzmann (1859-1934): They placed the more historical synoptic Gospels above the more mystical Gospel of John.

(c) Schweitzer's own period: He advocated a so-called eschatological approach as opposed to a non-eschatological one.

I will not explain these phases any further. I mention them here only to indicate that distinguishing phases in the history of theology was not a new phenomenon.

Through a careful analysis, the Swiss Roman Catholic theologian Hans Küng (b. 1928) has shown that the paradigm concept, which was first developed for the natural sciences, is entirely applicable to theology:

WHAT THEN *IS* THEOLOGY?

(a) As in the natural sciences, we find in the history of theology frequent periods of "normal science," characterized by a cumulative growth of knowledge, a solving of remaining "puzzles," and a resistance to all that might pose a threat to the dominating paradigm.

(b) As in the natural sciences, the consciousness of a growing crisis is the starting point in theology for a change in the dominant axioms, and ultimately for the development of a new paradigm.

(c) As in the natural sciences, in theology an earlier paradigm is only given up when a new one has become available.

(d) As in the natural sciences, we find in theology that, during the replacement of a paradigm, not only rational-scientific but also non-scientific factors play a role, so that this replacement has the character of a genuine *conversion*.

(e) As in the natural sciences, it is very difficult in theology to predict whether a new paradigm will be absorbed by the earlier one, whether it will replace the earlier one, or whether it will be stored in the archives for a time. If it is accepted, what started out as an innovation will eventually stabilize into a new tradition.

Coming back to the religious ground-motives, we realize that, in their pure form, the ground-motives of Greek antiquity and humanism could hardly give rise on their own to paradigms for theology because they could not avoid being mixed with the Christian ground-motive. Paradigms in systematic theology which are not purely biblical—insofar as purely biblical paradigms could ever exist—are necessarily mixtures of the biblical ground-motive with one of the purely secular ground-motives.

In this context, we must remember, though, that modern humanists are not pagans in the strict sense of the word, for pagans do not know God's special revelation. In the historical sense of the term, modern humanists are apostate Christians, or (physical or spiritual) offspring of apostate Christians. (It is important not to confuse modern humanists with humanists in the sixteenth century! At that time, they were all Christians, and the term "humanism" referred to a special interest in antiquity. For instance, Philipp Melanchthon was called a German humanist, and John Calvin a French humanist.)

Three General Paradigms

In the light of the mixtures mentioned, we can now distinguish three paradigms:

1. The *Scholastic* paradigm, based on the dualistic combination of the ground-motives of Greek antiquity and Christianity. This is the paradigm for the systematic theology of conservative Roman Catholicism. It is dominated by Thomism, the thought system of Thomas Aquinas (1225-1274), which is the normative philosophy and theology of the Roman Catholic Church, reintroduced in 1879 by Pope Leo XIII. It differs from the later paradigms particularly in two respects:

(a) It reads the Bible through the "glasses" of Aristotelian (i.e., ancient pagan) thinking, so that both pagan concepts and thought contents have pervaded its theology. For instance, the doctrine of transubstantiation (bread and wine changing into the body and the blood of Christ) would be inconceivable without the Aristotelian distinction between *substantia* and *accidentia* (the substance of bread and wine is transformed, but not the accidents).

(b) As a matter of fact, the Scholastic paradigm is not primarily based on Scripture but on "Sacred Tradition." Besides Aristotle, the church considered as authoritative the church fathers (especially Augustine), and particularly the conciliar dogmas and the papal doctrinal decrees.

This paradigm also had a powerful effect on early Protestant theology, both among the Lutherans (Martin Chemnitz, Johann Gerhard, Johannes A. Quenstedt, David Hollaz, and others) and among Reformed theologians (Theodore Beza, Amandus Polanus, William Perkins, Francis Gomarus, Gisbert Voetius, and others). Synodical decrees, with the Canons of Dort being the best known example, occupied here, *de facto* and *de iure*, the same place as papal doctrinal decrees.

2. The *scientistic* paradigm, based on the dualistic combination of the Christian and the humanistic ground-motives. This is the paradigm of systematic theology for liberal or modernist theology, marked especially by the results of so-called "higher biblical criticism" or the "historical-critical method." The products of a science that is considered to be neutral and objective, but is in reality rationalistic-

positivistic, dominate the view of Scripture. Typical ideas of the biblical ground-motive, such as creation, the fall, redemption, the Kingdom of God, the end of the world, etc., are retained but are transformed according to the demands of the ideals of the humanistic ground-motive: those of autonomous Man and of a manageable reality.

A priori, this ground-motive does not allow for the ground-idea of Scripture as the infallible and inspired Word of God. According to this type of thinking, this ground-idea cannot possibly ever be the result of scientific investigation. On the contrary, because of the error of a neutral, objective, unprejudiced science, this paradigm seeks, with the help of "modern scientific" investigation, to prove the contrary: that Scripture is *not* in fact the infallible and inspired Word of God.

3. The *Evangelical* paradigm, or whatever you wish to call it. I do not care very much about the name, as long as we know what is meant: the systematic-theological paradigm of that *traditional* theology that builds on the Apostles' Creed and the Nicene Creed, and that we therefore call *orthodox*, without quibbling about details. Negatively speaking, it is one paradigm that has largely escaped the effects of the Scholastic and humanist paradigms. Though this is a negative statement, it is crucial, because so much of what is called "orthodox" theology is in fact heavily affected by traditional Scholasticism, and sometimes also by the humanist paradigm. Here are some more positive characteristics:

(a) I call those theologians "Evangelical" in the broad sense of the word who are fundamentally faithful to the Bible's understanding of itself, that is, who believe of Scripture what it testifies about itself, namely, that it is the inspired Word of God (cf. 2 Tim. 3:16), not just the word of men (cf. 1 Thess. 2:13, even though this verse refers to preaching). Therefore, their starting point is not "modern" (autonomous, humanist, anthropocentric) Man, but one which is strictly theonomous, theocentric, and Christocentric (that is, it stands under God's law, placing God and Christ in the center).

(b) I call those theologians "Evangelical" in the broad sense who seek, as a matter of principle, to be led by the contents of Scripture, not by extra-biblical thought contents, whether they be Scholastic or humanistic. *Scriptura Sacra sui ipsius interpres*, "Holy Scripture is its own interpreter," as Thomas Aquinas said long ago (cf. 2 Pet. 1:20, "no prophecy of Scripture comes from someone's own interpretation"). These theologians do not study Scripture and Christian faith from perspectives that are foreign to it, but endeavor to understand it from its own center, without forcing it into conformity with a scientific system that is imposed upon it from the outside.

Is it realistic to assume that such a theology really exists, let alone that it *can* exist? Scientistic theology's view of science is founded upon a long-standing rationalist tradition in Western civilization. As a consequence, scientistic theology time and again consciously imposed upon Christian faith a secular view of reality and knowledge that is foreign to it, thus contaminating the Christian faith. However, theologians who want to remain faithful to Scripture often do the same, not because they deliberately apply foreign presuppositions but because they are hardly even aware of their own presuppositions to begin with. Consequently, they often adopt a worldview that is either Scholastic, biblicist, or secular, or else an eclectic blend of elements from all three. But "unintentional" sins (cf. Lev. 4) are still sins.

I can now expand my definition of an ideal Christian theology a little. This theology is not only faithful to Scripture's own self-understanding, but is capable of *critically accounting* for this faithfulness on the basis of philosophical presuppositions that are themselves in line with Scripture (see my *Wisdom for Thinkers*). Spiritual apostasy can manifest itself not only in scientistic theology but also in Evangelical theology insofar as the latter is usually an open fortress, with little *theoretically substantiated* resistance to all kinds of philosophical schools (Andree Troost). Therefore, a truly Evangelical systematic theology can only be designed and maintained on the basis of a thorough, coherent theoretical-philosophical view of reality and knowledge, rooted in the same biblical ground-motive as this theology itself. The latter phrase means that it must be based upon Scripture as accepted according to its own self-understanding as the divinely authoritative Word of God.

Orthodoxism

As I said before, the *scientistic* paradigm in theology is based upon the dualistic combination of the Christian and the humanistic ground-motives. It is the ground-motive of modernist or liberal theology. Its view of Scripture is dominated by a rationalist-positivist science, even though it may put the *emphasis*, for instance, upon religious feeling (Friedrich Schleiermacher), revelation and kerygma (Karl Barth), human existence (Rudolf Bultmann), or hope (Jürgen Moltmann). These various emphases point to various schools within the scientistic paradigm.

Of course, in School A the humanistic ground-motive may be working much more intensely than in School B. In fact, there is even a gradual transition from more Evangelical schools to more scientistic schools. In other words, there may sometimes be more scientism in Evangelical theology than we might expect, and more genuinely Evangelical faith in scientistic theology than we might expect. After a pre-critical and a (historical-)critical period, we may distinguish a post-critical paradigm, in which there is more room for the Evangelical approach, but hopefully without the latter ever regressing to the pre-critical period. That is, what we hope for is an approach that has absorbed the right lessons from the historical-critical period.

To be more specific: within scientistic theology I see the following phases, which are so clearly distinct that the transitions between them definitely remind us of scientific revolutions as described by Thomas Kuhn. We will not quarrel about terminology, but simply try to distinguish some of the most important phases in scientistic theology. We will see that this is mainly a theological history of the German-speaking world.

The first phase in Lutheran and Reformed theology, lasting from the Reformation to the Enlightenment, was a mixture of biblical and Scholastic thinking. It is interesting to consider this phase in the light of distinctions made by Swiss Reformed theologian Fritz Buri (1907-1995) without necessarily agreeing with all his evaluations of the various types of theology he distinguishes. Buri sees three possibilities for the relationship between reason and revelation in theology: (1) a "theology of reason" (see below for the discussion of Enlightenment Rationalism and Sensitivism), (2) a "theology of revelation" (see below for the discussion of Kerygmatism), and (3) a theology consisting of a synthesis of reason and revelation (see above for the discussion of Scholastic theology).

Scholasticism itself already had clearly rationalistic overtones, but in the eighteenth century an entirely new, liberal approach appeared, characterized by the rationalism of the Enlightenment of that time. While many see a stark contrast between early Protestant orthodoxism and Enlightenment liberalism, several authors have, as I have said before, clearly distinguished the continuity between the two because of the underlying rationalism. Theologians who shifted from early Protestant orthodoxism to Enlightenment liberalism had to make important changes in their thinking, but one thing did not change: the rationalistic methodology of theology.

Enlightenment Rationalism

In fact, the Enlightenment was not much more than the start of the final phase of Western rationalism which had been around for so long already. But now the difference was that rationalism was no longer limited to the thinking elite, for the Enlightenment popularized rationalism and scientism among the masses: science was to be the new god. The notion of powerful natural reason as such was nothing new; it had in fact characterized Scholasticism from the outset. Nevertheless, the German theologian Wolfhart Pannenberg (b. 1928) is right in speaking of a real *paradigm switch* between early Protestant orthodoxism and Enlightenment liberalism. Very simply put, the great difference was that early Protestant rationalism had tried to wrap all the truths of the Bible in its rationalistic concepts, except the great mysteries: revelation, inspiration, miracles, the virgin birth, the resurrection, the ascension, etc. Enlightenment liberalism no longer saw any reason to halt before these mysteries; why erect such a protective barrier around them? As a consequence, these mysteries too were squeezed into concepts considered acceptable before the tribunal of reason.

Enlightenment rationalism is characterized by a harsh anti-supernaturalism, that is, a fierce resistance to anything supernatural. Therefore, it declared the faith in revelation, inspiration, miracles, the virgin birth, the resurrection, the ascension, etc., to be outdated, because the modern mind could no longer accept such "irrational" ideas (note again the confusion with the suprarational!). The Enlightenment did take the moral value of Scripture seriously, but not its historical value. Reason alone, elevated to a near-divine status, was considered to be "infinite," just as God is infinite. This rationalism was marked in particular by a naïve, uncritical optimism. Is it not naïve to *a priori* take for granted that everything that exists, within or outside the universe, can be grasped by reason, and can be clothed in its concepts?

It was only with the great German philosopher Immanuel Kant (1724-1804) and his nineteenth-century successors Johann G. Fichte, Friedrich W. J. Schelling and Georg W. F. Hegel that German thinking became critical again.

We can distinguish three periods in this "liberal theology," which may be viewed as separated by paradigmatic revolutions (Hans Grass). The first period was characterized by the historical criticism of David F. Strauss, Ferdinand C. Baur, and Wilhelm Vatke.

The second period was marked by Albrecht Ritschl, who in his own way tried to overcome the antithesis between orthodox and liberal theology (see below for the discussion of Sensitivism). Other important figures were his followers, Wilhelm Herrmann (later a teacher of Karl Barth) and Adolf von Harnack. Besides this, we must mention the advocates of historical criticism in Old and New Testament theology (especially Julius Wellhausen), who relegated systematic theology somewhat to the background.

The third period was characterized by the History of Religions school (especially Hermann Gunkel), which attempted to understand the Christian faith by comparisons with other ancient religions.

In the twentieth century too, liberalism has had some important representatives, such as Rudolf Bultmann and Paul Tillich, though Hans Küng includes them, together with Karl Barth, in a single post-Enlightenment group. This simplifies matters too much, however; the differences among post-Enlightenment theologians are enormous.

Sensitivism

After Immanuel Kant, an entirely new phase in theology started with what I would like to call the subjective-Romantic *sensitivism* of the German theologian Friedrich Schleiermacher (1768-1834). This paradigm finds its starting point in the Kantian dualism of religion and science, corresponding with what Kant called "practical reason" on the one hand and "pure (i.e., theoretical) reason" on the other. This paradigm is characterized by a tendency to reduce religious experience to sensitivity and feeling. Religion is defined as the "feeling of absolute dependence," the immediate consciousness of something "unconditional."

This view strongly emphasized the personal religious-sensitive experience, feeling, intuition, tradition, and mysticism, over against reason and thinking. The immediate contact with the Infinite, rooted in feeling, was considered to be far more important than all dogmas, Holy Scripture, and even our belief in personal immortality. Personal religious life was viewed by Schleiermacher as wider than the Moravian pietism in which he had been raised because it includes the whole of social-cultural life. He also considered it to be deeper than the common aesthetic-intellectual sensitivity of Romanticism because the latter lacked an authentically religious dimension. Schleiermacher's "doctrine of faith" differed from traditional dogmatics—which he considered a set of "dry" objective doctrines—in that it emphasized subjective personal experience and viewed the person of Christ, church community, sin and redemption in terms of negative or positive consciousness of God.

Besides this, Schleiermacher wanted to develop for theology a sound scientific foundation like the ones developed for the physical and the historical sciences, in order to make it a genuine, mature science like the others. Moreover, his theology was empirical in that he ruled out all unhealthy scholastic speculations and limited theology to what was empirically known from religious experience. In these points, he remained in line with Enlightenment theology. However, the emphasis on the strictly empirical approach was also useful as an argument against (liberal) deism, which denied God's concern with the world: Schleiermacher affirmed God's immanent presence in this world and in human experience, and in this regard remained in line with traditional theology.

Because he created some kind of "mediation" between traditional and liberal theology, Schleiermacher has been described as *the* founder of modern theology. Faced with the chilly rationalistic climate of post-Enlightenment theology, he undertook a complete reconstruction of Christian theology. Since Schleiermacher, no serious scientific theology can get around him. According to Paul Avis, either you follow him, as Albrecht Ritschl, Wilhelm Herrmann and

185

WHAT THEN *IS* THEOLOGY?

Rudolf Bultmann did, or you fight with him, as Karl Barth and Emil Brunner did, or you enter into a dialogue with him, as Wolfhart Pannenberg does—but he cannot be avoided.

This transition from Enlightenment liberalism to Schleiermacher's sensitivism sounds exactly like a scientific revolution as defined by Thomas Kuhn. Karl Barth applied to Schleiermacher a few words that the latter had himself applied to Frederick the Great, King of Prussia: "He did not found a school, but an era." At the same time, Barth was Schleiermacher's greatest critic and opponent, so much so that we can say of Barth what he said of Schleiermacher. With Barth, a new theological paradigm began, although this did not *replace* the Schleiermacherian paradigm. (In this respect, theology differs from other special sciences, where newer paradigms usually replace older ones. In theology, the older paradigms usually remain, especially when there are church denominations attached to them!)

Schleiermacher clearly broke the power of liberal Enlightenment theology. At the same time, his approach smacked too much of liberalism: he did not see Scripture *objectively* as a record of divine interventions and a collection of divine statements, but *subjectively* as a record of human religious experiences. Therefore, he did not feel the need to take the Bible seriously in every detail. In his view, the yardstick for the believer is not the Bible but his own religious experiences. This is the very point where, a century later, Barth attacked Schleiermacher by returning to the *objective* datum of divine revelation. For Schleiermacher, the divine Word is not the Bible, but rather that which is within us, the believers—or, as he called it, the "Spirit" in us. For Barth, the divine Word is that which addresses us from "the outside"—God—through the Scriptures.

In the course of the nineteenth century we find these four main currents: (a) traditional Roman Catholic theology (having as its starting point the *church* and its authoritative tradition); (b) traditional Protestant theology (having as its starting point the *Bible* as God's Word); (c) Enlightenment liberalism (having as its starting point human *reason*); and (d) Schleiermacher's sensitivism (having as its starting point human religious *feeling*).

At first sight, points (c) and (d) seem to be very different; at least Schleiermacher himself thought they were. In fact, however, they are both forms of the "subjective" theology of "Christian consciousness," in which it is of secondary importance whether you locate this in human conscience, human feeling, or human reason. Traditional Roman Catholic and Protestant theology are forms of "objective" theology in which the theologian finds his starting point outside himself: in church tradition, or in the Bible.

The three Swiss theologians, Karl Barth, Fritz Buri and Hans Küng—the first two Reformed and the third Roman Catholic—also belittled the difference between Enlightenment liberalism and Schleiermacher's sensitivism. They viewed both of them as forms of "modernist" dogmatics (Barth), or of "the neo-Protestant type of intellectual religion (*Verstandsreligion*) in the broadest sense" (Buri), or as forms that broke away from Protestant orthodoxy (Küng).

Kerygmatism

We now come to the *kerygmatism* or *dialecticism* of Karl Barth (1886-1968). His theology was a clear step back towards traditional orthodoxy with its emphasis on the "objective" revelation of God, and thus on the unchangeable, unassailable message (Greek: *kerygma*) of God, away from rationalist and sensitivist thought. It is sometimes called "neo-orthodoxy," although Barth did not like that term.

In Barth's view, God is the "wholly Other," perfectly transcendent, not directly identifiable with anything in the world, not even the words of Scripture. Because revelation is the encounter with the "wholly Other," we cannot describe it. The only thing that the biblical authors did is to describe what they felt after that revelation came to them. And we ourselves can do no more than this when revelation comes to us. God cannot be taken as self-evident, as someone who simply is "there," as a "given" at our disposal, laid down in the words of Scripture (classical orthodoxy), or in our religious consciousness (Schleiermacher), or wherever. God can be found only in a true encounter, in which the infinite and eternal God confronts us, who are finite and temporal creatures.

Such an encounter is, on our side, neither predictable nor controllable. The Word from above overwhelms us, and shows the "wholly Other" to us in the "eternal moment." In this very moment, God's Word, that touched time and history in the person of

WHAT THEN *IS* THEOLOGY?

Jesus Christ, touches us anew. In this way, we hear the original Word itself, which traverses the distances of time, distances that form no barrier or hindrance for the course of communication from eternity (formulation of Alasdair Heron).

It is clear how this view formed a counterbalance to Schleiermacher. Barth accused him of having substituted Man for God, anthropology for theology. In this way, Barth complained, Schleiermacher ruled out the necessity of revelation and the authority of Scripture as the vehicle of God's Word, not to mention the necessity of faith, which Schleiermacher viewed as a general awareness of God rather than Man's obedient response to the "eternal moment" of God's Word.

At the same time, one of the most essential differences between classical orthodoxy and Barth's neo-orthodoxy must also be underlined. It lies in the emphatic distinction that Barth makes between the Bible and God's Word. Barth used the following famous words concerning these two: "Scripture is God's Word insofar as God lets it be his Word, insofar as God speaks through it . . . Thus, Scripture *becomes* God's Word in this event, and it is to its *being* in this *becoming* that the word 'is' refers in the phrase that the Bible is God's Word." In other words: "now and then, this or that Word spoken by the prophets and apostles and preached in church becomes *his* Word."

It goes without saying that I feel more at home with this view than with rationalist or even sensitivist (i.e., modernist) theology. At the same time, like many other Christians, I feel uncomfortable with Barth because he endeavors to do something that, in my view, is truly *impossible*: finding an intermediate position between the traditional-orthodox standpoint and the (alleged) results of higher biblical criticism; between the well-intended orthodox confession that all Scripture was inspired and the mild recognition that the biblical authors sometimes made mistakes; between the Bible as the infallible Word of God and the Bible as the fallible, defective word of men. A revelation cannot be from God when, as Barth suggested, it is at the same time, in its written form, irrelevant with respect to the physical world and historical events (points in which the Bible supposedly errs many times). But it is no wonder that it does so, for in Barth's view, Scripture is not God's revelation, although God *can* reveal himself through the human words of Scripture.

This is the Achilles heel of Barthianism, says British-American theologian Colin Brown (b. 1932). The early Barth emphasized the supernatural character of revelation so strongly that there seemed to be no room left for the natural world and natural events. And the later Barth was more interested in finding a theological interpretation for events than worrying about their historicity. In this way, he tried to make Christianity into an esoteric, otherworldly religion rather than one that has its roots in history. But if we think we can have divine revelation without a defense of its thoroughly historical foundation, Christianity evaporates. Unfortunately, Barth seemed to be indifferent to this objection.

We could say that, just as rationalist theology in the eighteenth and nineteenth century isolated and absolutized the scholastic domain of Nature (natural reason), Barthianism isolated and absolutized the Scholastic domain of Grace (including revelation). Interestingly, in this way both Enlightenment rationalism and Barthianism continued in spite of themselves to presuppose the Nature–Grace scheme of Scholasticism, instead of utterly refuting and rejecting it. This is what radical Christian philosophy and theology attempt to do.

New Paradigms?

It is not so easy to point out the rise in the second half of the twentieth century of a new paradigm that has the caliber of Barth's kerygmatism, while forming a sufficient counterbalance to it. I am not going to enter into this question very deeply; I will only list here some of the names that have been mentioned, such as the German-American theologian Paul Tillich (1886-1965), or the German theologian Wolfhart Pannenberg (b. 1928), sometimes called the "third force in modern theology," after Schleiermacher and Barth. But it is not yet clear whether his theology has the same stature as theirs.

Hans Küng has tried to present one single "post-Enlightenment, postmodern, contemporary paradigm," in which he includes kerygmatism, existentalist theology, hermeneutic theology, political theology, and liberation theology (including feminist, black, and third-world theology). In his view, the theology governed by this paradigm must be truthful, free, and critical. But it must also be both Catholic and Evangelical, both traditional and contemporaneous, both Christocentric and ecumenical, both theoretical-scientific and practical-pastoral.

Of course, the postmodern era has supplied us with candidates of its own for a new paradigm for theology. The American theologian Chester Gillis (b. 1951) suggests "pluralism," which introduces data from other religions into Christian thought. Next, there is the Yale School in theology, with, as its main figures, George A. Lindbeck (b. 1923), Hans W. Frei (1922-1988), and, from a later generation, Stanley Hauerwas (b. 1940). This so-called "post-liberal" movement believes that the liberal movement has gotten bogged down in mere anthropology and political agendas, while the Evangelical movement is wrestling with an acute identity crisis, hanging somewhere between fundamentalism and neo-Evangelicalism. It has been suggested that the dialogue between the Evangelicals and the post-liberals might miraculously give rise to some sort of common confession, which might imply a real *paradigm shift*.

From the viewpoint of radical Christian philosophy it is interesting to note that post-liberal theology highlights not only the role of human reason, but also that of the whole human being when describing the acquisition of theological knowledge and faith knowledge. We may also mention here James K. A. Smith (b. 1970) with his emphasis on the sensitive and social aspects of Man, as well as the significance of liturgical practices such as the Eucharist. It is too early to claim that such a movement actually involves a truly new paradigm which affects a considerable part of Christendom, including not only post-liberal, but perhaps even post-Evangelical sectors. Already now, some speak of a possible transformation of post-liberal theology.

This uncertainty can also be seen in other movements such as "weak theology," also called "non-dogmatic theology," in the wake of French philosopher Jacques Derrida's deconstructionism. It calls itself weak because of its anti-ideological, anti-totalitarian, anti-militant attitude toward theology. Important representatives are John D. Caputo (b. 1940) (who referred to Derrida's thought as a "religion without religion"), Gianni Vattimo (b. 1936), and Jeffrey W. Robbins (b. 1972). The idea of a "weak" theology is correlated with the idea of the "weakness" of God, who is not, as tradition would have it, an overwhelming physical power but "an unconditional claim without strength."

A third school worth mentioning is the British "Radical Orthodoxy" of John Milbank (b. 1952), Catherine Pickstock (b. 1952), and Graham Ward (b. 1955), originally referred to by Milbank as "postmodern critical Augustinianism." The movement has been influenced by Neo-Platonism, John Duns Scotus (c. 1255-1308), Karl Barth, and the French Jesuit and theologian Henri-Marie de Lubac (1896-1991) who emphasized the ancient Nature–Grace scheme. Recently, James K.A. Smith offered a significant critique of this school. He underlined the significance of the great French postmodern thinkers (Jacques Derrida, Jean-François Lyotard, Michel Foucault) for theology, and has—strikingly enough—made a connection with both the Reformed tradition and the Pentecostal movement.

Postmodernity and Orthodoxy

Because of their "relativism" and "pluralism," postmodern schools have often been considered by orthodox Protestants as a threat to their "absolute" theological theories. This seems to me to betray a kind of ignorance with respect to:

(a) The *postmodern mood* (including some healthy self-relativization and openness to other opinions), characterizing the *entire* Western culture. This is not to be confused with postmodern*ism* as a collective name for various secular philosophical schools.

(b) The battle that we wage, in common with postmodernity, against the strict *rationalism* of modernism, a struggle that creates room not only for irrational factors but also for supra-rational ones.

(c) The common battle against the modernist faith in *progress*. In the meantime, this faith has largely died out, although it still survives here and there in Marxism, and especially in "technologism" (for example: computer technology is "modern," while the Internet is, with regard to its contents, a typically "postmodern" chaotic mixture of wisdom and foolishness).

(d) The postmodern idea of truth. Dogmas are relative (being the work of humans), and truth in its immanent sense is pluriform. (But, as orthodox Christians would add, Truth in its transcendent sense, the truth in Christ, is absolute and unassailable for the dissecting lancet of reason.)

WHAT THEN *IS* THEOLOGY?

(e) The benefits of postmodern thinking. There is the idea that we should take ourselves a bit less seriously (cf. American philosopher Richard Rorty's [1931-2007] idea of *irony*), with as a very real consequence a rising interest in religion. Atheism for example, is typically "modern" (not "postmodern"). Religion is "okay" again; to quote the slogan of the Austrian-American philosopher Paul K. Feyerabend (1924-1994): "Anything goes."

(f) Postmodernity's close relationship with the philosophical hermeneutics of German philosopher Hans-Georg Gadamer (1900-2002), French philosopher Paul Ricœur (1913-2005), and others. All theological interpretation is "contextual" (determined by the context of both the text and the reader). That is, it occurs on the basis of paradigms which are not only rational, but also, and especially, supra-rational.

(g) The necessity for relativizing one's own (Western) norms and values, through which more respect for other cultures has become possible. This is a tremendous gain in mission and missiology.

(h) The necessity of emphasizing the similarities between the various church denominations, which are more important than the differences. This leads to less pretence and more openness toward a pluriform theology (possibly even one which is internally less consistent), more emphasis on feeling, experiencing, and acting than on (theoretical) knowing—in our terminology: a theology with as much emphasis on the sensitive, formative, lingual, social, aesthetic, etc. aspects as on the logical aspect.

Those who see the positive sides of postmodern thinking—which, again, is not the same as postmodernism—can only conclude that, in this respect as well, Dooyeweerdian philosophy was far ahead of its time. This is especially true of point (b) (the battle against rationalism, and the emphasis on the supra-rational); point (d) (the relative truth of theological dogmas and theories, and beyond them the absolute truth in Christ); and point (f) (all interpretation is "contextual," and ultimately supra-rational).

The Classical Reformational Paradigm

Within the classical-Reformational paradigm we can distinguish at least three "sub-paradigms" that may be considered to be both traditional and orthodox:

(a) The *Scholastic* sub-paradigm. This is the paradigm of early Protestant theology and of present-day conservative-orthodox Protestantism, whether Lutheran or Reformed, insofar as these still lean heavily upon the theology of their predecessors from the sixteenth to eighteenth centuries. In the nineteenth century, the German Reformed theologian Heinrich Heppe (1820-1879) was one of the most conspicuous representatives of this group. But, to a considerable extent, Abraham Kuyper (1837-1920) and Herman Bavinck (1854-1921) also fall into this category.

(b) The *fundamentalist* sub-paradigm. This is the paradigm of many Evangelical theologians, especially in North America. It is a striking mixture of the orthodox tradition and all kinds of modern positivistic and scientistic influences. Perhaps its most striking representative was the more conservative wing of the International Council of Biblical Inerrancy of the seventies and eighties, with men such as John Gerstner (1914-1996), James I. Packer (b. 1926), Norman L. Geisler (b. 1932), Robert C. Sproul (b. 1939), and Greg Bahnsen (1948-1995). I cannot help sympathizing with this paradigm because of the good intentions with which it was constructed. Its greatest problem is simply that it lacked a radical Christian-philosophical view of cosmic reality and knowledge, especially scientific knowledge.

(c) The *cosmonomic* sub-paradigm. This is the paradigm based on the radical Christian-philosophical view of reality and knowledge developed in particular by Herman Dooyeweerd of the Netherlands, with the support of his compatriot Dirk H.Th. Vollenhoven, Hendrik P. Stoker of South Africa, the American H. Evan Runner, and many others. It can be called "cosmonomic" in reference to the English name invented for Dooyeweerd's system of thought: "philosophy of the cosmonomic idea." This paradigm especially emphasizes the "cosmonomic idea," that is, the transcendental ground-idea of coherence, unity and origin, which, according to Dooyeweerd, underlies *all* philosophy and *all* special sciences. As a paradigm for theology, it has been developed in particular by the Dutch theologian and philosopher Andree Troost (1916-2008), the American theologian Gordon J. Spykman (1926-1993), the South African philosopher, Daniel F. M. Strauss (b. 1946), and myself, since I wrote my theological dissertation (Bloemfontein, 1993). The intention of this paradigm is to supply theology with a truly biblical basis, free from both Scholasticism and scientism (see points [a] and [b] above).

In the present survey, I have so far explained the philosophical presuppositions. Let me also mention some theological distinctions within orthodox Protestant thinking without elaborating them. My first example is *federalism,* the paradigm which has at its center the concept of the covenant. Neither Roman Catholic nor Lutheran theology ever developed a true covenant theology. This happened only in Reformed theology, so that it seems justified to speak, with Wentzel van Huyssteen, of a "Reformed paradigm." In the words of Vollenhoven, Scripture "views religion as a covenant (*unio federalis*), known to the human race even before the fall through Word-revelation." Of course, Scripture does not explicitly say anything of the kind. But this does not necessarily mean that this view is wrong. It is a typical example of a theological theory, or even paradigm, designed to account for the "scientific data" that have become available through Scriptural exegesis without being directly "derived" from Scripture.

I will examine federalism more closely in the next chapter. Here I will emphasize only its historical background. The classical Reformational paradigm arose as a consequence of the sixteenth-century Reformation, which was not only a psychical, socio-economic, cultural-historical, and pistical revolution, but it was also a scientific revolution as defined by Thomas Kuhn. It involved an upheaval of Roman Catholic thinking, and gave rise to an entirely new, Protestant paradigm. The Reformation did not destroy the Roman Catholic paradigm; it endures to the present day, simply because the Roman Catholic *Church* also endures to the present day. What is more, besides producing its own new paradigm, the Protestant Reformation also contributed indirectly to a reformation within Roman Catholicism itself, specifically, a renewal of the Scholastic (Thomistic) paradigm. Concomitantly, shortly after, the newly formed Protestant paradigm was itself strongly affected by the Scholastic paradigm, and adopted many elements from it.

The Dispensationalist Paradigm

My second example of an orthodox Protestant paradigm is the dispensationalist paradigm, characterized by premillenialism (the belief that Christ's second coming will take place *before* the millennial kingdom), and either a classical or a more moderate form of dispensationalism. Just as federalism distinguishes a number of different covenants in salvation history, dispensationalism distinguishes a number of various dispensations, i.e., epochs, each with its own specific divine features. In the words of American theologian Cyrus I. Scofield (1843-1921, well known through the best-selling Scofield Bible): "A dispensation is a time period during which Man is tested with regard to obedience to a specific revelation of the will of God." The Anglo-Irish theologian John N. Darby (1800-1882) is usually viewed as the founder of dispensationalism, while the American theologian Lewis Sperry Chafer (1871-1952) has given the most extensive exposition of it. All dispensationalists are necessarily premillenialists, but premillenialists are not always dispensationalists.

The dispensationalist paradigm arose through a "scientific" revolution in nineteenth-century Western Europe known as "the Réveil." Of course, the Réveil too was more than just a revolution in scientific theology. It was also a psychical, socio-economic, cultural-historical, and especially pistical revolution. The Réveil did not destroy the federalist paradigm—the latter has lasted up to the present. But besides producing its own new paradigm, the Réveil also contributed to a reformation within Calvinism itself, a movement known as Neo-Calvinism (Abraham Kuyper).

As I said, both the Reformation and the Réveil were primarily pistical revolutions. Insofar as they also implied theological revolutions, the new paradigms they produced were closely intertwined with the occurring pistical changes. Moreover, the Reformation and the Réveil were ultimately revolutions of a *transcendent-religious* character. They not only entailed a renewal in thinking, in social and cultural-historical development and in church life, but primarily a renewal of the heart in many—though not all—of those involved in these revolutions. This renewal led to a new (pre-theoretical) reflection upon faith, and this in turn caused the formation of the new theological paradigms. In the latter sense, the Reformation and the Réveil involved "scientific revolutions" as defined by Kuhn.

This becomes even more obvious when we look at the relationships between these theological revolutions and the philosophical climate of the time-periods in which they occurred. The Reformation cannot be viewed apart from the Renaissance. This comes to light especially in (a) its *nationalistic* character, resulting in the formation of national Protestant churches over against the "catholic" (i.e., worldwide, universal) church, and (b) its *individualistic* character, expressed by its great emphasis on the necessity of personal conversion and regeneration, the general priesthood of all believers, their personal relationship to God, and personal Bible study.

In a similar way, the Réveil cannot be viewed apart from Romanticism. Both are ardent, sincere, and passionate. Both cultivate susceptibility, exaltation, intense sensitivity, friendships, the common enjoyment of the things of the mind, nostalgia for the past (i.e., the time prior to the combated Enlightenment), the veneration of the original individual, the preference of faith to philosophy, the preference of the inspiring and uplifting to the rational. During the Réveil, the greatest renewal *within* the classical Reformed paradigm was brought about by Abraham Kuyper, whose views are for this reason often called "Neo-Calvinist." For the dispensationalist paradigm, John N. Darby was by far the most original and influential thinker. The American Reformed theologian Vern S. Poythress (b. 1946) summarized Darby's influence as follows: he taught (a) a sharp distinction between law and grace; (b) a sharp vertical distinction between the "earthly" and "heavenly" peoples of God, i.e., Israel and the Church; (c) a "literal" interpretation of prophecy in connection with the Jewish nation; (d) a strongly premillenialist emphasis and the expectation of prophecy's imminent fulfillment; and (e) a negative, separatist evaluation of the existing institutional church. It was particularly his premillenialism, but not his ecclesiology, which quickly began to characterize American dispensationalism.

The main differences between the federalist and the dispensational paradigms may be summarized in the following questions:

(a) Is there one people of God or two? In other words, is there one Church from Adam until the last day, or is there an everlasting distinction between Israel and the Church?

(b) Must we interpret the Old Testament prophecies literally, that is, mainly with regard to Israel, or must they be spiritualized and applied to the Church?

Could there be a third way? Should we advocate a combination of (a) and (b): a literal fulfillment of the prophecies, but ultimately one people of God (whether we call them "the Church," "spiritual Israel," or something else)? Could this even lead to an entirely new paradigm, in which the federalist and the dispensational paradigms are integrated, as Poythress and others have suggested?

How to Choose?

Finally, we arrive at a methodological question that is crucial for every systematic theology: how can we decide which systematic-theological paradigm out of the many that are available is to be preferred? The problems implied in such a decision are basically the same as those with respect to alternative scientific paradigms in all the other special sciences. Ultimately such choices are determined by the worldview of the special scientists concerned, which itself is governed by a religious ground-motive. In various special sciences I could mention striking examples of this (see the later volumes in this series). Just consider the significance of evolutionary theory in the life sciences, of psychoanalysis or behaviorism in classical psychology, of Marxism or Keynesianism in economic theory.

Starting from the principles of the *general* Evangelical paradigm, we ask ourselves how we can determine which (sub)paradigm is closer to biblical truth: federalism or dispensationalism? It is difficult to assume that *both* could be right. Theoretically, however, it is possible that both are partly right, or even entirely wrong. This means that the advocates of federalism and dispensationalism would do well to at least listen to each other attentively, in order to learn as much as possible from each other. Each paradigm runs the risk of inbreeding and a certain one-sidedness. Even if we are convinced that our own paradigm is closer to the truth than the other one, we can always benefit from delving into the other paradigm. We can even learn something useful from a study of scientistic paradigms if, on the basis of a radical Christian view of reality, we know at least how to tell the tares from the wheat.

Even for some gifted academic theologians such a cross-pollination seems to be very difficult. They have a simplistic view of this kind of confrontation between paradigms. One main reason for this is the time-honored Scholastic appeal to *loca probantia* ("proof texts"), and the naïve idea that: (a) their theological theories have been derived from such proof texts; and (b) a simple appeal to such texts will suffice to checkmate the opponent. They do not realize that proof texts and other "biblical data"—which they view as objective—always function within the boundaries of a paradigm. A certain point that seems to be a strong argument within A's paradigm may not impress at all within B's paradigm. On the contrary, it may even cause astonishment because the same point is sometimes used within B's paradigm as a counter-argument against A's paradigm. A striking example is Colossians 2:11-12, which is offered by both Baptists and paedobaptists as evidence for their respective views.

Therefore, a discussion is only useful if both parties at least ask themselves how a certain argument not only functions within their own paradigm but also in that of the opponent. Theologians who do not have a certain capacity for empathy would do better not to engage in discussion in the first place, if they do not want the debate to end with the opponents sniping at each other from unapproachable and unassailable fortresses. And even if theologians have a great capacity for empathy, they should not count on persuading their opponents easily. In the worst case, some orthodox theologians chide their opponents for being unwilling to give up their obviously wrong view and for disobeying the clear words of Scripture. Liberal theologian Paul Tillich (1886-1965) went so far as to assert that in some regards fundamentalism has "demonic traits"! This is not the proper way to develop better mutual understanding.

We should remember that both the federalist and the dispensationalist paradigms are very complex and all-encompassing in nature. In these paradigms, many different aspects of Scripture have been brought together into one coherent framework. Asking the federalist or the dispensationalist to give up his paradigm is asking him to give up many different views at the same time. Actually, it means that he has to build up his entire system of thought on a totally new foundation. In many cases, this even involves all kinds of practical decisions, sometimes including the move to another church denomination. Scientific paradigms do not stand on their own; ultimately, they are rooted in a transcendent-religious ground-motive. Therefore, a theological *paradigm switch* usually involves, among other things, drastic pistical, social and cultural changes, or, in other words, a kind of conversion.

Moreover, federalism and dispensationalism are both internally very coherent. If one tries to attack one element in such a paradigm, the other elements in it will immediately come to its defense. We accept the weak spots in our own paradigm—if we are even conscious of them—believing that the rest of the paradigm is so strong that it can afford those weak spots. At the same time, we believe that the weak spots in the opponent's paradigm are sufficient proof that it is wrong. However, if we try to shoot holes in the other's paradigm at those spots, it turns out that the opponent can easily withdraw into those parts of his fortress that he considers to be the strongest. Every theologian should have enough self-knowledge to know this from experience. If we try to interpret a Scripture passage to our own advantage, the opponent will either offer us his "superior" interpretation, or come with two or three other passages that he believes support his view. We soon discover that we are forced to interpret dozens of Scripture passages at once, whereas in reality we can only discuss them one by one.

Uncertainty

In a time in which the scientistic theological paradigm enjoys a large number of adherents, many conservative theologians feel anxiety. They experience a great need for a powerful, strongly coherent thought system. Withdrawing into such a shelter creates a feeling of safety. In times of uncertainty, many believers are more unable than ever to handle this challenge to their paradigmatic certainties. This is why many cannot afford to think through and re-evaluate their theological foundations in a truly thorough and critical way. They hasten to reject even the idea of doing so, and refuse to enter into the arguments presented. Sometimes they even resort to an attitude of arrogance or mockery—especially if they are theologians with a high reputation—just to cover up their own insecurity. Of course, this is true not only for federalists and dispensationalists, but also for any other brand of theology, whether orthodox or liberal. It is human to act in such a way—but that does not make it right.

Many Christians have great difficulty accepting that the proof texts they quote do not speak nearly as clear a language as they had always thought. As I said before, even experienced theologians sometimes seem to think that they "have only to let Scripture speak" in order to prove the correctness of their theological theories. Apparently, they do not realize that these Scriptures only speak in such a "simple" and "clear" way for them because they read them through the "glasses" of their federalist or dispensationalist paradigm—or whatever other glasses they have decided to put on. Things that concern salvation are simple and clear for all Bible-believing Christians. The reason is that these things are *not the fruit of theological investigation* but rather the fruit of the work of the Holy Spirit in their hearts, which applies the Bible's simple and clear testimony to their consciences. "[T]here is salvation in no one else [but Christ], for there is no other name under heaven given among men by which we must be saved" (Acts 4:12). Period. No further discussion or interpretation is needed.

Of course, the fundamental aspects of salvation can and must definitely become a study object for theology (soteriology). But my main point right now is that the knowledge of them is not the *fruit* of theological investigation but *precedes* and *underlies* such investigation, because these aspects are primarily of a transcendent-religious nature. Therefore, they are truly *fundamental*: they separate orthodox Christians from liberal ones, not on the level of rational-theoretical paradigms but on the level of the knowledge of the supra-rational, supra-theoretical, transcendent-religious heart (*fides qua*).

This is very different in the case of paradigms such as federalism or dispensationalism. These *are* the fruit of scholarly investigation, and as such, they are subject to theological criticism. Calling these things "fundamental," or discrediting Christians who think otherwise, is one important cause of sectarianism. In fact, the background of this attitude is scientism. People greatly overestimate their own theological abilities and findings, and elevate the latter to the level of *fundamental* truths of Scripture. They even allow these theories to disrupt common believers. Thus, strictly theological matters such as the central concept of the covenant, or of dispensations, are reduced to "shibboleths" (cf. Judges 12:6), reasons for church divisions, and tests to determine the orthodoxy of others.

As long as we do not understand the scientistic-rationalistic background of this objectionable attitude, we will never break free of such sectarian tendencies, and we will continue to create new church divisions (apart from the even worse divisions that are nothing but the result of personality clashes between revered leaders). Strictly speaking, theological theories are not—nor can they ever be—"fundamental truths." They are nothing but the free creations of the theologians' minds. To be sure, they must be designed in such a way that they account for the biblical data, as I have explained earlier. But it is not *a priori* certain that this is done correctly, or that there is only one right way to do it. Scientific theories are always fallible and faulty. Therefore, it is a sin to impose them upon common believers as "final truth." This important matter will be further dealt with in the next and final chapter.

Chapter Ten

THEOLOGICAL THEORY BUILDING & TRUTH

In this final chapter I will turn to a rather abstract subject which is not the easiest one in this book. Therefore, I hope that my readers are already more or less familiar with what I wrote in my book *Wisdom for Thinkers*, especially in chapters 9 and 10 (about theology and truth respectively).

Truth is a fascinating concept, even from an etymological point of view. It is related to German *Treue* and Dutch *trouw*, which mean "faithfulness" or "loyalty." It is also related to Danish, Norwegian and Swedish *tro*, which means "faith," a word which, it goes without saying, is related to "faithfulness." Interestingly, the Greek word *pistis* similarly means both "faith" and "faithfulness"; see, for instance, *pistis* in Gal. 5:22, which is translated as "faith" in the KJV and "faithfulness" in the ESV. In reference to God, *pistis* is rendered as "faithfulness" (Rom. 3:3), corresponding to Hebrew *èmet* or *amnah*. In reference to the believer, *pistis* is rendered as "faith" (Rom. 3:22-31), corresponding to the Hebrew *èmunah*. The words *èmet*, *amnah* and *èmunah* are all derived from the Hebrew root *'-m-n*, "being true" or "being faithful."

The word "truth" is also etymologically related to the word "trust" in the sense of "confidence," a word that is itself derived from Latin *fides*, "faith." This is an interesting cluster in quite a few languages: truth, faith, faithfulness (fidelity), trust, confidence. God is "truth" in the sense that he is both loyal and trustworthy. If you ponder these related terms, you will soon see that, to grasp the biblical meaning of "truth," the notion of scientific truth will not help you very much. Biblical truth and scientific truth move on different levels, so to speak. This is what I will try to explain in this chapter.

WHAT THEN *IS* THEOLOGY?

The Biblical Notion of Truth

The Hebrew word *èmet* can mean both "truth" and "faithfulness." Translators have to determine which rendering they prefer, for instance in Psalm 85:11, "truth" ([NKJV, ASV), or "loyalty" (CEF, GNB), or "faithfulness" (ESV, NI; cf. Deut. 32:4 and Ps. 31:5 in KJV and ESV). No matter how one translates it, the term is basically related to the transcendent-religious faith relationship between Man and God. God is "truth" in the sense that he is absolutely trustworthy in what he says and does, and deserves our unconditional and loyal confidence (Ps. 31:6; Jer. 10:10; Rom. 3:4, 7). Man too must be "truth," that is, faithful, trustworthy, worthy of the confidence of others (Exod. 18:21; Neh. 7:2; Ps. 45:4).

The biblical *Amen* means something like "True!", "Really!", "Sure!", and is related to *èmet*, "truth." In Isaiah 65:16, *Èlohey amen* literally means "God of the Amen," i.e., "God of truth" ([N]KJV, ASV, ESV), or "the one true God" (NIV), or "the faithful God" (GNB; cf. "the God who can be trusted," CEV). You see, it is not easy to translate terms like *èmet* and *amen* consistently!

Besides these lofty meanings, the Bible also uses "truth" in the everyday practical meaning of the word, that is, in the sense of "reality." This or that is "true" in the sense of really-being-so. When Joseph sent his brothers back to Canaan to fetch Benjamin so that they could demonstrate whether there was "truth" in them (Gen. 42:16), this implies in the more general sense the question of whether they were trustworthy men. More specifically it involved the question of whether it was "true" that they had a younger brother at home, that is, whether this was really the case. In Deuteronomy 22:20, the question is whether or not a certain girl has "truly," that is, "really" entered marriage as a virgin or not. Was it true or not? In 1 Kings 22:16, king Ahab urges the prophet Micaiah to tell him what is "true," that is, to tell him how things "really" are. In Isaiah 43:9, the nations say, *èmet*, i.e., "It is true," or, "It is really the case." In Daniel 8:26, it is said of a vision that it is "true," that is, it tells how things "really" are (cf. Dan. 10:1). When the woman in Mark 5:33 tells Jesus the full truth, she tells him how things "really" are; what she said was "right," corresponding with reality. When Paul commands us to tell the truth, he means that we have to tell how things "really" are (Eph. 4:25; cf. Rom. 9:1; 2 Cor. 7:14; 12:6; 1 Tim. 2:7).

In short, the two basic meanings of truth in the Bible are as follows: (a) It is truth in its practical *immanent* meaning of (knowledge about) the really-being-so of immanent things; or (b) it is truth in its practical *transcendent* meaning as referring to the transcendent-religious relationship between God and Man, that is, (knowledge about) the really-being-so of transcendent things. In both cases the *practical* idea of truth is involved, not a *theoretical-conceptual* one. It is this practical idea with which we are concerned in science, including theology.

There is a snare here that has to be carefully avoided. The truth of a theological theory (see below) aims at the biblical truth in its transcendent-religious meaning, but the two are not identical, *nor can they ever be*. Scientific truth involves a theoretical idea of truth, which can be trustworthy only if it is embedded in a radical Christian view of reality and knowledge. Only in this case is there the possibility of a link between theoretical-theological truth and practical-biblical truth. But even then, the two are never identical.

Theories of Truth

For a Christian, the matter of truth, particularly in its transcendent-religious meaning, is of primary importance in his entire life and work. Jesus himself testified that he had come into the world, "to bear witness to the truth" (John 18:37), and the Apostle John appeals to the believers to "walk in the truth" (2 John 4; cf. 3 John 3-4; cf. the contrast in John 8:44). People can be "girded with truth" (Eph. 6:14 NKJV), or "deprived of the truth" (1 Tim. 6:5; cf. 2 Tim. 4:4; Titus 1:14; James 5:19). For the Christian, no domain of life, including theology, is exempt from this demand for truthfulness, for standing and walking in the truth. Since the Christian's scientific work must also be marked by truth, he will be confronted with the question whether, and to what extent, his scientific work, theological or otherwise, yields any *truth* about his field of investigation.

For many scientists, including theologians, an affirmative

answer to this question is rather self-evident. Many of them believe that they can simply "start from the objective facts" in that part of reality they are investigating—for instance, the Bible— without realizing that they are entangled in a secular view of reality, which has been adopted especially by (neo-)positivism. This is the thought system that wishes to start from the so-called "positively given," the "objective" empirical facts (*sense data*) of reality. Many believing scientists are amazed to hear that a radical Christian philosophy of science necessarily rejects positivism, including notions such as "objective scientific facts" and "neutral, unprejudiced science." Many theologians can hardly believe that it is problematic to speak of the "objective facts of Scripture," and that it is not *a priori* self-evident that their theological theories represent truth about their field of investigation.

For systematic theologians, this problem is even greater than for natural scientists because for the former it is not the general custom to use the concept of "theory" in their discipline. Though we may not agree with their presuppositions, we can at least express our appreciation for philosophers such as William W. Bartley and Hans Albert, and theologians such as Wolfhart Pannenberg, Gerhard Sauter, Gordon D. Kaufman, Heinzpeter Hempelmann, David Tracy, Andree Troost, Danie Strauss, and Wentzel van Huyssteen. They have all drawn the attentions of theologians to the importance of the "theory of theories" for (systematic) theology. That is the theory, or theories, advanced by modern philosophy of science, about how scientific theories are formed in the first place, whether it be in theology or in any other special science, or even in philosophy of science itself, for that matter.

Let me give you an example of the importance of the philosophy of science for theology. Some philosophers and scientists firmly deny that science has anything to do with "truth" in any sense of the word. They argue that at best scientific theories have some validity as long as they have not been falsified. They are useful instruments for creating some coherence between certain observations, for making certain predictions with respect to reality, and for constructing certain machines in applied science. We will see later that this view is called *instrumentalism*.

Such a view has some obvious consequences for the theologian.

If his discipline is truly *scientific*, why would the instrumentalist argumentation I have just given not hold for him as well? If it is true that he is a *scientist*, then he designs theological theories that, according to this view, have nothing to do with truth (or "the" Truth). It is difficult to imagine that many theologians would accept this view. They usually resolve this dilemma by severing "sacred" theology in a Scholastic manner from the "profane" natural sciences—and the old Nature–Grace dualism pops up again! In this way, these theologians can claim that natural scientific theories may merely be "valid" (for a time), whereas theological theories are related to the permanent truth of God. However, if this Scholastic split is rejected—as we very strongly advocate—there is no reason why the view that scientific theories do not yield truth would not apply equally to theology, as it does for *all* special sciences.

One thing must be clear. The question concerning the possible truth of theological theories cannot be solved in an intuitive way, for instance, from some "biblical" or "believing" intuition, for it is clearly evident that this intuition can lead to conflicting answers. The question can be answered only within the framework of a Christian-philosophical view of reality, including a Christian-philosophical view of scientific theory building.

Three Theories of Truth

Throughout history, philosophers of science have developed various theories of truth. I am going to mention seven of the most important ones:

(a) The *pragmatic* theory of the philosophical school called pragmatism (Charles S. Peirce, William James, John Dewey) states that a logical judgment is true if it "works," or, if it is useful. Truth is not (only) the logical quality of judgments but (also) the quality of actions leading to the desired goal. What this could mean in theology is illustrated by the American philosopher William James (1842-1910) in his book *Pragmatism* (1907): "If the hypothesis of God works satisfactorily . . . it is true." If religious actions "work," that is, are useful for those who do them, they are "true." If believing the Bible brings benefit ("blessing") to people it is "true."

A theologian who is inclined to a pragmatic approach is Hans-

WHAT THEN *IS* THEOLOGY?

Dieter Bastian (b. 1930). One can have some sympathy for this approach because, in practice, people are hardly interested in "truth" unless they also have some benefit from it. Practical truth is not merely some abstract, objective matter but a relational matter. A major problem with the theory, however, is that "truth" as intended here could also be found in any other book, even a book of fairy tales. And conversely, if certain people assert that, to them, the Bible is not useful, or even causes them harm (for instance, by discouraging them with its claims that certain things they like to do are sinful), to them the Bible is falsehood.

(b) The *performative* theory of linguistic philosophers, such as the British philosopher Peter F. Strawson (1919-2006), states that we make a judgment true by agreeing with it. The description "true" or "untrue" is a performative action, that is, it makes the judgment involved true. For instance, "I promise you" or "I thank you" is not the description of a performance but is itself a performance. By saying that I promise, I am promising; by saying that I thank, I am thanking. In Christian life, examples of such performative statements are "I bless you" or "I baptize you." In the latter statement, a practical action—sprinkling with, or dipping in, water— is involved, but uttering the words makes this action a Christian baptism.

In theology, the performative theory seems to claim that Scripture is made true by agreeing with it. When people accept Scripture as the Word of God it becomes true for them. Here again, one can have some sympathy for this theory because one could ask what truth would concretely mean if there were nobody who recognized and accepted it as such. As I have said before, truth is a relational matter.

(c) The *existentialist* theory states that truth is not determined by the logical quality of the choices people make, but by the authenticity of their choices. This authenticity depends solely on the question whether or not people can make their choices freely and independently. What this could mean for theology has been made clear by theologians who were strongly influenced by existentialism, such as Paul Tillich (1886-1965) and Rudolf Bultmann (1884-1976). Tillich was inspired by this philosophy to formulate the existential questions of modern philosophy, which he relates to the symbols of the Christian faith. Man lives in "finite freedom," that is, in anxiety, and, in this situation, asks for a ground to stand upon, for a power (God, the Infinite Being) to whom he can entrust himself in order to realize his freedom, his potentials, himself-as-possibility. Truth is truthfulness with respect to the "New Being," which has appeared in Jesus.

Bultmann sees Christians as people whose eyes have been opened by the Christian *kerygma* to the fact that they have existed "improperly," that is, in an inauthentic self-understanding. This was the state in which they were rigidly closed off from true existence, that is, refused to choose or realize their as yet unknown but true and unique "being." The *kerygma* asked them to give up their inauthentic self-understanding, and to exist henceforth in the light of their prospective "proper being," that is, God. Christians are those who actively respond to the *kerygma*, and experience the possibility of concretely giving up their old self-understanding and existing in a "proper" sense, that is, out of God. Truth is truthfulness with respect to the challenge of the *kerygma* to lead a true life of freedom and love.

Here again, one can have some sympathy for this theory because it gives truth a much wider (*existential!*) scope than just the logical-rational aspects of it, as has traditionally been done so often. As an approach to practical Christian truth, it is therefore much more acceptable than traditional rationalism. The point is, however, that scientific theology as such is a logical-rational matter. There is a tremendous difference between practical, *existential* truth and theoretical, i.e., logical truth. Therefore, the question we are asking right now remains: Does theological truth have anything to do with the Truth?

Two Further Theories of Truth

Looking back at the three truth theories I have just described, I can easily explain why, to my mind, the pragmatic, performative, and existentialist theories are unacceptable in the framework of a Christian-philosophical view of reality and knowledge. The major problem with all three of them is that they are forms of subjectivism, that is, they see truth as something that is ultimately determined by Man, by what *he* finds useful, what *he* performs, or what *he* chooses existentially and authentically, respectively. Adherents of subjectivism can no longer recognize that there is—or could be—something like an objective ontic truth, consisting independently of our experience and of our relationship to that truth. This is a truth that addresses us from "beyond," and that remains truth, even if we do not respond to it, or respond to it in a negative way.

The two following theories do not fare any better because they too do not wish or dare to accept a relationship between truth and some cosmic reality "out there."

(d) The *redundancy* theory says that judgment A, which states that judgment B is true, is entirely identical with judgment B itself. It is superfluous to say, "The judgment 'the sky is blue' is true," for this is the same as saying, "The sky is blue." What this means is that, in this view, the term "truth" as such is a superfluous word. The term does not refer to anything in reality but is based upon a general conventional practice. "Is blue" refers to a feature of the sky, it is argued, but "is true" does not refer to a feature of any judgment whatsoever. Apparently, this truth theory too shrinks from relating "truth" to "reality" because of the problems that would result from such a conclusion (see below).

(e) The *consensus* theory states that something is true if it is more or less generally accepted among people. Truth is never an individual possession; the individual person claiming in opposition to the masses that *he* possesses the truth simply deceives himself. Truth is always the possession of a community. In this view again, there is no relationship between "truth" and "reality," and surely no room for absoluteness: truth changes as the consensus changes. Especially in politics, this theory is important: in a democracy, something is "true" when at least fifty percent call it true.

Actually, not many philosophers will hold a *pure* form of this theory. Besides, most philosophers subscribe to a different theory of truth, so that even by its own standards the consensus theory cannot be true, because among philosophers there is no consensus about it. The theory does not protect us against wishful thinking, against badly informed multitudes, against widely accepted deceptions such as astrology and numerology. Democracy is good, not because it leads to any form of truth but because it keeps the powers in balance (see my *Power in Service*).

The Coherence Theory of Truth

Let us now look at the two theories that in philosophy have played, and still play, the greatest role:

(f) The *coherence* theory. This theory says, "A judgment is true if and only if it is coherent (or consistent) with the other judgments in a certain thought system." Truth does not lie in separate judgments but in the continual and coherent integration of judgments in a system. We do not say that truth *is* but that it *becomes*, and completes itself only in the progress of thinking. This theory is found especially in rationalism and German idealism (Baruch de Spinoza, Gottfried W. Leibniz, Georg W. F. Hegel, Francis H. Bradley), but also in the writings of various logical positivists (Otto Neurath, Rudolf Carnap, Carl G. Hempel), and in the philosophy of science, where it appears especially in Thomas S. Kuhn and related thinkers.

Here again, we can make a distinction. The consistent adherents of the coherence theory will never appeal to "experience" or "reality." However, more metaphysically minded adherents are not ashamed to assume some relationship between the thought system involved and "reality."

The consistent adherents of the coherence theory use what I would call a weakened criterion of truth. In their view, truth is nothing more than "logical validity." Something that is "true" is true only within the context of a theory; a judgment is true if it is coherent with the other judgments in a theory. As such, this coherence theory is very important for correct theory building, also within theology. As the Swiss theologian Emil Brunner (1889-1966) says, not only must theological statements not contradict revelational truth, they must not contradict each other either. A theory is consistent (coherent) if no judgment in that theory conflicts with any other judgment in that theory. Such a theory is "true" in the sense of the weakened criterion of truth; it is *internally* true but not necessarily anything more than that.

If this criterion of truth were right, a scientific theory could never demonstrate the truth of a judgment in the *ontic* sense, that is, in terms of the really-being-so of things "out there." The judgments within a theory, or the philosophical presuppositions on which the theory is based, are *ontically* either true or untrue in the sense that either they do or they do not correspond with reality (*external* truth). To be sure, one could maintain the coherence theory by pointing out that the philosophical presuppositions involved do not belong to a certain scientific theory as such. However, they do belong to the underlying paradigm, which itself is rooted in a pre-scientific worldview. Moreover, in our view, all presuppositions are ultimately rooted in the existential, transcendent-religious (anastatic or apostatic) faith choices that are made in the scientist's heart. This means that ultimately, beyond all our (practical and theoretical) reflections, we are, on a transcendent-religious level, interested in the question of whether our views correspond with reality, whether "things are really that way" as we assert in our theories.

The coherence theory certainly has some relativizing value *within* the framework of our theoretical thinking. First, we do not claim that a certain theory is true in the sense that *all* judgments within that theory correspond with reality. Second, theoretical judgments are based upon a certain abstract distance from reality so that in the full, integral sense they never *could* correspond with reality (I will explain this below). It is not theoretically but only supra-theoretically that we know *a priori* of an objective (observer-independent) reality. This is the point where the coherence criterion falls short. The question of the external coherence of theories involves our pre-theoretical beliefs, in which we possess the transcendent-religious faith certitude that our practical view of reality corresponds with reality itself.

The coherence theory suffers from the same problem as *all* theories of truth: it attempts to assess the problem of truth on a purely theoretical level, whereas radical Christian philosophy asserts that this is *a priori* impossible. Ultimately, the question of truth—as well as the possible truth of scientific theories, among which are included theological theories—can only be solved on the transcendent level, as I will try to explain in more detail below.

The Correspondence Theory of Truth

(g) The *correspondence* theory says, "A judgment is true if, and only if, it corresponds with a state of affairs that is independent of human experience." In simpler terms, a judgment is true if it corresponds with reality. This theory was defended in Greek antiquity (by Plato and Aristotle in the fifth and fourth centuries B.C.). It was afterwards held by thinkers such as the French philosopher René Descartes (1596-1650), and the British philosopher John Locke (1632-1704), and it flourished in the empiricist and positivist traditions.

Modern adherents of the correspondence theory have adopted either an ontological view ("a judgment is true if and only if it corresponds with the reality described") or an epistemological view ("a judgment is true if and only if it corresponds with the empirical data involved"). Later, we will inquire a little more into this, as well as the coherence theory, and consider their possible relevance for theology.

For the reasons mentioned at the close of the previous section, the correspondence theory as a *theory* is just as unsatisfactory as the coherence theory. First, it offers too little because it is limited to the domain of the logical. For instance, it does not take into account that a correspondence between judgment and fact may be *logically* true but for other (e.g., *moral*) reasons may be untrue. If a patient by worrying about his health develops a physical ailment of which he is unaware, it is logical for the physician to tell him that he has this ailment. Therapeutically, however, it is a lie. The therapeutic truth is that the doctor tells him that he has nothing to worry about, in order not to aggravate his situation (cf. the "little white lies" in Exod. 1:18-19; Josh. 2:4-5; 2 Sam. 17:20; in all these cases it would have been *immoral* to tell the *logical* truth).

This is why various philosophical schools have tried to design truth theories that escape from the logical limitation of the current theories. Whenever a correspondence theory is adopted, then it is sometimes one that claims a correspondence between behavior in general (not just logical-rational behavior) and states of affairs. Dooyeweerd has expressed this more accurately by stating that, besides logical truth, there is also historical-formative truth ("this or that is historic or ahistoric behavior"), social truth ("this or that is social or asocial behavior"), aesthetic truth ("this or that is beautiful or ugly"), juridical truth ("this or that is just or unjust"), and ethical truth ("this or that is morally good or bad") (see below). None of these is logical truth because the historical-formative, the social, the aesthetic, the juridical, and the ethical each have their own modal qualities and cannot be reduced to the logical.

Second, the opposite objection against the correspondence theory as a *theory* is that it offers too much. It rightly assumes that there is an external, observer-independent reality, but it forgets that, as a *theory*, it has no independent access to that reality in order to determine whether our scientific theories correspond with it. The certainty that there is an extra-mental, observer-independent reality is not theoretical at all. It is a *pre-theoretical*, or rather *supra-theoretical*, even *supra-rational* faith, which to my mind is ultimately of a *transcendent-religious* nature. We *believe* in the existence of the world "out there" because we believe in the God who created our sense organs, and does not deceive us through them. There is no "theory" whatsoever involved in this existential certitude.

The "theoreticalization" of practical thinking, including Christian-believing thinking, is quite disturbing, as I indicated earlier. To mention some Christian thinkers, the Dutch-American philosopher and theologian Cornelius Van Til (1895-1987) wrote about the "theory of reality" that the Bible allegedly contains. The American theologian Norman L. Geisler (b. 1932) claimed that the correspondence theory is indirectly "taught" by the Bible. The American theologian John S. Feinberg (b. 1946) states as his opinion that the Bible writers presuppose a "theory of truth," namely, a form of the correspondence theory.

This is a typically scientistic confusion between, on the one hand, a philosophical correspondence *theory* and, on the other hand, the everyday experience of Man who, in immediate relationship with reality, is unaware of any theories. The Bible writers were not even *aware* of the (theoretical) *problem* of whether or not their description of reality actually *corresponds* with that reality. This is not because they were primitive but because a correspondence *theory* presupposes the *theoretical distance* between reality and thinking. This distance simply does not *exist* in practical thinking, not only in biblical times but also today among the most "modern" humans.

Thus, a Christian philosophy of science necessarily *transcends* both the coherence and the correspondence theories. In other words, the question about the relationship between scientific theories and the reality of our study field can be answered in the affirmative—but only if we understand that theoretical thought always has to be fed back to our practical thinking, and especially our transcendent-religious thinking. Only in our faith do we have true (existential) knowledge of creational reality. Theories, including theological theories, contain at best certain "truth elements." These will only be unfolded if, in the *supra*-theoretical faith attitude, they are related to creation in its integral fullness, unity, and coherence, and hence to the Creator as the Root and Ground of this creation.

Scientific Truth

Assuming that you have read chapter 10 of my book *Wisdom for Thinkers*, I shall briefly summarize what I have said there, and am going to apply that now more specifically to theology.

The view that philosophical and scientific theories, no matter how flawed and provisional, are approximations of cosmic reality is called (scientific) *realism*. The view that scientific theories are just useful, convenient instruments, which do not tell us anything about the true nature of reality is, as I said, called *instrumentalism*. When the revolutionary work of the German scholar Nicolaus Copernicus (1473-1543) on the movements of the celestial bodies appeared in 1543, the German Lutheran theologian Andreas Osiander (1498-1552) claimed in a foreword that Copernicus' theories had to be taken (to use our terminology) in an instrumentalist sense. That is, in Osiander's view, these theories said nothing about how our solar system really worked. In order to understand that subject, one had to turn to the Bible (see, e.g., Ps. 104:5, the earth does not move).

The Italian cardinal Roberto Bellarmino (1542-1621) argued in the same way with respect to the theories of the Italian natural scientist Galileo Galilei (1564-1642). Similarly, the British Anglican bishop George Berkeley (1685-1753) strongly defended an instrumentalist view with respect to the theory of gravity of the British natural scientist Isaac Newton (1643-1727).

The interesting question one might ask at this point is whether these theologians—Osiander being a Lutheran, Bellarmino a Roman

WHAT THEN *IS* THEOLOGY?

Catholic, and Berkeley an Anglican—as well as many theologians after them, would have been prepared to take an instrumentalist standpoint with respect to theological theories as well! Why should one be an instrumentalist when it comes to natural scientific theories and a realist when it comes to theological theories? As I have said before, the only reason for this would be the well-known Scholastic prejudice: the alleged dualism between *grace*, to which sacred theology belongs, based upon God's Word-revelation, and *nature*, to which profane (secular) philosophy and the other sciences belong, based upon the light of natural reason alone. As soon as one gives up this dualism, and takes instrumentalism for granted, one is confronted with the highly interesting conclusion that theological theories too have to be viewed as just practical instruments, which tell us nothing about the really-being-so of the world.

However, especially in the early twentieth century, people began to realize that instrumentalism is not so self-evident after all. First, this viewpoint cannot explain the fact that theories can give rise to risky predictions, which moreover often come true (as happened with Einstein's theory of relativity). Second, how can one explain that certain theoretical "fictions," such as Kekulé's discovery of the ring structure of certain molecules (e.g., benzene), can now be made visible in an almost direct way with the help of an electron microscope? Third, how can instrumentalism explain the tremendous success of technology if the physical theories on which the latter is based in some way or other have nothing to do with the "really-being-so" of nature?

The substantial objections against instrumentalism did not lead to a return to old realism because the latter had turned out to be too naïve. It was clear by now that theories are not simply copies, images, pictures, representations of reality, as had been thought not only by the natural scientists but also by the theologians. If that were the case, how could one explain that no single theory has a permanent character, but that all theories, even the best established—even theological theories—are in the long run replaced, or at any rate fundamentally modified? At least *something* had to be learned from instrumentalism, which had claimed that, for every set of observational data, in principle a large—perhaps even an infinite—number of theories is in principle conceivable.

All these possible theories may be "good," not because they reflect reality, but because they involve a meaningful and consistent interpretation of the observational data *and* allow for a further testing of this interpretation. But how can we ever know whether one of them tells us the (full) truth about the study field concerned, and how can we trace that one single theory?

Critical Realism

The newer, so-called "critical" or "qualified" realism combines the insights of old realism (theories have "something" to do with reality) and instrumentalism (theories can never be called [definitive] representations of reality). It is the view that theories cannot be "drawn" (adopted) from reality as such, but are invented, created, designed by scientists to explain the observational data. This realism maintains, however, that theories which fulfill academic criteria indeed have to do—no matter in what restricted and preliminary sense—with the "really-being-so" of reality.

The term "design" reminds me of an interesting remark made by Karl Barth: "Dogmatic theology as such does not ask what the apostles and prophets have said but what, 'on the basis of the apostles and prophets,' we ourselves must say." In our terminology, systematic-theological theories are not descriptions of the facts, but responses to the facts. These responses are not drawn from the Bible but designed by us.

To illustrate critical realism, we can think of the example that I dealt with in the previous chapter: federalism *versus* dispensationalism. Both theories fulfill the conditions, that is, both explain the biblical data in an effective way, and both contain creatively designed theoretical ideas that offer possibilities for further exploration. But in principle there might be many more theories capable of achieving the same result. As long as we remain unaware of these other theories, we might try to learn from both federalism and dispensationalism. But even some combination of the two can never be presented as the final truth concerning the matter. Theologians will keep studying, revising, and improving, and sometimes they will see very different pathways that they might like to tread. Critical realists believe that, in continuing to do so, we may be confident that, in the long term, we will be closer to the truth about our field of investigation than we were before.

This character of theological theories is still not well understood by some theologians. For instance, as recently as 1998, the American theologian Millard J. Erickson (b. 1932) still described what he considered the definitive theological method entirely in terms of the hopelessly outdated method of induction developed by the British philosopher Francis Bacon, (1561-1626), involving the objective collection of observational data, which are then combined to form theories or models. No philosopher of science, Christian or otherwise, would accept such a methodology today, simply because we now realize that there *is* no such thing as objective observation. Just like any other science, theology does not start with observations—you would not know *where* to start— but with *problems*, which arise from earlier theories, doctrines, or dogmas. Problems are solved, not by means of theories that allegedly *follow* from scientific facts but, by means of theories that are *designed* to explain scientific facts—facts which are themselves always embedded in scientific theories. The proper pathway in science is not from facts to theories, but primarily from theories to facts, and subsequently back to theories.

Nowadays, theologians who are aware of the philosophy of science have also seen the great benefits of a critical-realist approach to theology. The South African–American theologian Wentzel van Huyssteen (b. 1942) and the British theologian, N. T. ("Tom") Wright (b. 1948) are among those who recognize, on the one hand, that science is based on the hypothesis that "objective" laws do exist, and that the main goal of science is the discovery of these laws. On the other hand, they realize that the *formulation* of these laws is "invented," and subsequently undergoes further refinement or is finally refuted, in a critical way. Think about this fine balance between discovering and inventing!

However, what is lacking in such theologians, as well as in many philosophers of science, is the insight that we need *more* than critical realism when it comes to science in relation to truth. For instance, where critical realism as such provides no justification for the correspondence *theory*, radical Christian philosophy has a *pre-theoretical* justification for our faith in the "objective" empirical world, a transcendent-religious faith that underlies all knowledge. To my mind, we have here the key to the problem as to how we can transcend the whole conflict between (traditional and critical) realism and instrumentalism, or between the correspondence theory and the coherence theory. Every fact can be truly known only in the integral coherence of the whole empirical reality, which is not possible without the transcendent orientation of this reality toward its Creator.

Supra-Theological Truth

Scientistic theology is at best aware of certain "truth elements." There are at least two reasons for the fact that it contains such elements at all. First, even if people do not always recognize it, the acquisition of knowledge is subject to the law of God, and this law cannot constantly be avoided. For instance, orthodox and liberal theologians are subject to the same laws of logic, and if these laws are obeyed it is virtually impossible to evade truth altogether.

Second, scientistic theology is historically rooted in the orthodox historical tradition, and therefore may still contain many truth elements from the past. Conversely, this means that, because of these truth elements, orthodox theologians can still learn much from scientistic theologians. Just like all secular scientists, these theologians owe their scientific achievements, historically speaking, to a faith originally based upon Scripture: the faith in the coherence, the uniformity, the knowability, and the law-order of cosmic reality.

At the same time, we remember that logic with its laws is not enough to bring us to a universally valid, that is, *full* truth. This is because the logical aspect of truth, *as an aspect*, can really be grasped only in *coherence* with all other modal reality aspects, that is, with the integral structure of the entire immanent-modal empirical reality. Therefore, theological truth—as *logical* truth—can never be the *full* truth. I point to the following reasons for this (cf. chapter 10 in my *Wisdom for Thinkers*):

(1) Theoretical truth is *specialized* truth in that it refers to only one specialized, abstracted modal aspect of our full, practical experience of reality. Thus, theological knowledge refers only to the pistical aspect of truth. It is necessarily one-sided, detached,

abstracted knowledge, and thus never identical with the full, practical faith knowledge of the heart.

(2) Theological truth is exclusively *logical* truth ("this is logically right or wrong"), not to be confused with *pistical* truth ("this is certain or uncertain, credible or incredible, worthy or unworthy of our faith, or our confidence"). Pistical truth is part of our everyday practical truth, whereas theological truth is theoretical truth.

(3) Logical truth, pistical truth, and all other kinds of truth, can only be grasped in a *supra*-modal idea of the fullness, unity, and origin of this modal diversity of cosmic reality.

(4) In its turn, such a philosophical idea of truth is only possible through the supra-philosophical, transcendent-religious knowledge of the Truth in the believing heart, in submission to the divine revelation in Christ and in Scripture, and through the power of the Holy Spirit.

I cannot emphasize enough that there is no gap, nor can there ever be any gap, between some "supernatural" truth of Christian faith and some "natural" truth of (usually secularized) thinking. Such a gap can only exist on the basis of the Scholastic Nature–Grace dualism, which we utterly reject.

The Fullness of Truth

In the Christian view of the heart, the logical function arising from the heart is only one of many functions. Therefore, Truth, in its transcendent-religious meaning, cannot be enclosed in abstract, theoretical thought, including theological thought. On the contrary, this Truth is the supra-logical, supra-modal knowledge of the transcendent-religious heart. As a result of regeneration and the enlightenment of the Holy Spirit, this heart is under the guidance of the revealed truth of the Scriptures, and is oriented toward, and filled with, him who is the Truth, the Christ of the Scriptures.

From this heart, this transcendent fullness of the Truth shines through all functions of Man's immanent-modal life, and through all his theoretical work, including theology. Not only is theology *about* the truth of Christ, but Christ is the Truth (John 14:6), also *for* theology.

God's Word is the "word of truth" (2 Cor. 6:7; Eph. 1:13; Col.

1:5; 2 Tim. 2:15; James 1:18) because only on the basis of this Word can true knowledge of reality be possible. And the Holy Spirit is the "Spirit of truth" (John 14:17; 15:26; 16:13) because only in the power of this Spirit is true knowledge of reality possible. It is this truth in its transcendent-religious fullness that gives each form of immanent, modally qualified truth its meaning, validity, and certainty. The fact that we are "of the truth" (John 18:37; 1 John 3:19) guides our subjective understanding of the empirical world.

Of course, we are always aware that sin may be a serious hindrance for a Christian understanding of the truth. This happens when the heart falls back into the grip of apostate ground-motives. To be sure, many thinkers who are influenced by some non-Christian ground-motive—such as Scholasticism, scientism, rationalism, or positivism—have discovered *relatively true* states of affairs within empirical reality. But that does not change our basic conviction that all relative truths within immanent reality are ultimately true only in the *fullness* of Truth, revealed by God in Christ.

Not even the simplest linguistic statement about the Bible can ever be isolated from the whole of created reality, and thus from the meaningfulness of that reality as located in Christ. Where this is not seen, "theological truth" is narrowed into "logical correctness" or abstract truth elements within a context that as such does not "stand in the truth" (John 8:44). Every immanent, relative truth "becomes" truth in the fullest sense only if it refers beyond itself to the transcendent meaningfulness of the Truth in Christ. Conversely, this meaningfulness of the Truth must shine through all human thinking, including theological thinking.

"I am the way, and the truth, and the life.
No one comes to the Father except through me" (John 14:6).

CONCISE BIBLIOGRAPHY

Aulén, G. 1960. *The Faith of the Christian Church*. Trans. Eric H. Wahlstrom. Philadelphia: Muhlenberg Press.

Avis, P. 1986. *The Methods of Modern Theology: The Dream of Reason*. Basingstoke: Marshall Pickering.

Barth, K. 1969–1988. *Church Dogmatics*, Vol. I,1-IV,4 (14 vols.). Edinburgh: T. & T. Clark.

Bartley, W. W. 1964. *The Retreat to Commitment*. London: Chatto & Windus.

Bavinck, H. 2003-2008. *Reformed Dogmatics*, Vol. 1-4. Grand Rapids, MI: Baker.

Bloesch, D. G. 1971. *The Ground of Certainty: Toward an Evangelical Theology of Revelation*. Grand Rapids, MI: Eerdmans.

Brümmer, V. 1981. *Theology and Philosophical Inquiry: An Introduction*. London: Macmillan.

Caputo, J. D. 2006. *Philosophy and Theology*. Nashville, TN: Abingdon Press.

Chafer, L. S. 1983. *Systematic Theology*. 8 vols. Dallas, TX: Dallas Seminary Press.

Clouser, R. A. 1999. *Knowing with the Heart: Religious Experience and Belief in God*. Eugene, OR: Wipf & Stock.

Dooyeweerd, H. 1960. *In the Twilight of Western Thought: Studies in the Pretended Autonomy of Philosophical Thought*. Philadelphia: Presbyterian & Reformed Publishing Company.

Dooyeweerd, H. 1984 (repr.). *A New Critique of Theoretical Thought*, I: *The Necessary Presuppositions of Philosophy* (1953); II: *The General Theory of the Modal Spheres* (1955); III: *The Structures of Individuality of Temporal Reality* (1957). Jordan Station: Paideia Press.

Erickson, M. J. 1998. *Christian Theology*. 2nd ed. Grand Rapids: Baker Book House.

Fowler, S. *What Is Theology?* Blackburn (Australia): Foundation for Christian Scholarship.

Frei, H. W. 1992. *Types of Christian Theology*. New Haven: Yale University Press.

Grenz, S. J. & Franke, J. R. 2001. *Beyond Foundationalism: Shaping Theology in a Postmodern Context*. Louisville, KY: Westminster John Knox Press.

Guarino, T. G. 2005. *Foundations of Systematic Theology*. New York: T. & T. Clark International.

Holmes, A. F. 1977. *All Truth is God's Truth*. Grand Rapids, MI: Eerdmans.

Kuhn, T. S. 1970. *The Structure of Scientific Revolutions*. 2nd ed. Chicago: University of Chicago Press.

Lewis, C. S. 2009. *The Great Divorce*. San Francisco: HarperOne.

McGrath, A. E. 2001. *A Scientific Theology*. 3 vols. London: T. & T. Clark.

Michener, R. T. 2012. *Postliberal Theology: A Guide for the Perplexed*. Edinburgh: T. & T. Clark.

Oliphint, K. S. 2006. *Reasons {for Faith}: Philosophy in the Service of Theology*. Phillipsburg, NJ: P&R Publishing.

Oliphint, K. S. & Tipton, L. G. (eds.). 2007. *Revelation and Reason: New Essays in Reformed Apologetics*. Phillipsburg, NJ: P&R Publishing.

Ouweneel, W. J. 2014a. *Wisdom for Thinkers: An Introduction to Christian Philosophy*. Jordan Station, ON: Paideia Press.

Ouweneel, W. J. 2014b. *Power in Service: An Introduction to Christian Political Thought*. Jordan Station, ON: Paideia Press.

Phillips, T. R. & Okholm, D. L. (eds.). 1996. *The Nature of Confession: Evangelicals and Postliberals in Conversation*. Downers Grove, IL: InterVarsity Press.

Plantinga, A. 2000. *Warranted Christian Belief*. New York: Oxford University Press.

Plantinga, A. & Wolterstorff, N. (eds.). 2009. *Faith and Rationality: Reason and Belief in God*. Notre Dame, IN: University of Notre Dame Press.

Possenti, V. 2001. *Philosophy and Revelation: A Contribution to the Debate on Reason and Faith*. Aldershot: Ashgate.

Poythress, V. 1987. *Understanding Dispensationalists*. Grand Rapids, MI: Academie Books.

Scalise, C. J. 1996. *From Scripture to Theology: A Canonical Journey into Hermeneutics.* Downers Grove, IL: InterVarsity Press.

Smith, J. K. A. 2006. *Who's Afraid of Postmodernism?: Taking Derrida, Lyotard, and Foucault to Church.* Grand Rapids, MI: Baker Academic.

Smith, J. K. A. 2009. *Desiring the Kingdom: Worship, Worldview, and Cultural Formation.* Grand Rapids, MI: Baker Academic.

Smith, J. K. A. & Olthuis, J. H. (eds.). 2005. *Radical Orthodoxy and the Reformed Tradition: Creation, Covenant, and Participation.* Grand Rapids: Baker Academic & Brazos Press.

Spykman, G. J. 1992. *Reformational Theology: A New Paradigm for Doing Dogmatics.* Grand Rapids, MI: Eerdmans.

Stone, H. W. & Duke, J. O. 2006. *How to Think Theologically.* 2nd ed. Minneapolis, MN: Fortress Press.

Vanhoozer, K. J. 2005. *The Drama of Doctrine: A Canonical Linguistic Approach to Christian Theology.* Louisville, KY: Westminster John Knox.

Vanhoozer, K. J. & Warner, M. (eds.). 2007. *Transcending Boundaries in Philosophy and Theology: Reason, Meaning and Experience.* Aldershot: Ashgate.

Van Huyssteen, J. W. V. 1997. *Essays in Postfoundationalist Theology.* Grand Rapids, MI: Eerdmans.

White, J. E. 1994. *What Is Truth? A Comparative Study of the Positions of Cornelius Van Til, Francis Schaeffer, Carl F.H. Henry, Donald Bloesch, Millard Erickson.* Nashville, TN: Broadman & Holman Publishers.

SCRIPTURE INDEX

WHAT THEN *IS* THEOLOGY?

INDEX OF NAMES

INDEX OF SUBJECTS

Printed in the USA
CPSIA information can be obtained
at www.ICGtesting.com
LVHW010037281223
767563LV00002B/122